IMAGE TRANSFORMATIONS
OF THE BRAIN-MIND

IMAGE TRANSFORMATIONS OF THE BRAIN-MIND

EXPERIENCING THE EMERGENT SUPERVENING SELF

GLEN A. JUST

IMAGE TRANSFORMATIONS OF THE BRAIN-MIND
EXPERIENCING THE EMERGENT SUPERVENING SELF

Cover image by Ruby Li-Just

iUniverse books may be ordered through booksellers or by contacting:

iUniverse
1663 Liberty Drive
Bloomington, IN 47403
www.iuniverse.com
844-349-9409

ISBN: 978-1-6632-3356-1 (sc)
ISBN: 978-1-6632-3357-8 (e)

Print information available on the last page.

iUniverse rev. date: 12/10/2021

CONTENTS

PART I
GENESIS AND IMAGE TRANSFORMATIONS
OF THE PHENOMENAL-SELF

PART II
PLASTICITY OF THE PHENOMENAL-SELF
IN DREAMS AND HALLUCINATIONS

PART III
TRANSFORMATIONS OF THE
PHENOMENAL SELF

ABOUT THE AUTHOR
AND TEXT

Glen Just is a retired professor from the Minnesota State University System. He has spent his professional life teaching, researching and administering programs in the social and behavioral sciences as they relate to offenders and the mentally ill in America's Criminal Justice System. He is retired and lives with his wife Ruby in Kennewick, Washington.

Image Transformations of the Brain-Mind is his latest book that addresses basic questions about SELF and CONSCIOUSNESS. Previous books: *Autobiography of a Ghost* (2009*), Mind of the Mystic* (2011), and *Dream, Creativity & Mental Health* (2012) provide the historical base and empirical background for *Image Transformations of the Brain-Mind.*

Dr. Just has two major concerns—how dreams and altered state experiences help explain how the mind emerges from its fetal beginning and matures through adulthood to enable free will (the Supervening-SELF) and how sensory image transformations of the brain-mind lead to subjective experience. This book shares numerous insights into:

- Virtually transformed sensory images that feel like a little person (homunculus) in our brains.
- How the Physical-SELF is transformed into the Virtual-SELF.
- How the SELF in dreams feels just as real as it does in waking.
- The author's dream classifications according to type of sensory experience.

- Transformative brain-mind images that underlie altered mental states and various religious experiences.
- How dream memories and the 24-hour mind become waking déjà vu experiences.
- Psychological and philosophical questions of autonomy and determinism.

ACKNOWLEDGMENTS

This book would never exist without J. Allan Hobson's friendship, personal time, and encouragement. His criticisms of this book's first draft (2014, 610 pages) resulted in total reorganization and rewriting.

Isabel Alfonso's careful readings and numerous suggestions over multiple drafts added much needed clarity to the final text. As a soul-mate of self-hypnosis, Isabel has been a bright light on a dark street. I thank Allan for introducing me to Isabel.

My friend, former student, and still active family therapist mentor Richard DeBeau has also read through various drafts. I am indebted to his insights while remaining unable to add all the clarity of text he seeks.

My friend Judith Whitehead has helped edit three separate drafts. Her suggestions have left their imprint on the majority of this book's pages.

OVERVIEW

Transformative Imaging

The major objective of Image Transformations of the Brain-Mind is to review the sensory imaging processes that support and generate virtual and phenomenal representations of self, body, and world.

I explain how the brain dynamically transforms sensory images at two levels—primary and secondary. The human brain reimages primary sensory images at our secondary level of consciousness to create all manner of virtual and phenomenal entities, such as "ghosts," a pantheon of "spirits," and the self itself.

Imaging at our secondary level of consciousness is dynamic and represents a bidirectional transformative process. Dynamic complexity at our secondary level of consciousness also means that concepts of virtual images can be and are transformed back into primary percepts. At the level of secondary consciousness, I will explain how concepts derived from belief and suggestion are concretized and personified in dreams and hallucinations, as well as being the source of such entities as presence and possession. Simply stated, I argue that transformative imagery lies at the heart of humanity's secondary level of consciousness; that is, what makes humans human.

Lucid Methodology

Learning to employ lucidity across states of consciousness is the method I use to explore bidirectional sensory image transformations between primary and secondary consciousness[1]. I argue that subjective, first-person analysis, combined with "hard science's" empirical methods, generates insight into virtual and phenomenal processes of the brain not possible with either method alone[2].

By lucidly observing the contents of dreams and hallucinations[3], I explore the bidirectional image transformations occurring between primary and secondary consciousness that generate our virtual world of both representative and illusory entities.

Being lucid across states of consciousness naturally begs the question, "What is the self?" Lucidity in dreams means that we are able to be in a dual state of consciousness—we dream and observe the dream simultaneously[4]. I argue that lucid control in dual states of consciousness demonstrates the active role of an autonomous self. I also clarify the relationship between the autonomy of our higher-order brain functions and the automaticity of core brain dynamics.

Comparative Neuro-psycho-phenomenology

Thinkers and researchers from philosophy, religion, psychology, and neuroscience have long wrestled with questions of what is the "self" and what are the mechanisms of its existence. I propose that reimaging of primary sensory stimuli at our secondary level of consciousness is the mechanism that creates an autonomous-self.

Image transformations at our secondary level of consciousness exemplify the plasticity of both our physical and virtual self-image transformations. I present numerous self-experiments, as well as spontaneous examples of sensory image transformations, to help clarify the critical role these transformations play in phenomenal-self and consciousness content constructions.

Internationally known professionals such as Gerald Edelman, Thomas Metzinger, Allan Hobson, Evan Thompson, and Manfred Clynes and Jaak Panksepp argue for the incorporation of first-person phenomenal research with the "hard sciences." Let me start this adventure with a quote from Jaak Panksepp and Manfred Clynes[5]: "It is long past time to join the best aspects of the two disciplines into a synthesis which I would call 'Comparative Neuro-psycho-phenomenology.'"

Analysis that attempts to reduce subjective sensory experiences to cell biology and biochemistry alone does not support a methodology that sufficiently addresses the bidirectional image transformations observed in dreams, hallucinations, and related altered states of consciousness. Integration of subjective and objective methods in consciousness research presents a means to overcome the limitations of reductionism[6].

Throughout the following pages, I maintain that transformative sensory imagery is the most neglected component of Clynes and Panksepp's envisioned synthesis. I further agree with them that ". . . objective neural anchor points are routinely missing for concepts . . ." like Freud's Oedipus complex[ibid], or self as illusion. I employ the lucid method of observing and manipulating image transformations in dreams and other altered states to ground percepts and concepts to "objective neural anchors."

It is my goal that at the end of this book the reader will be better able to interpret how the self develops from womb to tomb, as well as being in possession of new insights that will further help clarify the image transformations and self-processes in their dreams and hallucinations. I end by defining the self itself.

SOURCES: PART I: OVERVIEW

Just, G. A. (2009) Autobiography of a Ghost. Mankato, MN: Eagle Entertainment USA; (2012) Dreams, Creativity & Mental Health. Mankato, MN: Eagle Entertainment USA.

Just, Glen A. (2015). Convergence of Subjective and Objective Methodologies in Consciousness Research, in Advances in Psychology Research. Volume 103, Hauppauge, NY: Nova Science Publishers, Inc.

Hobson, J. A., & Just, G. A. (2013) "Lucid Hallucinations."

In Hallucinations, Causes, Management and Prognosis, Ed. Sofia Alvarez. Hauppauge, NY: Nova Science Publications.

Voss, U., Holzmann, R., Tuin, I., & Hobson, J. A. (2009) Lucid Dreaming: A State of Consciousness with Features of both Waking and Non-Lucid Dreaming. Sleep, 32 (9), 1191-1200.

Clynes, Manfred & Panksepp, Jaak, eds. (1988) Emotions and Psychopathology, p. 45. (New York: Plenum Press): 45. 7.

Churchland, P. S (2000) Neuro-philosophy at Work. New York: Cambridge University Press; (2013). Touching a Nerve: The Self as Brain. New York: Norton.

PART I

Genesis And Image Transformations Of The Phenomenal-Self

The major question addressed in Part I is how the phenomenal-self emerges developmentally as a virtual, functional, and autonomous process. The brain must control chaos at two levels: At the primary level—neuronal "noise" generated by a multitude of brain processes and maintenance functions and, at the secondary-level, the phenomenal integration of visual, tactile, and auditory sensations that permit meaningful interactions with social and physical environments[1,2,3,4].

From a first-person perspective, I combine lucid analyses across states of consciousness that include dreams, hallucinations, and various trance states with dream and empirical research in neuroscience and related disciplines. I have been a lucid dreamer since 5-years of age and a manipulator of dream and altered state content for over 60-years. *Image Transformations of the Brain-Mind* sets forth a preliminary model that combines subjective and objective research methods that address fundamental issues of self-image transformations.

Maintaining lucidity across states of consciousness is a subjective research method that permits observation of bidirectional sensory image transformations between primary and secondary levels of consciousness. I provide numerous observations of how transformative imaging (TFI) across states of consciousness offers insights into phenomenal self-processes. Thus, as the book progresses, the stage is set to examine the interrelationships between primary and secondary image transformations, how the phenomenal-self emerges and functions, how memory associations are transformed in dreams and hallucinations, psycho-genic transformations, and free will.

Sources: Part I: Genesis and Image Transformations of the PhenomenalSelf

1. Hinton, G. E., and van Camp, D. (1993). Keeping neural networks simple by minimizing the description length. Proceedings of COLT-93,5-13.
2. Hobson, J. Allan and Friston, Karl J. (2014) Consciousness, dreams, and inference: the cartesian theatre revisited. J. Conscious. Studies. 21, 6-32.
3. Hobson, J. Allan, Hong, Charles C.H., and Friston, Karl J. (2014) Virtual reality and consciousness inference in dreaming. Frontiers in Psychology. Volume 5, article 1133.
4. Whitney, David, & Fischer, Jason, et al., (posted online Apr. 07, 2014). Brain's 15-second delay shields us from hallucinogenic experience. Reuters/Eddie Keogh.

CHAPTER 1

❧

Self

Self is not Illusion

Self is not a specific set of neurons like other parts of the brain, such as the amygdala. As a shifting set of neurons, it is heuristically helpful to think of the self as a process. Self as process uses different cells in different configurations over any period of time. Self relies on, or perhaps I should say accesses, memory to maintain continuity moment-to-moment.

Processes in our higher cortical centers are actively involved in neuronal stability through visual image averaging over a 10-15 second interval[1]. David Whitney, the senior author of this research stated: "What you are seeing at the present moment is not a fresh snapshot of the world but rather an average of what you've seen in the past 10 to 15 seconds". (This blended "snapshot" is called a continuity field). The continuity field "smoothes" what would otherwise be a jittery perception of object features over time. Essentially, it pulls together physically but not radically different objects to appear more similar to each other. This is surprising because it means the visual system sacrifices accuracy for the sake of the continuous, stable perception of objects.

According to Whitney and Jason Fischer, the continuity field is an advantageous mechanism because it excludes "visual noise." The brain uses this mechanism to reduce complexity and avoid neuronal overload. Note that this is neuronal complexity, not complexity of the quantum variety. It is a brain chaos reduction mechanism at higher levels of sensory integration. What is more, without such brain development humans would find the world an unsteady and frightening place to be. It might be similar to a person on hallucinogenic drugs experiencing sudden changes of color, a play of shadows, and splashes of light. It would be just too overwhelming to live like this on a daily basis—a severe ordeal for the psyche [Ibid].

The continuity field is modulated by attention. Note the active interplay between a non-conscious process, visual blending, and attention which reflects active involvement by the self. These findings mesh with Hobson's protoconsciousness theory, which suggests that synaptic pruning is simplifying learned experience[2]. This simplification process conserves energy and stabilizes the brain as a system. Thus, we are better able to handle surprise and shock as we navigate our everyday environments.

Researchers such as Whitney, Fischer, and Hobson help us realize the degree to which the brain is creating a virtual reality of the world that we humans navigate. Combining Whitney and Fischer's top-down research with Hobson's bottom-up analysis helps clarify how the self manages its own top-down behavioral processes. Thus, multiple primary and secondary processes are responsible for removing chaos from our visual encounter with environment.

Michael Gazzaniga in *The Mind's Past* says ". . . we do know about the fiction of our lives: [I] have written this book about how our mind and brain accomplish the amazing feat of constructing our past and, in so doing, create the illusion of self, which in turn motivates us to reach beyond our automatic brain"[3]. I accept Gazzaniga's treatment of the self as a process that gives rise to all our human capacities—ability to develop culture, express creativity, as well as direct and build our futures. He uses the term "interpreter" to refer to the brain device central to this evolutionary emergent capacity: "The brain device we humans possess, which I call the interpreter, allows for special human pursuits. It also creates the impression that our brain works according to "our" instructions, not the other way around"[3]. I think we are confusing the general reader when we say that self is an illusion and then call it our "interpreter."

However, in general agreement with Gazzaniga, self as a specific brain configuration is an illusion, but self as a distributed process is not.

In agreement with Gazzaniga, since the late 1950s, I have called this brain device my "controller". Conceptualizing the self, whether we call it an "interpreter" or "controller" as being capable of actively directing brain processes unleashes its therapeutic potential. This argument has been a central thesis to my various writings.

Gazzaniga follows the interpretation of Benjamin Libet's work that the brain's higher cortical centers follow the automatic output of our brain's core dynamics. Libet found that neuronal sets activate in our brains before higher order consciousness becomes aware of these actions[4]. Thus, the argument emerged that free will is an illusion. However, it is my position that Libet's research is only part of the story.

In contrast to the Libet and Gazzaniga position that free will is an illusion, I follow a Niklas Luhmann interpretation that reverses the direction of structure and function[5]: Developmentally, the self comes to function as a semi-permanent and dynamic brain process and memory is transitory. I'm also assuming that there is constant two-way, bidirectional, interaction between the self and memory. I'm viewing self as a developmental process that takes on long-term structure in much the same way as we learn social roles. Consequently, with dissociative identity disorder (DID), what was formerly called multiple personality, there can be more than one self that emerges and acts. This interpretation of DID generally follows Gazzaniga's *The Social Brain*[6].

I conceive of the phenomenal-self exercising the autonomy of free will as the meta-organizer of the brain's automatic processes. Autonomy of action is the evolutionary level that sets us apart from other animals. In dreams, we observe the brain's core dynamics acting in Libet-fashion—automatically. In lucid dreaming, we note the phenomenal-self observing these automatic actions. In dream programming (scripting), we observe the phenomenal-self directing, and redirecting, the automaticity of the brain's core dynamics. It is my thesis that the brain's automatic, transformative imaging helps create the Libet illusion that there is no free will, and the self is not in control. Whitney's and Fischer's "continuity field" also calls the Libet interpretation into question. The brain is experiencing a lot of activity over a 10-to-15-second time period.

Applying Luhmann's interpretation of structure-functionalism, consciousness with its focused component we call self is the brain's semi-permanent process that draws on the available content of memory moment-to-moment. And in my interpretation, the brain's core dynamics reflect Libet-like responses while our higher order cognitive centers direct our purposeful behavior.

Lucidly observing bidirectional sensory image transformations in dreams, hallucinations, and trance states critically challenges a reductionist interpretation that the brain's higher cortical centers are simply processing core-brain dynamics. In other words, transformative imaging between primary and secondary levels of consciousness has not been adequately entered into analysis of neuronal behavior when Libet-like responses are considered in isolation from the larger system.

The self as a permanent, virtual process helps clarify how our personalities can be maintained when various parts of our physical brain have been altered. The self as virtual process also helps us understand how personality can be expressed so differently in different social situations; The self is context dependent—at any given moment, the self in its "now" state is felt as though it were a physical thing. The consciousness of the self is a "now" state of cognition and feeling which is actively coupled with the environment.

The phenomenal-self aspect of secondary consciousness as a dynamic system draws upon memory moment-to-moment to compare "now" experiences with past memories. The above interpretation contrasts with Libet-determinism; thus, I'm arguing that the self functions as an active, autonomous agent capable of globally directing human actions.

Self as Focused Consciousness

Consciousness viewed through a transparent skull looks a lot like sheet lightening walking across a hot, stormy summer sky. Except— the accompanying electrical charges take on a focus much like a searchlight. Neuronal discharges skip from one part of the brain's sensory modules to another. All of this busy electro-chemical activity supports subjective self-awareness called you and me. Continuity of the self is memory-dependent. Long-term memory is necessary for a self that maintains awareness of itself through time. Long-term memory is the looking glass that reflects and maintains our identity—the changing, but "now" stable state continuity of the self over time.

These complex biochemical processes permit us to be aware that we are separate beings on this pale blue dot called Earth. The self that is aware of being aware in this metaphorical description is a moving light beam reflecting in its own memory mirror. It is the ability of the brain's higher cortical centers to re-image sensation that is occurring in our dynamic core that makes possible complex social life, the arts, and the pursuit of science. The human mind is not a mystery of extraterrestrial stuff. The human mind of secondary consciousness is virtual process derived from a three-pound piece of meat—a very marvelous piece of meat that is.

How does a three-pound piece of meat exercise free will? Most of the scientific community says free will doesn't exist; Sam Harris being a prime example[7]. Free will and consciousness are hot button terms in the brain sciences and philosophy[8]. Until recently treating consciousness and free will as researchable subjects would dry up grant money or result in loss of university tenure.

Bruce Hood's *The Self Illusion: How the Social Brain Creates Identity*[9] is typical of contemporary perspectives. For most of us, it seems strange to have so many professionals tell us that the self we feel every waking moment of our lives is not real. How is it possible to use the mind for self-healing if it's an illusion? By treating my phenomenal-self as an active agent, I was able to control nightmares, and later apply these controls across states of consciousness. Controlling what happens in various states of consciousness is no small matter for those of us who have suffered posttraumatic stress (PTSD), hallucinations, and OCD.

Whatever the complexity of biology--creating self, it is a functional set of neurons that can act back upon other sets of neurons. Self is not an organ in the brain. It is not even a single network of brain cells in accord with contemporary opinions[10,11,12]. My ideas about my nose are not concrete things physically located in my nose. My thoughts about writing this book are not located outside of my body. Are my thoughts only real when I've put them on paper and the reader can physically observe them? Are my thoughts only real when their neuronal correlates are observed with recording devices such as fMRI or PET?

In private, prominent researchers are beginning to admit that they too believe that the mind is not only real, but also that it can be causative. If I use my mind to program a dream, or to fly off in virtual space to the beginning of time, is this not a demonstration of mind acting back on itself? If I can control sensation, such that you can stick a pin in my hand without my feeling pain, is this not the phenomenal-self blocking automatic discharges in interconnected neural networks? Mind-over-matter is metaphor for one set of neurons acting on another set of neurons. In the examples of dream programming and blocked pain, mind as secondary consciousness (phenomenal-self) is the meta-cognitive capacity of one set of the brain's neurons acting on another set of neurons to generate autonomous actions—free will!

If accomplished meditators quiet the brain's noise, and this neuronal synchrony is confirmed with brain imaging[10], is this not mind-over-matter according to the above interpretation? Let us refine working definitions of "will" and "free will" rather than obscure the potential of our own subjective states. Mind as process is never detached from its supporting neurons. The self as a brain organ or specific set of neurons is illusion, but then we started with this assumption.

Historically, shamans and clergy performing exorcisms didn't have a clue about the brain's transformative imaging. Nevertheless, they devised working procedures to remove "evil spirits", (that is, to alter subjective brain states) from controlling our bodies and minds. Simply, the phenomenal-self acts on belief and shamans and clergy use these beliefs to exercise virtual demons that feel real. I'm suggesting that "objective" science is not being objective when it denies the functional effects of transformative imaging; that is, when transformative imaging turns belief into experiential reality; or neuronal image transformations into its phenomenal-self.

In 1759 Rene' Descartes explained the mind as immaterial "soul," which contemporary neuroscience now understands as self, as something that was separate from the body[14]. "Soul" was external to body and existed in the spiritual world of God, and mysticism. As science developed through The Enlightenment, there was a major backlash against immaterial explanations of soul (vitalism). Eventually, mind as concept went out of vogue, and ceased to be considered as a researchable variable. Even though we have come to understand mind (self) as a functional process, we are still struggling to get past this historical backlash and related terminology.

Self as a Co-Creation of Secondary Consciousness

Primary consciousness is associated with our brain's dynamic core functions of organismic maintenance and species survival. In the course of evolution, automatic functions in the dynamic core permitted animals to search for food, engage in physical protection, and reproduce. No higher-level cognitive awareness is necessary for basic survival. At our human level, we also have these basic dynamic core capacities and primary process emotions. However, evolution has given us a secondary level of consciousness—we can identify ourselves in the mirror. I've made the distinction with phenomenal-self and core-self dynamics to represent primary and secondary levels of consciousness. I took the position in *Dreams, Creativity & Mental Health* (2012) that the mirror reflections of the physical-core-self by the phenomenal-self require a major increase in the number of brain cells. This interpretation resonates with Stephen J. Gould's argument that language and its correlated capacities is a byproduct of a "big brain[15]".

Homo sapiens experience the phenomenal-self at the secondary level of consciousness and the brain's core dynamics as physical-entities. Thus, I assume that emerging language complexity and self-processes evolved concurrently. From this perspective, a transformative process emerges whereby words come to represent concepts—re-imaged percepts—at the secondary level. Thus, I suppose the elephant can manipulate concepts without language[16], such as mourning over its dead. For additional insights into thought without language read Oliver Sacks marvelous book, *Seeing Voices*[17].

Transformative imaging permits humans to hold two sensory elements simultaneously: for example, the phenomenal-self, viewing it's physical-self in dreams. The phenomenal-self is separately generated at our secondary level of consciousness as a dispersed functional entity; while all the sensations of primary consciousness become associated with the physical-self.

In math, this primary to secondary imaging process reflects the relationship between numbers and numerals[18]. This distinction between primary and secondary consciousness, two different levels of hierarchical brain modular functionality, permits virtual creations in the brain called the phenomenal-self, "spirits," and multiple selves. Secondary consciousness enables a *"Mind to Go Out of"* as argued by Hobson and Voss[19]. Thus, mental illness arrives in the course of evolution as a virtual biological emergent—as a psychogenic process. Awareness of being aware requires mentally holding images of the phenomenal and physical selves simultaneously. Simply, mirror recognition is one set of neurons recognizing or acting on another set of neurons to create virtual products. No *Ouija* board game here! Stated differently, ability to hold two images simultaneously creates a dynamic relationship that enacts as a virtual being. Thus, if we focus on the self as a thing it disappears.

At the primary level, core brain dynamics are usually expressed without conscious control or awareness by our higher-order-phenomenal-self. At the secondary level, the phenomenal-self is a shifting set of neurons that is dependent on memory. The marvel of this dual imaging process supports the emergence of a virtual, functional entity—the phenomenal-self, which can act back upon and control neurons in the brain's core dynamics. We are both automatons (primary consciousness) and free spirits (secondary consciousness) according to this interpretation. To get a better handle on free will read Ryan and Deci[20]. For a quick, succinct, and readable three page understanding of free will read Eddy Nahmias[21].

The Time Continuum of the Phenomenal-Self

Humans, dolphins, elephants and some other higher primates have mirror recognition. Dolphins call each other by name, even after 20 years of separation. Elephants appear to mourn over their deceased loved one. Question: What does this have to do with the formation of the self? Answer: Being aware that we are aware (having a separate identity) is an evolutionary level of development that permits mirror recognition on the part of higher-order primates, some other mammals and birds. We humans are not alone in this sentient universe of self-awareness.The emergence of human-level awareness is not something exclusive to our species. Earth is not the center of creation, and self-awareness emerges in the course of evolution by degrees.

Imaging by our higher-brain centers, those more recently evolved parts of our brains, permits mirror reflections (also referred to as memory content) of our physical and virtual selves to form consistently over time. The "now" of consciousness (the self) uses memory content of past events to compare and project possible future events. Thus, the "now" state of consciousness can use memories from the past to project the future. Sentient beings evolve to live in a time continuum, which permits humans to experience changes occurring throughout the cosmos. Time awareness begs an understanding of the laws of physics and the processes of biochemistry.

At any given moment in time our self-image changes depending on our particular focus, physical size, moods, state of consciousness, energy level, and any number of other factors. The key however is that self-images are always felt intimately, as feeling is always a part of our "now" state of consciousness. Self-images change a little moment-to-moment, and they change quite a bit over the decades. But self-images are always present in any state of consciousness. Self-images might be distorted but they are still present if we are conscious. Self-images are stored in neurons, and neurons remember even though they are being continuously pruned and reconfigured; thus, there is both continuity and change over time that permits each of us to feel like the same person, even with radical changes brought about by accident and trauma.

The phenomenal-self and physical-self reflect our "mental" and physical changes over time. And as expressed in our dreams, our phenomenal-self also reflects maturation of cognitive-emotional growth and decline. This is an ongoing dynamic relationship between primary and secondary levels of consciousness. It is a dynamic and not a linear process.

Personal example: Virtual creation over time

In my imagination, I'm looking into a glass jar that holds my brain and seeing global sheets of electrical energy moving constantly. I see the phenomenal-self's searchlight as it goes on and off. I see the searchlight supported by a multitude of waking sensations. I see the searchlight of aged vision diming while other sensations of hearing, touch, taste and smell keep the searchlight seeking, seeking! Thus, the summer of consciousness becomes the autumn, becomes the winter of my being.

This virtual creation of neuronal processes exists as output on the part of a shifting, dynamic pattern of brain cells. Is it any wonder that physiological research has not been able to find the organ of consciousness? Is it any wonder that lack of physiological research in years past brought Descartes[14] to the conclusion that consciousness was in the mind of God? Imagine Descartes' conclusions if he had understood the psychological mechanism behind the *Ouija* board. Does the reader believe that physiological correlates of consciousness alone will explain the autonomy of the self?

The self appears to be configured as a fluid neuronal structure in an open dynamic system. The self is a constantly changing set of our brain's neurons, which by necessity must pay attention to the "now" moments of its environmental relationships. The self as consciousness feels, and it feels as though it were an organ of substance. I think it is misleading to call this process an illusion. Is the dynamic interaction of yeast with other ingredients in dough an illusion? Is the process of heat changing water into vapor an illusion? These processes produce what is called phase changes in the physical sciences. A conceptual shift is necessary if we wish to capitalize on the therapeutic potential of the phenomenal-self—the self that is a process and not a thing.

Physiologically, the phenomenal-self emerges from brain neurons as an electro-chemical process. Stop this process and the phenomenal-self is no longer present. If I define the self as illusion, I stop analyzing process. If I stop the analyzing process, I miss the transformative-phase changes from which self is created. If I dismiss the phase changes from which self is created, I enter a state of denial, which says that our sense of self is simply a bunch of automaton cells doing their own thing. And blind materialism reigns! Lucidly observing image transformations in dreams and hallucinations focuses attention on the automaticity of the brain's primary consciousness and the autonomy of the phenomenal-self at our secondary level of consciousness. Conclusion—psychologists, philosopher, and neuroscientists have more dynamic interpretations if they incorporate image phase-changes of the phenomenal-self in their analyses.

The Phenomenal-Self is Phase State Change

Interpreting self-processes of mind as fiction denies a more complete inquiry into the virtual, psychological and social development of one of nature's most profound accomplishments. Systems biology and complexity theory offer a different perspective[22,23,24].

If the self is the product of brain cell electro-chemical processes, then human-level subjectivity is the dynamic systems output of this collective energy exchange. System biology supports system psychology, which in turn offers insight into the origin of the self, consciousness, and free will. At the physical level, gain or loss of energy turns H_2O into a solid, liquid, or gas— phase state changes. But note (I suggest with tongue-in-cheek) that the phase change of H_2O into a gas is fiction, an illusion.

Meinard Kuhlman has emphasized that understanding physics requires that we look at relationships between particles rather than at the particles themselves[25]. This is the case for chemistry as well when hydrogen and oxygen combined become water. Following this emergent pattern across nature from physics, through chemistry to biology helps us heuristically re-conceptualize the forces of nature. In like fashion, biochemistry that we call sensation in the brain's core dynamics creates consciousness. Thus, the reimaged and focused searchlight of bio-chemical consciousness eventually emerges as self. And, as I've been arguing, transformative imaging is central to our understanding of how the self emerges as a phenomenal entity.

Magic is *Self [Coming] to Mind*—to quote the title of Antonio Damasio's book by the same name. Paraphrasing Einstein, the magic of self is not spooky action at a distance.

Sources: Chapter 1: Self

1. Whitney, David, & Fischer, Jason, et al., (posted online Apr. 07, 2014). Brain '15-second delay' shields us from hallucinogenic experience. Reuters/Eddie Keogh.
2. Hobson, J. A. (2009) REM sleep and dreaming: towards a theory of protoconsciousness. Nature Reviews Neuroscience 10 (11), 803-813.
3. Gazzaniga, M. S. (1998) The Mind's Past. Berkeley: University of California Press.
4. Libet, B. Neural time factors in consciousness and unconscious mental functions. In Toward a Science of Consciousness: The First Tucson Discussions and Debates (S. R. Hameroff, et al, Eds.). Cambridge: MIT Press, 1996, pp. 337-347.
5. Luhmann, Niklas. (2013) Introduction to Systems Theory. Ed. Dirk Baecker. Cambridge, UK: The Polity Press
6. Gazzaniga, M.S. (1985) The Social Brain: Discovering the Networks of the Mind. New York: Basic Books. (p. 90)
7. Harris, Sam. (2012) Free Will. New York: Free Press.
8. Thompson, Evan. (2015) Waking, Dreaming, Being. New York: Columbia University Press.
9. Hood, Bruce. (2012) The Self Illusion: How the Social Brain Creates Identity. New York: Oxford Press.
10. Ricard, M., Lutz, A., & Davidson, R.J. Mind of the Meditator, Science, (Nov. 2014), 39-45.
11. Metzinger, Thomas. (2009). The Ego Tunnel: The Science of the Mind and Myth of the Self. New York: Basic Books.

12. Edelman, Gerald (1987) Neural Darwinism: The Theory of Neuronal Group Selection. Philadelphia: Basic Books.
13. Windt, Jennifer M. (2015) Dreaming: A Conceptual Framework for Philosophy of Mind and Empirical Research. Cambridge, MA: The MIT Press.
14. Descartes, R. (1637) The Philosophical Works of Descartes, rendered into English by Elizabeth S. Haldane and G. R. T. Ross, vol. l. New York: Cambridge University Press (1970).
15. Gould, Stephen J. Exaptation: A crucial tool for an evolutionary psychology. Journal of Social Issues 47 (1991): 43-65.
16. King, B. J. "When Animals Mourn." Scientific American; July, 2013.
17. Oliver Sacks. (1989) Seeing Voices: A Journey into the World of the Deaf. LA: U. of Calif. Press.
18. Lakoff, G., & Nunez, Rafael E. (2000) Where Mathematics Comes From: How the Embodied Mind brings Mathematics into Being. New York: Basic Books.
19. Hobson, J. A., & Voss, U. (2011) A Mind to go out of: reflections on primary and secondary consciousness. Consciousness and Cognition, 20(4): 993-997.
20. Ryan, R. M., & Deci, E. L. (2006) Self-regulation and the problem of human autonomy: Does psychology need choice, self-determination and will? Journal of Personality. 74, 1557-1585.
21. Nahmias, Eddy. Why we have Free Will. Scientific American (Jan. 2015, 77-79).
22. Deacon, T. (2012) Incomplete Nature: How Mind Emerged from Matter. New York: W. W. Norton & Company.
23. Ackoff, Russell L., & Emery, Fred E. (2006) On Purposeful Systems: An Interdisciplinary Analysis of Individual and Social Behavior as a System of Purposeful Events. New Brunswick, USA: Aldine Transaction.

24. Lewis, M. D. (2005) Bridging emotion theory and neurobiology through dynamic systems modelling. Behavioral and Brain Sciences, 28, 169-245.
25. Kuhlman, Meinard. Quantum Physics: What is Real? Scientific American; August, 2013.

CHAPTER 2

The Brain's Psycho-neuro-phenomenological Configurations

Transformative imagery operates as the key component of my dynamic systems model and is the centerpiece of how the phenomenal-self emerges and is sustained. The phenomenal-self as a virtual entity can act meta-cognitively to control and direct dreams, hallucinations, as well as other states of consciousness. In subsequent chapters, I will provide examples of how the contents of the phenomenal-self can be modified to possess the "Other," become the "Other," or disappear as a virtual entity.

Sensory image transformations of the phenomenal-self are wonderfully explicit in both pre-and post-literate societies. We observe a huge range of imagery constructions in the contents of consciousness from shamanism to modern day exorcism. This huge range of the brain's phenomenal configurations speaks loudly to the autonomy of self, and the presence of free will.

In the framework of transformative imagery (TFI), "ghosts," having visions, being possessed by "spirits," and experiencing all the episodes of shamanism, acknowledge the plasticity of the self as a virtual, phenomenal construction of the brain's neurons. TFI suggests that religious experience, such as "spirits," is an inevitable, epigenetic expression of the brain's transformative imager. The phenomenal-self is an emergent, metacognitive mechanism that acquires permanent functions at our higher cognitive levels. Being lucid across states of consciousness supports the phenomenal-self being a metacognitive agent.

Lucidity in dreams and hallucinations also acknowledges the difference between primary and secondary consciousness as one part of the brain-mind observes another. Thus, human consciousness cannot be discussed only at one level. As a metacognitive entity, the phenomenal-self, in any state of consciousness, attempts to integrate all of the image transformations it experiences.

I extend "belief" to the whole of our subjective reality. At our higher cortical levels, the brain's transformative imager operates on meaning derived from language and culture, not empirical logic. Simply put, the brain's image generator transforms sensation both top-down (cognitively) and bottom-up (affectively). By lucidly observing dreams and hallucinations, we can follow this bidirectional transformative process. This innate, genetically determined transformative process, I contend, is the un-cracked nut at the core of the theist-a-theist debate.

Self-reflective thinkers throughout the ages have sought answers to humankind's most fundamental phenomenal experiences. Modern science continues to reveal the natural origin of "spirits," "ghosts," and a pantheon of ethereal "beings." To logically say that humanity's phenomenal experiences are illusions according to third-person scientific explanation misses the point. Logic does not guide phenomenal, first-person, transformative imaging. Identifying the natural origin of image transformations, such as "ghosts" and "spirits," can potentially move us beyond the endless debate between theists and a-theists. Consequently, I embrace the emerging neuroscience of religious experience [1] that recognizes genomic and epigenetic mechanisms that generate the variety of sensory image transformations of the phenomenal-self.

In *Mind of the Mystic* (2011), I viewed religious belief and spirituality as being epigenetic products of a genetic algorithm. In this book, I am discussing transformative imaging as the mechanism that turns the subjective meaning of sensation into "concrete" entities, the mechanism that sustains the formal social organization of spirituality we call religious institutions. From this perspective, human religiosity is a "normal" and probably inevitable epigenetic phenomenon. In other words, the brain's natural, transformative imaging processes are at the core of religious experiences. Logic is a later application applied to institutionalized religion, for example, St. Augustine's writings.

I like Thomas Metzinger for both his insight and writer's clarity: "Religious belief is an attempt to endow your life with deeper meaning and embed it in a positive meta-context—it is the deeply human attempt to finally feel at home. It is a strategy to outsmart the hedonic treadmill"[2]. A compatible message of the natural origin of spirituality is found in Stuart Kauffman's *Reinventing the* Sacred[3]. In my interpretation of Kauffman, we can remove the destructive aspects of radicalized religious dogma by naturalizing our understanding of how our sense of a religious spirit is an integral part of biology. I have been and am arguing that an understanding of how the brain transforms sensory images is central to this naturalizing process.

Metzinger addresses our human capacity to create phenomenal-selves: "The fact that we can actively design the structure of our conscious minds has been neglected and will become increasingly obvious through the development of rational neuroanthropology"[4].

Let me indulge one more quote from this sage philosopher-researcher that emphasizes the plasticity of the brain's neurophenomenological configurations: ". . . there is an enormous number of possible neural configurations in our brains and [a] vastness of different types of subjective experience. Most of us are completely unaware of the potential and depth of our experiential space. The amount of possible neurophenomenological configurations of an individual human brain is so large that you can explore only a tiny fraction of them in your lifetime"[5].

However, I want to be clear about my interpretation of Metzinger's ". . . vastness of different types of subjective experience." The content of one's waking experiences is vast, and the content of dreams and hallucinations is vast. And the variety of phenomenal-selves is vast. But in my experience, the forms of consciousness states are restricted to the channels by which sensory experiences are processed. Nevertheless, all forms of consciousness states that I have experienced and am discussing utilize sensory image transformations. Transformative images are expressed as select sensory forms, such as hallucinations, OBEs, possession and presence, dreams, speech without cognitive control (glossolalia), automatic writing, shamanic possession, and a slate of phenomenological-self models.

Gradually neuroscience is placing each form of these states of consciousness under the microscope of research. The historical, mystical interpretations of the phenomenal-self are shrinking as the human brain gradually gives up its secrets. We no longer think the earth is flat; and from my perspective, possession is not a supernatural but an alternative, "natural," state of consciousness. Now permit me to compare dream content with dream form following Allan Hobson's research. He maintains that dream forms violate waking experiences of (1) time, (2) space, (3) muscle activation, (4) movement, and (5) logic. The content manner in which these violations can occur are vast, but the five forms just listed are not[6].

In parallel fashion to dreams, hallucinatory sensory form can be experienced singularly as sight, hearing, touch, or any combination of our senses[7]. The waking, controlled hallucination that I call my "Genesis Journey" was mostly visual with the exception of hitting the plasma wall at the beginning of cosmic time. Speaking-in-tongues (glossolalia), employs sound only. When I became the shamanic bear, I used *self-identification* with another body[8] to feel the power of the bear. I then entered this virtually created bear into my consciousness and substituted it for my physical self. When the ghost followed me up the stairs, I could feel it trying to enter my body—no visuals needed; when it stood over my bed, I could hear it breathing. The hallucination of Moses in my classroom was visual only.

Is it a sign of strength or weakness to control states of

consciousness? Such a large percentage of the world's children have their early years slathered in myth; and unfortunately for so many, these myths continue into old age. In 21st Century America we increasingly drown child development in pharmaceuticals and myth. Perhaps pharmaceuticals are an improvement over body-slamming kids on cement floors in psychiatric wards, although in terms of outcome, I fail to see much difference.

Subjective World Modeling

I'm briefly recapping subjective world modeling in the following section. Our waking brains organize images into action sequences that represent our ongoing relationship with the outside world. These sequences reflect our real-time movement through social and physical space. All of these images depend selectively on how we focus attention on our surroundings. Movement in our uniquely imaged world, from morning 'til night, creates our moment-to-moment subjective reality. As Llinas says, motricity is at the core of consciousness [9]. Thus, physical involvement of clients can be incorporated into therapeutic strategies [10]. In terms of monism, the self is always embodied as brain-mind [11]. Interpreting dreams and hallucinations as just other virtual creations of our brains takes away the feeling of bizarreness. Meta-consciously, I just remind myself that I'm in different states of consciousness. It's relatively irrelevant that I'm stressed, anxious, overtired, or recovering from broken ankle surgery. Knowing that hallucinations or visions are phenomenal creations of the brain-mind permits me to explore how to control them, eliminate their negative effects, and turn trauma into outright fun. As we become students of our own states of consciousness, there is great motivation to explain the "what" and "how."

As we transition from infancy to adulthood, we get more adept at predicting what we can't see. We learn to predict what is "going to happen around the corner" and out of sight. From limited visual cues or voice intonations, we learn to anticipate another person's emotional state. We fill in the missing parts of the mountain lion that is mostly hidden in the trees. We look at a box and imaginatively "see" the parts that are not in view. And if we have good spatial ability, we can visually rotate the box in our minds. The "mind's eye" literally sees what is out of sight.

Thinking about our relationship to the outside world, we discover endless examples of how we virtually create something that is not materially available to our physical eyes or ears. We rely on this ability to survive and go about our daily living. We believe that the virtual images of the world that we create in our dreams are real while we are dreaming [11, 12]. Awake, we also believe that how our brain-mind reproduces the world is the way the world really exists. However, we must use the methods of science to overcome subjective reality, e.g., the world is not flat, we are not the center of the universe, and microorganisms are making us ill not "evil spirits."

The infant's brain has to learn the distinction between which face is mom's and which is grandma's, this is my toe and not my nose, and a million other things. As the child attaches words to objects-in-environment, the global world becomes increasingly refined into specific elements. It is little wonder that objects and words can be recorded in one neuron [13].

The phenomenal-self is not a body part like our heart or lungs. The phenomenal-self forms as a developmental process. Neurons gradually form self-organized, functionally integrated patterns from experience and memories [14, 15, 16, 17]. In this explanation, I'm also generally supporting Thelen and Smith's dynamic systems model of human development [18]. This set of processes continues to change lifelong, but brain architecture supporting related processes can be damaged, broken, or destroyed. The phenomenal-self is also a marvel of evolution.

The formation of selves is complex and not totally understood. At lower cortical levels, there are primary-process emotions and control mechanisms that run all of the body's survival and maintenance functions [19]. At higher cortical levels, there is metacognitive awareness with focus on the phenomenal-self [20, 21]. In this conception, the phenomenal-self sits at the top of the brain's evolutionary hierarchy, oversees the organism's total relationship to environment, and offers partial autonomy of thought, movement, and control.

Following Gerald Edelman's logic [15], the self is a special configuration of brain cells supported by brain chemistry. The self is not an immaterial something that resides externally to the brain. The phenomenal-self always feels like an integral part of our physical body, except in pathology. Nevertheless, the self performs as a real, functional entity. And due to physical-mental monism of the brain-mind, the virtual, phenomenal-self disappears when its supporting neurons die.

The brain's neurons generate a virtual, phenomenal-self that only exists as long as the physical brain stays intact. In comparative fashion, a steam engine converts liquid water by introducing heat to produce steam. Consciousness, so to speak, is a dependent, electro-chemical product of cells converting energy [11, 22, 23]. however, this conversion process is a marvel of self-organizing, complex, transformative imaging neurons [24]. To be functional, the human brain must generate a special organization of cells that can act back upon other groups of neurons. We call this special configuration of dispersed cells across the various brain modules the phenomenal-self. Thus, bio-chemical processes support cellular action to form transformative sensory images that feel physical.

Our self as bio-chemical process disappears when we are in coma, under anesthesia, deeply asleep, or dead. Historically, treating the processes that generate the self as a real body part or, in Descartes' case something that was non-material and external to our body, created all kinds of confusion. Knowing that the self is a product of biochemical neuronal processes permits us to both foster and manipulate the contents and processes that generate our dreams and hallucinations. Image transformations that are the phenomenal-self, as well as the contents of consciousness, realize the vast potential of Metzinger's experiential brain space.

The proto-self of a newborn is more potential than reality. Self as a virtual entity grows along with our physical body. Initially our newborn self is reflected by our basic urges—eating, drinking, breathing, and filling our diapers. As newborn helplessness gives way to movement, ability to turn over, crawl, and then walk, the phenomenal-self grows in parallel. The concrete world of primary sensation gradually becomes increasingly abstract as we pass out of infancy. And with the growth of language, our individual world becomes more specifically defined and interrelated as we enter school and learn the complexities of our social environment.

As infants and young children, we feel the sensations of our bodies, and gradually experience the virtual creation of the phenomenal-self as a thing of substance. We feel the phenomenal-self as an essential part of who we are. Biological development, combined with environmental interaction, makes children natural essentialists. Realizing that the phenomenal-self is a virtual process, dependent on stimulation, fundamentally changes how we perceive children's socialization and formal education; and how we perceive the social order.

The intricate processes that create human subjectivity demand a conceptual framework that can handle the complexities of human-level evolution. The phenomenal-self is expressed in seemingly endless variations through gene-environment interaction. A phenomenal, autonomous, virtual self reflects the neuronal plasticity that allows *Homo sapiens* to dominate the globe.

Genetic plasticity supports the seemingly endless variations of how self is expressed through gene-environment interaction. Add the multitude of factors influencing embryogenesis and the post-partum socio-physical elements that affect our brain's development, and the word dynamic is not up to the task.

A sophisticated analytical framework is necessary to handle nature's most complex experiment—the creation of a brain that can

25

know and heal itself[7, 10, 24]. This framework includes systems biology and system dynamic theories from sources such as *The Origins of Order*[16], *Incomplete Nature*[25], *A Dynamic Systems Approach to the Development of Cognition and Action*[18], *Neural Darwinism*[15], *Being No One*[26], and *Mind in Life*[27]–to stress a few examples.

Systems biology incorporates dynamic analysis of all of our brain's modules and their evolutionary history. Complexity of emerging biological structures over millions of years supports a new level of development—cellular biology creating the virtual processes of our phenomenal-self. Dynamic systems psychology and physiology support the interpretation of psychogenesis that I've attributed to the formation of the phenomenal-self.

Science has yet to tease out all the intricacies of the human brain. How do all these automaton-like brain modules work to create the phenomenal-self as a functional entity capable of independent action? As knowledge of cellular and bio-chemical brain processes accumulate, we gradually come to understand how we humans can be self-aware. Unfortunately, human consciousness (subjectivity) was not considered to be a meaningful area of research throughout most of the 20th Century. Fortunately, a new emphasis on consciousness studies began to emerge in the 1980s.

Regarding human subjectivity, Allan Hobson says: "[We] need to work on a science of subjectivity. In order to utilize first-person data, we need to be both cautious and versatile[28]". From personal communications over the past six years and *Dreaming as Virtual Reality*, I'm reasonably sure that Hobson feels as I do—human subjectivity should be plumbed through a combination of studies in biology, physiology, neuroscience, psychology, and sleep/dream research.

It seems strange that so many thinkers and researchers should skirt the issue of human subjectivity. The assumption that human subjectivity cannot be affirmed or denied is increasingly outdated. Jaak Panksepp and Lucy Biven make a very strong case for animal subjectivity. Panksepp says: "The evidence is now overwhelming that all mammals have intense experiences when the ancient networks of their emotional brain are directly manipulated [29]."

Being aware of how the phenomenal-self gradually forms and matures provides insight into how changes occur in our dreams and hallucinations as we mature from infancy into old age. The study of dreams and hallucinations provides insight into the processes supporting the self [30]. Anything interfering with the biology that develops and maintains the phenomenal-self can distort how we think, feel, dream, and experience [31]. Understanding how the phenomenal-self forms and persists as process provides insights that we can apply across the lifespan and in all our musings across the professions.

Feeling our phenomenal-self as though it was a physical part of our brain is not really strange if we stop momentarily to consider how we react to sensory input. I experience emotion hearing great opera, at a physical level I feel the dynamic play of color with sunsets and sunrises, and I sense your presence. Virtual creations of the phenomenal-self are everywhere, and we feel them. When feeling stops, so does consciousness. Human-level subjectivity of secondary consciousness is probably the greatest gift that nature offers.

In summary, I've emphasized the importance of knowing how the higher cortical centers of our modular brains endlessly strive to integrate all of our sensory experiences (Panksepp's SEEKING System [19]). I've briefly followed various aspects of human maturation to acknowledge that we create a virtual world that we treat as though it were the real world. I've stressed that the phenomenal-self is a process of virtual creation that seems to be as much like an object as our heart does. These are core aspects of subjectivity that brings focus to our sense of possessing both corporeal and virtual selves: A phenomenal-self that feels corporeal but is a process.

For many of us, getting a handle on self as process might require rethinking ideas that we individually grew up with. Much of the world, including myself, has grown up thinking of self as an organ-like thing in our brains. Others have grown up thinking of self or "soul" as something spiritual or supernatural. Neuroscience confronts us with the reality that self is a virtual process that must always be supported by neurons. Now, I want to consider what is the relationship between the phenomenal-self and personality.

The Phenomenal-Self and Personality

The phenomenal-Self is conceived as a process of secondary consciousness that begins to form in the womb from a genetically given architecture [15, 32], matures and changes lifelong, and is capable of supervening over primary brain-mind processes. The phenomenal-self, so to speak, is the semi-permanent meta-role configuration that oversees our moment-to-moment relationships with our social and physical environments. It is a set of functional neural-biological processes in command of secondary consciousness. Always, neurons and biochemistry form the basis from which our phenomenal-self emerges and functions. Now let me tease out the differences between the phenomenal-self and personality.

Recent research by Roberta Riccelli and colleagues have identified five major personality types with neuro-brain imaging [33]. First, I'll review Riccelli and colleagues ground-breaking research, and then contrast personality with the phenomenal-self. Riccelli and colleagues found that five major personality types are formed from macro-level brain structures. They are: Individuals with high levels of *neuroticism* have increased thickness and reduced folding of the cerebral cortex. This brain structure is associated with a tendency to be in a negative state. *Extraversion* is associated with sociability and enthusiasm. *Openness* to ideas and experience, which is associated with creativity, curiosity, and novelty. These individuals had increased cortex folds and reduced thickness. *Agreeableness*— tendency to altruism and cooperativeness. *Conscientiousness*, which is a measure of self-control and conscientiousness.

I want to quickly note that Riccelli's, et. al, research is not saying that biology is the sole determinant of our personalities. Gene expression in the womb is subject to a multitude of factors from the mother's emotional state to environmental chemicals. Epigenetic factors in infancy and early childhood also help determine how life-experiences interact with our genomic inheritance. However, identifying these five basic personality types with brain structure is a major step forward with classification and potential early interventions with neuroticism.

Brain structures change as we age, and neuroticism predisposes us to develop neuro-psychiatric disorders such as autism and Alzheimer's disease. Luca Passamonti from the Department of Clinical Neuroscience at the University of Cambridge observes: "Linking how brain structure is related to basic personality traits is a crucial step to improving our understanding of the link between the brain morphology and particular mood, cognitive or behavioral disorders[ibid]."

Neuroscience is now linking brain morphology with personality traits and behavioral predispositions. This does not mean that we emerge from the womb predetermined. It does mean that we need follow up research to determine the extent to which the natural plasticity of the brain is subject to modification both before and after birth[34]. Riccelli and colleagues have taken a major step that can potentially lead to new and improved clinical interventions in neuro-psychiatric disorders. Now let me add clarity to the relationship between the phenomenal-self and personality.

The five basic personality types being presented are built on identifiable brain structures associated with the thickness and folding of the cerebral cortex. In contrast, the phenomenal-self is conceived as a dispersed set of neurons and processes that exist across the brain. Brain morphology predisposes self-expression to one of the five basic personality types. Personality types influence and guide us in our daily interaction with our social world, but also play a major role in how we perceive and interact with our physical world.

Personality types as specific brain configurations synergistically suggest modifications in how we classify "normal" versus pathological symptoms. In contrast, the phenomenal-self must have greater dynamic variability (neuronal plasticity) because it functions as if it is dispersed across areas supporting secondary consciousness, thus, subject to greater modification due to social influences. I will later explain how belief and bidirectional image transformations shape how we perceive and experience the world across states of consciousness.

In summation, personality types are associated with specific brain structures and the phenomenal-self is not. Genetics and epigenetic processes of personality formation are part of *Homo sapiens* evolutionary history. The phenomenal-self is an entity that is influenced by personality traits but is plastic to the extreme across cultures and how idiographic transformative sensation and images are generated and processed.

The following section adds additional clarification to my transformative view of the phenomenal-self using Niklas Luhmann's concept of structural-functionalism.

Using Niklas Luhmann to Interpret the Self and Its Memory

Following Luhmann, I'm reversing the traditional view of structure and process in dynamic systems theory in the following explanation of the phenomenal-self [35]. Historically, the social sciences thought of process as something that stems from structure. For example, the brain's structure of neuronal networks supports processes that become consciousness. Technically, this is a valid observation that needs to be teased apart.

Applying Luhmann's interpretation, consciousness as phenomenal-self-process can function as the semi-permanent, dynamic component of the brain, which in turn is supported by neuronal structure and related biochemical processes. Heuristically speaking, the brain's structured content of acquired memories supports the dynamic processes of focused phenomenal-self-consciousness. The phenomenal-self is capable of generating a past and future by accessing memory. Developmentally, memories accumulate over time, and start forming in the fetus. In this view, self and memories emerge together, as being dynamically interactive.

Development of the phenomenal-self as the autonomous part of secondary consciousness is the mechanism coordinating the organism movement in social and physical space. Thus, structures built by the developing fetus, infant, and adult center and draw upon learned experiences (memories) accumulated over time to evaluate the organism's ongoing relationship to environment. This process is an open system, dynamic interpretation of how human-level awareness and behavior emerges in the course of evolution. In brief, adding transformative imagery to a Luhmann-derived interpretation provides a simplified overview of my *Transformative-Dynamic Integrated Systems Model* (TDIS) [36].

Recapping: self-processes acquire a permanent quality, and what was previously perceived as structure being permanent (memory), is inverted and temporary. Memory is temporary in the sense that it is accessed moment-to-moment by the self as a guide to motricity. Memory is also temporary in the sense that it is constantly being changed and updated. Once I incorporate this paradigm shift in my thinking the confusion of self as a dispersed, ever-changing process evaporates. For related interpretations of self-processes, see Humberto Maturana and Francisco Varela [14].

Increasingly, brain science provides new information that destroys old myths and, at the same time, serves to deepen nature's mysteries. Neuroscience doesn't have all the answers about the self, nor of consciousness, dreaming, or hallucinations. But there is enough information for us to direct and control much of these virtual processes. Current knowledge permits us to rise above our anxieties and myth-driven fears. And control over states of consciousness permits exploration of this vast range of human subjectivity. The vast potential of our species *humane* growth lies before us. I am only one amongst a growing number who believe that knowledge of how our brains create reality is necessary for the survival of our species.

Our Virtual World

Children move in and out of fantasy play with ease. They practice many social roles from being princes and princesses to robots. Virtual role practice prepares us for life in the social world. At our secondary level of consciousness, virtual role practice is an integral part of how the phenomenal-self comes to acquire its socio-cultural configurations.

At our primary level of consciousness, where we acquire skills and behavioral competencies, mental practice can help hone motor routines found in sports, music, and complex physical routines. Sportsmen and women hone skill competencies by employing virtual routines. Mental practice integrates and consolidates skills in a manner similar to actual practice. Watch athletes at the Olympics and you will see these preparatory rituals repeated again and again. And then we have skill refinement in dreams.

Personal Case Study: Bike-riding as a self-process example

Research is increasingly supporting the idea that a major function of dreams is to integrate and consolidate experience [37, 38, 39]. Let me revisit my bike riding dream: I hadn't ridden a bicycle for about 30 years but began again upon retirement. I felt unsteady on my wobbly bike and had to reacquire my balance. Bike riding dreams began after a couple of weeks with supernormal abilities appearing in late morning episodes. I rode my dream bike over impossible terrain with ease. Mountain ledges were easily conquered, as were slopes and rugged terrain that would challenge a mountain goat. Typical of my dream-self, I noticed the disbelief of my dream observers. Notice how my phenomenal-self projects its own beliefs onto dream observers. The phenomenal-self can view its-self as self, or its-self as the "Other." Dream-self role plays a lot, and similar to waking roles, identity of the phenomenal-self appears to be reinforced 24/7.

As a quick aside, I want to call attention to what I perceive as the special type of memory consolidation occurring in this dream. My waking consciousness rides down city blocks one at a time. I stop appropriately, ride on the side of the road or in bike lanes; and I observe traffic, children, and animals. Neuronal conditioning in dreams does not follow this pattern. The focus of conditioning in my dreams appears to be that of honing groups of brain cells to fire automatically. And after a few weeks of biking practice, I ride effortlessly. I have internalized a fixed action pattern (FAP). Fantastic bike riding feats in these dreams are correlated with my actual skill acquisition, not with Freudian latent thoughts.

Responding consciously to our environment is slower and takes more focused energy than automated behavioral routines do. I assume that from an evolutionary point of view it's inefficient for a 24-hour mind to just shut down from dusk to dawn. Thus, dream imagery appears to be fine tuning skills on the brain's master templates. Dream imagery supports impossible scenarios that might be life threatening if I actually tried them on my daytime bike. Dreaming does, however, prepare us for tomorrow. Dreaming appears to help us prepare for a huge range of scenarios that goes beyond the single example of daytime biking.

Dream practice from this point of view gives us neuronal options for eventualities that have not yet happened. My biking dream elaborates the functionality of dream imagery as neuronal patterns are modified, embedded, and strengthened. This is a functional, not a waking logical preparatory sequence. Thus, dream learning is correlated with real-time functional activity.

To summarize this section, the brain provides an architecture on which we construct a virtual world and virtual, phenomenal-self. Dreaming is a process that carries over and helps embed behavioral routines in memory. At our secondary level of consciousness, an autonomous, phenomenal-self emerges as an ongoing, changing mechanism supported and maintained across the brain's global workspace. In Luhmann-like fashion, the self as process becomes the semi-permanent metacognitive agent that guides use throughout our lifetime. Memory upon which the phenomenal-self depends is an ever-changing substrate that is modified every dreaming night.

The Illusions in Dreams and Dual States of Consciousness

Feeling detached from our bodies can be triggered by oxygen deprivation, drugs, alcohol, physical trauma or direct electrical stimulation to the brain. Historically, people without knowledge of how the brain actually works associated feeling detached from their bodies with forces in their perceived spirit world. The effects of being out-of-body are dramatic regardless of our personal interpretations.

Once we begin to master the processes that create our virtual world, we are forced to rethink our childhood myths, and self-destructive beliefs. We stop believing our brain's illusion of being in direct contact with the physical world. With tongue-in-cheek, dear reader, the only time we are in direct contact with the world is when we're out-of-body.

We are in a position to play with these "magic," subjective imaging processes knowing that our brains transform input into vision, hearing, and touch across sensory modalities. Of most significance, however, is the realization that our brains can create all these virtual images without external stimulation. Lucid dreams/hallucinations can be our royal road to self-discovery.

The historical mysteries of dreams and hallucinations or visions are gradually yielding to science. I can attest that knowledge of how this all works in no way diminishes the psychological impact. What changes is admiration for the wonderful, complex brain that creates the human mind. Realizing that the brain can create *de novo* images of all sensations opens the door to creative manipulation of the content of many different states of consciousness.

Individually, when we transition from one state of consciousness to another, we can experience being in two states at the same time. Becoming possessed means that auto-created feelings transition from felt-presence to felt-possession. When we possess, say a totemic bear in what is called a shamanic trance, we enact a separate, virtual state of consciousness. Speaking-in-tongues (glossolalia) is a neuronal state that activates another configuration of brain-modules. This pattern of virtual creations repeats across what I define as different "forms" of consciousness states. Note that the contents of consciousness states are dependent on imagery transformations across sensory modalities.

We can replace anxiety with joyful anticipation and the excitement of discovery once we master major states of consciousness. It's a "wow" experience the first time we fly in a dream; it's even a bigger "wow" when we fly off the planet or zoom to a distant galaxy. It is "mind-blowing" when we activate this virtual imaging system during waking moments.

First compare the effects of observing our own dreams. As lucid dreamers, superhuman performances amaze us. But they no longer seem strange once we realize that this is just another act of creating virtual images in our brain. Knowledge that all of our brain's images, 24-hours a day, are virtual creations encourages a sense of compassion for people who are traumatized by uncontrolled, altered state imagery.

Personal Case Studies: Dream imagery and aging

At 85 years, I most often have dreams where I levitate or fly short distances. I also occasionally initiate above-earth and into-space flight that surpasses that of a childhood dream. I ask myself why my dream-mind now picks driveways and large buildings. I suspect that my ageing body, and growing concern with balance and heights, has something to do with both my joint waking and dreaming sense of vulnerability. I'm very conscious in my dreams that my body is no longer the owner of youthful agility. Typically, but not always, I only become a superhero in my dreams if I age regress. This is dream logic: Apparently, agility associations are being stored in my brain with my youthful prowess.

I demonstrate my ability to jump long distances in some of these dream scenarios. I'll jump over a 50-foot driveway, or at the extreme I'll jump over my driveway, travel past my neighbor's driveway as well, before I land. I tell my dream body not to jump further than that lest observers discover that I can fly. Again, this kind of thinking is common dream logic [40].

In a second, frequent dream, I'm in a large building and climbing around the rafters. A missing beam or some other obstruction blocks my progress. Evil forces might be pursuing me, or I might only be showing off. If a beam is missing, I fly over to the next handhold or ledge continuing without pause on my way. I frequently check to see if other people are aware of and admiring my super abilities. They usually are. "Egos" have free reign in our dreams. "Egos" can be deified in our visions. *Egoism lights up our dreams and visions like a streetlamp on a dark night.*

From age eight, and into my adult dreaming years, I flew around the planet and into outer space. I was fearless about heights both while awake and in my dreams. This all changed when my body aged and my physical abilities declined. Declining balance has changed my waking comfort on tall buildings and mountain ledges. I was surprised when this caution became part of my dream life. Nevertheless, my "Genesis Journey" to the beginning of time took place in my mid-60s. If you are an older reader, be prepared for similar changes in your dreams. My physical ability, and my relationship to environment, is automatically incorporated into my dreams. What currently gets incorporated in my dreams depends on my subjective, waking self-image. Note that this waking-dreaming relationship suggests a metacognitive awareness—an awareness that the phenomenal-self can and does transcend states of consciousness. A question for the therapist: How can we apply these insights and self-therapy processes to dissociative personality disorder?

Uncensored dream-selves are like those of a small child showing off a newly acquired skill. Dreamers commonly report their "egos" as nakedly self-centered as mine. My dream-self is not any more special than yours. I interpret these egoistic urges the way I interpret being hungry. Raw physical urges and emotions have direct expression in our dreams—dreams do not routinely censor primary emotions. Addicts of all kinds experience the controlling effects of habitual urges firsthand as they seek another "hit."

Dream Logic

Higher order logic is disconnected when we dream. All that polite stuff we learned when growing up fails to check our basic dream urges and emotions. Our sex and hunger drives are as fundamental to our physical makeup as breathing and thirst. Minds are controlled by neurons that support biological and emotional needs, not by "spirits," and not by logic.

Lucid dream observation means that our half-awake brain has access to waking logic while observing superhuman dream feats. While dreaming lucidly, we can remind ourselves that we are dreaming and continue to enact whatever supernormal feats we chose. We are logically being illogical. Managing dual states of consciousness permit us to fully enjoy these illusions.

Skipping back to my toddler out-of-body experience in the hospital, I projected out-of-body automatically. As adults, we can use various techniques to leave our body in both dreaming and waking states. However, as a child, my body and mind always felt like they moved together across various state of consciousness. The monism of brain-mind dictates that mind and body are experienced as moving through space and time together.

I was afraid to fly more than a few feet above the ground or over water until I was seven years old. As children, our virtually constructed world is terribly concrete. The Easter Bunny and Santa Claus are just as real as Uncle Fred. The line between "pretend" and external reality is as thin as a razor's edge. Thus, children's minds are rich with boundless possibilities to imagine things and mix fact and fiction. All of these developmental differences affect how and what we dream or even hallucinate.

Logic distortion in our dreams reminds us that what we think is normal depends on our history, state of consciousness, and the chemical state of our brain. Similarly, we shouldn't be surprised to find logic distortion when our brains are steeped like a tea bag in drugs or pharmaceuticals. Recovering drug addicts commonly experience a variety of brain-imaging distortions firsthand. Knowing how the brain is affected by its own chemistry or externally ingested chemicals, psychologically prepares us for these reality shifts. Awareness can prevent suicide.

Our waking minds demand logic that is tuned to perceived reality. But perceived reality always depends on belief, and how the different modules of our brains are physically communicating across different states of consciousness. I suspect that a lifetime of lucid dreaming adds a reality dimension to my dreams that non-lucid dreamers might not experience. My growing familiarity with dream research enhances respect for my own individuality. Dream forms (so aptly clarified by Allan Hobson) tell us that logic is disconnected, time and space is violated, and muscles are detached [40]. Further, dream content can have tremendous variation between individuals and across cultures. Remember as you analyze your own dreams that dream content is subject to individual beliefs and how our subjective interpretations are transformed into imagery.

Sources: Chapter 2: The Brain's Neurophenomenological Configurations

1. McNamara, Patrick. (2009) The Neuroscience of Religious Experience. NY: Cambridge University Press.
2. Metzinger, Thomas. (2009) The Ego Tunnel: The Science of the Mind and the Myth of the Self. New York: Basic Books: 211.
3. Kauffman, S. (2010) Reinventing the Sacred: A New View of Science, Reason, and Religion. New York: Basic Books.
4. Ibid, Metzinger, (2009), 218
5. Ibid, Metzinger, (2009), 217
6. Hobson, Allan. (1988) The Dreaming Brain: How the Brain Creates both the Sense and the Nonsense of Dreams. NY: Basic Books.
7. Just, Glen (2009) Autobiography of a Ghost. Mankato, MN: Eagle Entertainment USA.
8. Furlanetto, Tiziano., et al. The bilocated mind: new perspectives on self-localization and self-identification. *Human Neuroscience.* 08 March 2013. https://doi.org/10.3389/fnhum 2013.00071.
9. Llinas, R. R. (2002) i of the Vortex: From Neurons to Self. Cambridge, MA: A Bradford Book, The MIT Press.
10. van der Kolk, Bessel. (2014) The Body Keeps the Score: Brain, Mind, and Body in the Healing of Trauma. New York: Viking.
11. Hobson, J.A. (2009) The neurobiology of consciousness: Lucid dreaming wakes up, International Journal of Dream Research, 2 (2), pp. 41-44.
12. Hobson, J. A. (2016) Dreaming as Virtual Reality: A New Theory of the Brain-Mind. Clarendon: Oxford University Press.

13. Baars, Bernard B. J. & Gage, Nicole M. (2010) Cognition, Brain, and Consciousness, 2nd Ed. New York: Elsevier, Academic Press.
14. Maturana, Humberto R., & Varela, Francisco J. "Autopoiesis," in Autopoiesis and Cognition: The Realization of Living (Dordrecht:Reidel, (1980), 59-134.
15. Edelman, Gerald (1987) Neural Darwinism: The Theory of Neuronal Group Selection. Philadelphia: Basic Books.
16. Kauffman, S. (1993) The Origin of Order. New York: Oxford University Press.
17. Walker, M. P. (2009) The Role of Sleep in Cognition and Emotion. Annals of the New York Academy of Sciences, 1156: 168-197. Doi: 10.1111/j.1749-6632,2009.04416.x
18. Thelen, Ester; & Smith, Linda B. (1996) A Dynamic Systems Approach to the Development of Cognition and Action. Boston: MIT Press.
19. Panksepp, Jaak & Biven, Lucy. (2012) The Archaeology of Mind: Neuroevolutionary Origins of Human Emotions. New York: W. W. Norton & Company.
20. Arbruster, B. B. (1989) Metacognition in Creativity, 177-182.
21. Schooler, Jonathan W. meta-awarenes, perceptual decoupling and the wandering mind. *Cell Press*, vol. 15, Issue 7, July 2011, pp. 319-326.
22. Friston, K. (2009) The free-energy principle: A rough guide to the brain, *Trends in Cognitive Science*, **13** (7), pp.293-301; Friston, K. (2012) A free energy principle for biological systems, *Entropy*, **14**, pp. 2100-2121.
23. Lee, Jonny. A problem of scope for the free energy principle as a theory of cognition. Philosophical Psychology. Pub. Online: 11 Jul 2016.
24. Hobson, J. A. (2014) Ego Damage and Repair: Toward a Psychodynamic Neurology. London: Karnac.
25. Deacon, T. (2012) Incomplete Nature: How Mind Emerged from Matter. New York: W. W. Norton & Company.

18. Ibid, Thelen & Smith. (1996).

15. Ibid. Edelman. (1987).

26. Ibid, Metzinger, (2009). Being No One: The Self-model Theory of Subjectivity. Boston: MIT Press.

27. Thompson, Evan. (2010) Mind in Life: Biology, Phenomenology, and the Sciences of Mind. Belnap, Harvard University Press.

28. Hobson, J. A. (2016) Dreaming as Virtual Reality: A New Theory of the Brain-Mind. Clarendon: Oxford University Press.

29. Ibid, Panksepp & Biven. (2012), 391.

30. Windt, Jennifer. (2015) Dreaming: A Conceptual Framework for Philosophy of Mind and Empirical Research. Cambridge, MA: The MIT Press; The immersive spatiotemporal hallucination model of dreaming. Phenomenology and the Cognitive Sciences, June 2010, Vol. 9, Issue 2, pp. 295-316.

31. Kaplan-Solms, Karen & Solms, Mark. (2000) Clinical Studies in Neuro-Psychoanalysis: Introduction to a Depth Neuropsycyology. New York: H. Karnac Books Ltd.

32. Hobson, J. A. (2009) RE sleep and dreaming: towards a theory of protoconsciousness. Nature Reviews Neuroscience 10 (11), 803-813.

33. Roberta Riccelli, Nicola Toschi, Salvatore Nigro, Antonio Terracciano, Luca Passamonti. Surface -based morphometry reveals the neuroanatomical basis of the five-factor model of personality. Social Cognitive and Affective Neuroscience, 2017; nsw175 DOI: 10. 1093/scan/nsw175.

34. Tyssowski, Kelsey M., et al. Different Neuronal Activity Patterns Induce Different Gene Expression. *Cell Press*, DOI: https://doi/10.1016/j.neuron.2018.04.001.

35. Luhmann, Niklas. (2013) Introduction to Systems Theory. Ed. Dirk Baecker. Cambridge, UK: The Polity Press.

36. Just, Glen A. (2012) Dreams, Creativity & Mental Health. Mankato, MN: Eagle Entertainment USA.

37. Walker, M. P. (2009) The Role of Sleep in Cognition and Emotion. Annals of the New York Academy of Sciences, 1156: 168–197. doi: 10.1111/j.1749-6632.2009.04416.x.
38. Hobson, J. A., & Friston, K. J. (2012) Waking and dreaming consciousness: Neurobiological and functional considerations. Progress in Neurobiology, 98(1), 82-98.
39. Tononi, Giulio, & Chiara Cirelli. "Perchance to Prune." Scientific American; August, 2013.
40. Ibid, Hobson. (1988).

CHAPTER 3

Metaphorical Image Transformations

Image transformations that we can observe in dreams and hallucinations occur at two levels in the brain—primary and secondary. Initial sensory image transformations, such as light into color or air vibrations into sound, have traditionally been called qualia in philosophy. Secondary image transformations occur further downstream in the brain and are organized around subjective meaning[1]. What we initially perceive are primary sensory image transformations that we call sight, sound, or touch. What the brain constructs at our secondary level of consciousness is typically referred to as concepts.

How the brain moves from primary to secondary imaging and back again (from secondary concepts to primary percepts) is the critical question under consideration. My previous books provided background for the observation of bidirectional image transformations in dreams and hallucinations in my autobiography (2009), in altered states of consciousness (2011), and the relationship between physiological mechanisms and transformative imagery (2012). In this section, I want to reemphasize that transformative images (TFI) are fundamental to the interpretation of dreams, hallucinations, and psychogenic illnesses. (I more fully develop the relationship between psychogenic illness and transformative imagery in other works.)

Historically, the brain's secondary transformation of sensory images has been labelled illusion, delusion, fantastical creations, dream nonsense, and psychotic images. Thus, transformative images have been given all kinds of mystical and religious interpretations. It is through long-term analysis of dreams and hallucinations that I tease apart these various meanings of transformative imagery. With TFI consilience, however, I attempt to cut across the vagaries of historical, cultural, and disciplinary language.

First, let's explore observations of transformative imaging in dreams? Building on the subjective nature of dream imaging requires consideration of processes taking place in both our higher cortical centers and the brain's core dynamics. From personal experience, suggestion and belief activate processes that call forth new images across all of the senses—sight, sound, touch, taste, and smell. I will spend little time in this book with taste and smell as primary senses; however, as dream analysis demonstrates, the brain can create taste and smell *de novo*, from scratch, as it does with visual, auditory, and kinesthetic sensations.

I conceptualize transformative imagery as a central component of the brain's "software" that is running on its neuronal hardware. In agreement with Evan Thompson, I use the language of mechanics and cybernetics with the terms software and hardware even as I reject the computer-computational model that attempts to explain our brain as an information processing machine[2]. Automatic processes in our brain's core dynamics are the automaton correlate of machine computation. However, unlike computers, humans have higher cortical centers that can autonomously direct, re-direct and control these automatic processes. More pointedly, computers do not transform sensory images according to belief, biochemical-mood, or subjective meaning.

The Oxford American Dictionary (1980) defines metaphor as "the application of a word or phrase to something that it does not apply to literally, in order to indicate a comparison with the literal usage as the evening of one's life." An example might be: evening is a literal time of day, but evening of one's life is the metaphor. In the language of dreams, metaphor is the sensory transformation that is created by our brain's automatic imager. In dreams, bottom-up metaphorical transformations turn emotions into visual, tactile, and auditory images. For example, in my broken ankle dream transformative imaging turned pain into bad guys. A top-down, metaphorical dream transformations turned the concept "hole" into a concrete entity in which as a 5-year-old child I suspended myself in a dream submarine.

Thus, primary images (qualia) are the literal "something" in dreams, which is compared to the evening of one's day. Secondary, transformative visual images of bad guys are the metaphorical representations of the literal something that is ankle pain. In both image transformations, there is a literal something that is not being referenced. The confusion in dream metaphor image transformations is that the literal something that is being referenced (e.g., pain) has undergone transformation into a visual something and been personified (e.g., bad guys). Thus, pain to personified bad guys is a kind of metaphorical synesthesia.

I'm using dream metaphor to recognize the special way our imaging generator transforms primary sensations (emotions) and secondary images (feelings) into things. (I'm following Damasio's *The Feeling of What Happens* in my distinction between emotion—primary affect and feeling—secondary affect). Metaphorical image transformations occur with visual, auditory, and felt sensations. Ankle pain that hurts becomes dream visuals of bad guys, a loud sound in my house becomes a gunshot in my dream and being hot and sweaty leaves me in a dream world full of various watery scenes.

In my use of transformative imagery, I'm addressing both primary and secondary image transformations that can be under the control of the self at either a conscious or non-conscious level. Of necessity, the self must come to maturity accommodating the brain's mechanics from which it emerges. Consciously or non-consciously transformative imaging occurs automatically. In my reading of Freud, he imposed reified linguistic mechanisms to substitute for the normally nonconscious and invisible processes of transformative imaging. As I've demonstrated with dream programming (scripting), regardless of the sources stimulating sensory transformations in dreams, the self can learn to direct or re-direct them[3].

Without long-term dream analysis, metaphorical imaging is usually experienced at a nonconscious level. In altered states of consciousness, whether dreaming or hallucinating, the self typically takes image transformations at face value, as it does when awake. Without lucidity, the self tends to interpret sensation as being veridical within any of its given states of consciousness.

Following Allan Hobson's protoconsciousness theory[4], I conclude that the brain starts developing primary sensory maps (templates) in the womb, and that these maps are the fundamental structures around which all subsequent sensory input is organized, compared, and modified. Maps as I'm using the concept are groups of neurons that become active through stimulation. Thus, specific maps are not genetically given, nor do they just occur automatically. Neurons require use in order to record sensory experience, avoid pruning, grow, and make dendritic connections.

According to the metaphorical image transformation hypothesis, primary image templates across our senses underlie literal references such as pain and colors, and what is being compared is the metaphor—secondary image transformations. For example, pain in my healing right ankle is a sensory image that has been built around a primary neuronal map. This image is metaphorically transformed by my dreaming brain into bad guys torturing me. Sensation is made concrete and observable in our dreams and hallucinations through these transformative processes. In effect, for the phenomenal-self to be socially active in dreams, it must personify its sensory pallet. Language specificity both helps concretize and personify our physical and animated social world.

Lakoff and Johnson refer to sensory images, such as front and back, up and down, inside and out, as "Metaphors We Live By[5,6]." I use their concepts of metaphor as primary sensory images that begin to form in the womb and, from these maps all subsequent images are formed, reformed, and transformed. Recall that bi-directional metaphorical transformative imaging taking place in our dreams and hallucinations applies to any of our emotions or thoughts. Also, note that I also assume that primary neuronal templates efficiently build complexes of associated memories on this fetal architecture. Associations created by neurons and dendrites are energy efficient. The brain doesn't just fill up by adding new content; the brain builds on and rearranges its developmental files. In other words, the brain gets rid of stuff it doesn't use as it rearranges neuronal connections and builds new, updated memories. The memory capacity of our 3-pound brain is now thought to equal the entire content of the Internet[7] The prodigious and instant image creations experienced in dreams and hallucinations is supported by this Internet comparison.

The careful reader will also be aware that getting rid of superfluous neuronal connections builds the brain's capacity to abstract. Ability to abstract means that pruning superfluous neuronal connections day-to-day while building experience brings into relief what is most functional to the developing child or adult. Furthermore, this neuronal abstracting process that we observe in dreams is metaphorical by definition.

The "hole" in my Japanese submarine nightmare is the secondary image constructed top-down from meaning derived from language by my brain's image generator. My five-year-old brain heard ship's "hold" as "hole." Thus, attribution of meaning determined the content of the transformed images. As a virtual dream image, my phenomenal-self was able to escape into this "concretized" hole. In my experience, nowhere is the structural and functional role of the phenomenal-self as clear as it is in dreams.

In terms of protoconsciousness theory, the architecture of fetal proto-imaging must be forming an image that distinguishes between its body and its outside environment. Thus, I'm following Lakoff and Johnson's metaphor analysis, the primary fetal image of "hole" is derived from the inside of a container. The developing fetus already has an outside environment. As an example, "hole" as a primary fetal map is the substrate upon which a 5-year-old's brain later images a hole in a dream submarine.

As a secondary image derivative, "hole" has as many metaphorical references as our higher cortical developmental history provides— the empty space in my love-starved heart, or a break in the clouds. Nevertheless, my transformative image generator instantly forms whatever "hole" is subjectively relevant to the narrative script unfolding in my dreams or hallucinations. Transformative imaging as a hypothesis stresses the importance of subjective meaning to the organism. Thus, an additional nail is hammered into the coffins of strict behaviorism and related computational theories of the brain.

In my submarine nightmare, "hole" is a place for a small child to hide. Fear is the source of its metaphorical image transformation. Bottom-up metaphorical image translation in dreams turns emotional elements into concrete visuals and felt sensations. Top-down imaging transformations turn ideas, thoughts, and concepts into concrete visuals, and felt sensations. Thus, I interpret primary metaphors as the building blocks around which all of my sensory images are derived. And, I'm attempting to demonstrate that under guidance of the phenomenal-self our transformative image generator can operate bidirectionally[8], bottom-up and top-down across states of consciousness.

I ask the reader to imagine how anyone can become familiar with transformative imaging that is only available in first-person observations without dreaming lucidly. Try using third-person technology such as functional magnetic imaging (fMRI) to reveal these transformative processes. Nevertheless, we need fMRI-type research to triangulate subjective meaning with brain physiology.

Lucidly observing dream characters, like my real Chinese spouse, Ruby, experientially suggests that there is some type of primary racial template around which her dream features are constructed. Pre-and-post-sleep, and daydream dual state imaging can morph and shift the same as dream imagery. Comparing imagery in various states of consciousness suggests access to a common set of primary image templates, as well as a common transformative imager. Additionally, we observe that image transformations are energized by belief and subjective meaning[9].

However, note that lucid observation of dreams and hallucinations helps clarify the phenomenal-self's role in secondary image transformations. What our secondary image transformations create from womb to tomb, across states of consciousness, depends on our higher-order, subjective interpretation of sensory input—how the brain attributes meaning to experienced sensory stimuli. Thus, it is not the complexity of neuronal connections alone that determines human level consciousness; that is, the "connectome[10]".

I'm arguing that computers will never have human-level consciousness until they can duplicate the sensory image transformations under discussion. More pointedly, to have human-level consciousness computers must be built to duplicate primary emotions and then have the ability to transform emotion into secondary feelings and imagery.

The Elements of Sensory Dream Metaphor

In review, fetal REM can be observed at about 30 weeks of gestation. Infant awareness of the mother's voice[11,12,13], music preferences and tastes[14] suggests emergence of some type of self-organizing neuronal network that controls primary imaging. I assume that newly emerging neuronal structures form proto-images that represent all of our senses, not only the visual. Also, these newly emerging neuronal structures must be preparing the fetus to spatially experience its after-birth environment, and to coordinate movement.

I recognize that nature endows us with an architecture—neuronal maps—upon which to build this proto-imaging capacity. I've stressed that these early maps of sensory images appear to become the building blocks around which later, more refined images can be formed, maintained, and changed. I further assume that language plays a critical role in the later refinement of images; a point I've stressed with my "hold/hole" example.

Now I'll connect the functional neuronal groupings of proto-imaging with dream metaphor. I'm starting with the assumption that proto-images become the core maps upon which all later, more complex sensory data will be organized. How does long-term dream analysis lead to this interpretation?

Personal Case Study: Dream image of my Chinese spouse, Ruby

I seem to have a visual, proto-image, memory template of people of European-appearance with whom I grew up. With few exception, I spent the first 18-years of life with people of European appearance, and these images dominate my primary memory files.

When I first arrived in China for a three-year teaching stint, all Chinese looked alike. Of course, this is an exaggeration, but generally correct. It took me a full year to separate Chinese students according to their finer features. Conversely, my Chinese students told me that all European people look alike to them. Shifting our predominant racial environments requires time to overcome what appears to be primary image imprinting. From this perspective, physical-social stereotyping is a natural byproduct of how the brain's neuronal architecture organizes imagery. Thus, racial stereotyping is not just a social phenomenon. Epiphenomenally, we all stereotype other racial groups. Dream analysis indicates that in-group identification is a byproduct of how neurons record sensory information.

In my dreams, Ruby is a European-appearing composite: A person whose physical image changes from dream to dream. My dream characters do not appear to be of Asian or African origin; although an African or Asian image may occasionally appear. I recognize Ruby by my dream feelings, not by her physical appearance. Emotion and feeling in dreams take precedence over transformative imagery, not cognitive experiences. Note the interpretive confusion that results if I expect dream Ruby to look Asian, or dream imagery to be like a photograph. Or if I assume I'm free of racial stereotypes. However, visual stereotyping does not automatically lead to discrimination. Adding to the confusion, dream images of Ruby change from dream to dream. Lucidly focusing on Ruby's physical features, while dreaming, will also elicit facial morphing. Nevertheless, Ruby's dream image is typically a European-looking composite. Emotion is the dominant element that helps me identify Ruby and the dream's meaning. The dream character I'm interacting with or making love to resides in its own physical-emotional map. I identify dream characters by clues contained in these dual physical-emotional composites.

Uniquely to my personal history, dream Ruby is being recomposed physically on a European map. She is being visually misrepresented, but emotionally true to life. This is the dual emotional-physical aspect of dream character metaphor. Now, let me focus on dream metaphor that emphasizes emotion only. Again—Ruby! (I believe the above interpretation of memory templates partially addresses what Freud called the latent and manifest content of dreams).

Personal Case Study: Emotional-based images in dreams of Ruby

My dreaming brain accesses an emotional memory file I label "Irritating Women." I'm using memory file to represent how my brain appears to organize emotional associations of women in my life whom I've found irritating. In similar fashion, if I go to bed in a state of anger, a plethora of images appear in my dreams of people and situations that have previously made me feel angry. My memory associations reflect this global aspect of feelings.

Ruby has good reason to worry excessively due to her experiences in Post-Revolutionary China. She went through a number of years when her parents were sent to the country, resulting in hardships for the entire family, which included a broken back for her father. Ruby also interrupted an attempted stoning of her grandfather by instigations of the Red Guard when she was 8-years-old. In waking life, after a certain amount of excessive worrying on her part, I become irritated and, following my dream prompting, intervene to stop her agitation. My dreams have flagged the point where my tolerance levels are being exceeded—a kind of built-in marriage counselor.

My composite, visual images of Ruby are not literal, but the subjective feelings are. I know who she is by how I emotionally react to her, not by identifying words, such as "the love of my life." To paraphrase Temple Grandin's words, the "acting self" is organized around dream metaphor, and the "thinking self" is dictionary metaphor[15]. I think of this duality as something that is both cognitively and emotionally integrated. However, I logically separate cognitive and emotional imagery in order to better interpret my dreams.

Brain chemistry plays a large role in dream analysis[16]. Chemistry-guided animal behavior before frontal lobes created dictionary definitions[17], or secondary transformative imaging. Biochemically speaking, love is not defined by words; love is an emotional state of being. To emphasize the biochemical point, how does your dreaming brain image the effects of any neurotransmitter such as dopamine, norepinephrine, or acetylcholine? What do chemical shifts in global brain states feel like when we go from a dreaming state of consciousness with cholingergic dominance, to a waking state with aminergic dominance[18], or in a dual state of consciousness when we are half awake and half asleep[19,20]? So often, waking logic is illogical when it ignores brain chemistry and related transformative imaging.

Let me further clarify my use of cognitive dream metaphor before I tie various components of dream imagery and memory associations together. Creative elements of cognitive dream metaphor are more abstract and represent a shift from primary to secondary cognitive and emotional images that support and underlie cognitive associations. (In agreement with Antonio Damasio[21], and neuroscience generally, I'm assuming that there is always an emotional element in cognitive units employed in thinking).

My brain associates writing books with similar activities from my teaching background. Writing elicits dreams where I'm in the classroom lecturing, holding academic discussions or wandering half-lost around a university campus. Actual physical settings, former teaching colleagues, and students populate these dreams. My dream memory associations connect with my entire history as a teacher-writer-thinker. Thus, I note efficient neural processing where pruning and reorganization of neurons and dendrites has and is occurring functionally.

If the material I've been writing about is clear, I give meaningful dream lectures that can be incorporated into what I'll write about when awake. If I'm struggling with how to express something clearly, my dream lectures can seem like nonsense. In either case, I know my mind is processing and struggling with my new book. Below is a specific example from 30 October 2013.

Personal TFI example from my teaching background

I've been struggling with reorganization of this book and, almost daily, I rewrite or move sections around. I find this aspect of writing highly irritating. I have a table of contents beside my computer that looks like a 3-year-old has been scribbling. A dream version of my book's organization has been appearing repeatedly for over a month. I taught as a full-time professor for 20-years. Each term, I'd create or modify course outlines. In my current dreams, I'm associating organization of this book with those course outlines from my teaching history. In the following dream, my classroom is large with what appears to be over 100 seats.

There are three entrance/exit doors. Sometimes my desk, not a lectern, is elevated on a stage; other times the entire room is on one level. The course I'm teaching is introductory. I have a 3-ring-binder full of notes. I search through my notes and cannot find today's lecture. I mentally review material that should be covered and decide to "wing-it." In some dreams, I start lecturing; in others, I engage in discussion. Some dreams end before I can begin the class. I didn't initially realize the source of my memory associations for these dreams until weeks of similar dreams. We more fully appreciate how brains make associations when we follow our dreams over time.

Complex thoughts become metaphorical dream images by recreating scenarios from our histories, such as my teaching example exemplifies. Dreams also metaphorically transform the emotional reactions to life's struggles into concrete visual images. In somewhat of a reverse fashion, real-life associations drawn from memory become images as the dreaming brain wrestles with problem-solving: For example, reorganization of this book becomes associated with course outlines and old teaching environments. The self seems to be searching through its memory files for answers. As Jaak Panksepp argues, our "SEEKING system" is a primary component of our core-self dynamics[22].

This almost inexplicable process is a more complex set of memory associations than I wish to unravel here. The short version, however, is that my nonconscious brain organizes my waking thoughts by putting my dream-self in similar social and physical environments stored in associated memories. Thus, in my dreams, I lecture, hold discussions, write on blackboards, and read from text. However, during my waking moments, I'm only writing this book.

The brain appears to store information efficiently by building on preexisting neuronal templates. When we attempt to find causal waking relationships, we come up empty-handed, or contrive Freud-like explanations. However, when I interpret dream images associated with the classroom, I quickly realize that my brain is wrestling with materials for my new book, not exploring old teaching memories.

I more fully appreciate dream associations when creative product emerges. Dream interpreters have difficulty if they always expect to directly associate dream imagery with waking events or try to find waking cause and effect relationships. Metaphorical dream image transformations are often as complex, or more complex, than my teaching example. Thus, finding more direct waking relationships is often a lost cause.

A Gestalt-type thematic pattern is represented in both cognitive and emotional dream scenarios. In both cognitive and emotional thematic patterns, I "feel" the correctness of an idea, or the emotional integrity of a person. When life's scenarios occur according to my subjective expectations, they feel "right." From this point of view, "feeling right" acknowledges an emotional component being part of all sensory images. Thus, the emotional content of concepts recorded in neurons makes them feel right.

Following my dreams over the decades reminds me that emotional elements permeate even my most cognitive thoughts. When we stop feeling, we no longer have primary consciousness. When we stop transforming primary sensory images, human-level secondary consciousness disappears. Partial disruption of secondary consciousness occurs when we stop being able to connect feelings with relevant elements in our external environments. The world then feels bewildering and illogical.

The Holism of Sensory Dream Images

Visual sensory images are formed by 30-plus centers in the brain. The binding process that instantly forms composite characters in dreams is efficient and functional. Dream images of physical people, places, and things are not true to life; emotional images appear to be. Emotions are metaphorically turned into concrete visuals. As sensory binding occurs, all of these processing components are put together further downstream in the brain. Mentation that supports thought is experienced as abstract, visual processes for some of us; for others—word associations. For the Temple Grandin's and others like her, concrete abstractions dominate.

Building on the notion that all images have emotional content, I observe metaphorical transformation of feeling into concrete entities in my dreams that are central to my self's experiential world. Most critically, emotions turn into dream visuals and are assigned authors. Thus, dream characters become concrete, metaphorical image transformations of my emotions. In parallel fashion, during waking moments when we hallucinate, this transformative imaging process can turn auto-created physical sensations into felt "things" that can be perceived as if they are possessing us. Note the complexity of these brain processes—we auto-create a sensation, hold the sensation in memory, and then add concrete attributes of possession. In this dual cognitive-emotional aspect of consciousness, our transformed images can create visual hallucinations that can be single picture or movie-length stories.

I would miss these critical metaphorical image transformations if I didn't analyze dream content over an extended period of time. In summation, transformative imaging in dreams automatically turns emotion into concrete personifications. To be observed, personifications require an author—some "one" has to be observing. When a parallel of this transformative process occurs during waking hours, we subjectively experience another "presence" or feel as if we're being possessed by someone or something else[23]. These are aspects of dreams commonly missed in the laboratory.

Thoughts and cognitive images appear as words for some types of brains, as visuals for others. For instance, Einstein first visualized gravity and later transformed it into words and formulae. I too am an abstract visual thinker and often struggle to transform my visuals into words. Thus, I'm drawn to dictionary metaphor during my waking moments.

Transformative Dream Generation as a Source of Creativity

I'm looking forward to research that compares dream imagery to the dominant type of imagers we are: Visual or word, different types of sensory pattern organizers, or a combination of types. I suspect that people whose brains organize with words will have greater difficulty moving across and controlling various states of consciousness—a testable hypothesis. I speculate that neuronal distance from primary image templates is related to different types of creativity. In other words, the less convoluted access is to primary image templates, the greater is our level of creativity—another testable hypothesis.

Let me contrast my use of "Types of Imagers" with Perrine Ruby's research at the Lyon Neuroscience Research Center in France[24]. Ruby uses the term "Types of Dreamers" to mean "types of dream re-callers." Simplifying his research findings—people who sleep lightly recall more dreams than sound sleepers do. My cognitive-writing dreams make all kinds of nonconscious associations with physical landscapes, books, lectures, and discussions that "feel" academic. Thus, thoughts that I struggle with during the day are transformed in my dreams into an entire associative learning environment of school, books, lectures, and discussions. Sometimes these dream processes generate meaningful dream lectures, which in turn lead to waking epiphanies. At other times, the dream's physical learning environment occurs without insightful discussions or lectures. Commonly, the dream sequence continues for a number of nights until I resolve my problem.

The image transformations that occur with dream metaphor start with primary images in my neural networks transforming sensory and emotional elements into various kinds of secondary images. This transformative process appears to lie at the heart of creativity. Meaning: new neuronal connections that were not there when I went to bed are made in my dreams. Here's the critical point: what we call "creative ideas" derive from secondary image transformations as the result of new network connections. In my experience, dream lucidity encourages creative image transformations by connecting neuronal channels between primary and secondary consciousness. Automatic transformative imagery then becomes available to waking consciousness—another testable hypothesis.

I find it useful to think of the metaphorical image transformations in dreams as being dynamically generated from the primary templates upon which new memories are being written as old memories are being modified or discarded. Dream imaging is thematic in that so many different memory associations can be attached to the same core neuronal patterns. In one sense, they are abstract Gestalt-like patterns where proto-imaging templates are transcended and connect numerous specific examples. Consequently, I'm viewing creative thought as a form of neuronal reconfiguration, which can lead to new image transformations. In my lucid dream examples, we can learn to embellish and guide these images with active self-intervention. It's fun to lie in bed in a dual state of consciousness guiding an existing dream plot into new territory.

Transformed proto-image templates are thus hypothesized to underlie the initial processes of thematic abstractions, as well as Gestalt-like patterns, from which dream transformative imagery is derived. Thus, I hypothesize that photographic images are only retained in memory when they have strong emotional associations or represent special imprinted memories, such as those associated with trauma.

Creating a dream image, such as I do with my spouse, occurs by mixing and matching image elements from memory. Critically, thematic associations—physical and emotional—and our reactions to dream characters remain even as facial and bodily features change. Transformative features of our image generator, derived from ever changing neuronal templates, apply to all manner of substance—landscapes, people, a specific location, written materials, and a myriad of other things. Nevertheless, images such as Ruby's transform from dream scenario to dream scenario; while at the same time, the way I feel about her remains the same. As Norman Doidge observes, *The Brain that Changes Itself* is highly plastic[25].

My Ruby example in which my dreams mix and meld sensory information supports the protoconsciousness work of Hobson and Friston[26], as well as that of Lawrence Rosenblum, a professor at the University of California, Riverside. Quoting Rosenblum:

"Scientists have known for a few decades that certain brain regions integrate information from distinct senses. One region might, for example, meld visual information with somatosensory perception, such as touch and temperature. It now turns out that multisensory perception is a much more prevalent aspect of the brain's neural architecture than researchers realized, suggesting that the brain evolved to encourage such sensory cross talk"[27].

In my experience, the extent to which sensory information has been melded in the brain is more fully appreciated when we follow transformative imaging processes in our dreams. Information is not only melded in the Hobson-Friston and Rosenblum sense; information is transformed to meet the needs of subjective reality— belief and suggestion. We humans subjectively create meaning and then turn subjective meaning into concrete visuals in our dreams and hallucinations.

What is illogical to waking consciousness, such as my dreaming of riding a bike with superhuman skills, is metaphorically correct if my busy neurons are fine-tuning skills. I understand the underlying basis of dream metaphor, transformative imaging, as my brain's way of efficiently integrating and consolidating cognitive and emotional materials in my neural networks. Twenty-four hours, daily, my brain-mind is a meaning-maker.

In dreams, there is a type of cross-sensory processing that occurs with transformative imaging—a kind of synesthesia, if you will. This overarching process of metaphorical image transformation suggests researchable avenues of exploration as neuroscience unravels the intricate connections in various types of synesthesia itself. The phenomenal-self is busy creating virtual reality moment-to-moment. All manner of synesthesia can result when cross-talking sensory modalities employing transformative imagery get "wired" the wrong way.

In sum, dream metaphor is a process whereby new images, such as Asian Ruby, are derived from existing neuronal templates, such as the European. Moment-to-moment dream transformations reflect skill and image refinement that builds on existing coarser-grained primary patterns. And as noted, language specificity helps refine these coarser-grained patterns. Dream metaphor includes the attachment of new feeling elements to existing emotional architecture, and the concrete things to which our emotions have become associated. The language used to interpret dreams is metaphorical as defined. Note that secondary image transformations permit complex human emotions and emotional controls that are probably not possible for mammals and birds that are dependent on primary imaging alone.

Personal Case Study: A dream about classifications

On 2 June 2013 during an afternoon nap, I had a dream about classifications. I was in discussion with a number of other people and pointed out that yellow things go in yellow holes and white things in white holes. This is seeming nonsense as I saw no objects but was merely referring to "things." I awoke and, as I was pouring myself a glass of water, I realized that I had not finished my present, real-life book section on dream metaphor. I recalled that dreams of my spouse Ruby always image her as a person of European racial background. Thus, I was reminded that my racial stereotypes are derived from some type of primary neuronal templates—they are not only cultural constructions.

Image transformations in my afternoon nap were referring to Chinese (yellow things) and Europeans (white things)—a straightforward, metaphorical reminder that on first blush seemed like nonsense.

Much like Gestalt patterns, dream image transformations bring focus to a person's immediate physical and emotional state. Primary image files that began to form in the womb as proto-images appear to become the referential base for later cognitive and emotional image development. This analysis also suggests that the pregnant woman's emotional state, via body chemistry, might be influencing primary emotional templates in the developing fetus—biochemistry has its own neuronal conduits for chemical signaling.

The holism of sensory dream images takes the total person into consideration—developmental age, sexual orientation, and situational influences such as anxiety, stress, and physical trauma[28]. In other words, the major influences that make each one of us unique determine the content of transformative, metaphorical images that appear in our dreams. Our entire developmental history shapes a dynamic set of epigenetic neuronal processes. The neural content of our personal history determines the transformative images that emerge in our dreams and hallucinations. Hence, interpreting imaging across states of consciousness requires a psycho-neuro-phenomenological perspective.

The language of dreams is confusing if we cross-reference different published sources. Much of the confusion rests with occult and mystic interpretations. However, a good portion of the confusion resides with dream analysis by different disciplines—psychology, sleep and dream labs, neuroscience, philosophy, and religion. I've attempted to cut through a small part of this interdisciplinary confusion by combining bottom-up research with top-down deductive reasoning supported by transformative imaging analyses across states of consciousness.

I'm suggesting that better mental health by controlling dreams and hallucinations requires consideration of the image transformations that I've been discussing. Better mental health follows acquisition of knowledge that goes beyond the occult and popular dream "pulp fiction" that is so prevalent in American culture. Knowledge of transformative imaging processes can potentially help us to set aside these popular and occult interpretations.

Sources: Chapter 3: Metaphorical Image Transformations

1. Neisser, Ulric. (1966) Cognitive Psychology. NY: Appleton-Century-Crofts: 299.
2. Thompson, Evan. (2010) Mind in Life: Biology, Phenomenology, and the Sciences of Mind. Belnap, Harvard University Press.
3. Just, G. A. (2009) Autobiography of a Ghost. Mankato, MN: Eagle Entertainment USA.
4. Hobson, J. A. (2009) REM sleep and dreaming: towards a theory of protoconsciousness. Nature Reviews Neuroscience 10 (11), 803-813.
5. Lakoff, G., & Johnson, M. (1980) Metaphors We Live By. Chicago: The University of Chicago Press.
6. Lakoff, G., & Johnson, M. (1999) Philosophy in The Flesh: The Embodied Mind and Its Challenge To Western Thought. New York: Basic Books.
7. Salk Institute. Memory capacity of brain is 10 times more than previously thought. http://www.eurekalert.org/path releases/2016-01/si-mco012016.php.
8. Zheng, Chenguang and Colgin, Laura Lee. Beta and Gamma Rhythms Go with the Flow. DOI: http://dx.doi.org/10.1016/j.neuron.2014.12.067.
9. Pace-Schott, Edward F. Dreaming as a story-telling instinct. Frontiers in Psychology, doi: 10.3389/fpsyg.2013.00159.
10. Seung, Sebastian. (2012) Connectome: How the Brain's Wiring Makes Us Who We Are. Boston: Houghton Mifflin.

11. Partanen, Eino. Babies Learn to Recognize Words in the Womb. Brain and Behavior, 27 Aug. 2013.
12. DeCasper, A. J., & Fifer, W. P. (1980) Of human bonding: new-borns prefer their mothers' voices. Science, 208(4448), 1174-1176.
13. Kisilevsky, B. S., Hains, S. M., Lee, K., et al. (2003) Effects of experience on fetal voice recognition. Psychological Sciences, 14(3), 220-224.
14. Kisilevsky, B. S., Hains, S. M., Jacquet, A. Y., Granier-Deferre, C., & Lecanuet, P. P. (2004) Maturation of fetal responses to music. Developmental Science, 7(5), 550-559.
15. Grandin, T. & Panek, R. (2013) The Autistic Brain: Thinking Across the Spectrum. New York: Houghton Mifflin.
16. Hobson, J. A., & McCarley, R. W. (1977) "The brain as a dream state generator: an activation-synthesis hypothesis of the dream process." Am. J. Psychiatry 134, 1335-1348.
17. Panksepp, Jaak & Biven, Lucy. (2012) The Archaeology of Mind: Neuroevolutionary Origins of Human Emotions. New York: W. W. Norton & Company.
18. Hobson, J. A. (1988) The Dreaming Brain: How the Brain Creates both the Sense and the Nonsense of Dreams. NY: Basic Books.
19. Voss, U., Holzmann, R., Tin, I., & Hobson, J. A. (2009) Lucid Dreaming: A state of Consciousness with Features of both Waking and Non-lucid Dreaming. Sleep, 32(9).
20. Hobson, J. A., & Just, G. A. (2013) "Lucid Hallucinations." In Hallucinations, Causes, Management and Prognosis. Ed. Sofia Alvarez. Hauppauge, NY: Nova Science Pubs.
21. Damasio, A. R. (2010) Self Comes to Mind: Constructing the Conscious Brain. New York: Pantheon.
22. Ibid, Panksepp & Biven. (2012).
23. Ibid, Just, G. A. (2009)

24. Ruby, Perrine. http://www.dailymail.co.uk/sciencetech/article-2562551/Can-You-remember -dreams-Researchers-uncover-people-recall-morning.html#ixzz2toScwihW.
25. Doidge, N. (2007) The Brain that changes Itself: Stories of Personal Triumph from the Frontiers of Brain Science. New York: Viking.
26. Hobson, J. A., & Friston, K. J. (2012) Waking and dreaming consciousness: Neurobiological and functional considerations. Progress in Neurobiology, 98(1), 82-98.
27. Rosenblum, L. D. "A Confederacy of Senses." Scientific American, Jan. 2013, 73-75.
28. Cartwright, R. D. (1977) Night Life. Englewood Cliffs, NJ: Prentice-Hall, Inc.

PART II

Plasticity Of The Phenomenal-Self In Dreams And Hallucinations

Part II reviews and demonstrates how the effects of suggestion, belief, mood, and language create content in dreams and hallucinations. I present my personal classification of dreams and focus on how different types of sensory stimuli influence dream content. Lucid analysis of dream content is a first step to unravel how image transformations are generated by specific forms of sensory stimuli.

Brain and mind are not separate entities. Brain-mind is a single monistic entity maintained by biochemical and cellular processes. There are no homunculi or nonmaterial entities in brain-mind. Nevertheless, as a single monistic entity, the brain-mind as self can be in a dual state of consciousness. As noted, dream lucidity is a dual state of consciousness where one part of the self is observing while another part is engaged in some type of action.

Allan Hobson and Robert McCarley's research[1] on the biochemistry of dreams and Hobson's elaboration of dream forms in the 1970s and 1980s shifted attention away from Freudian dream content analysis. Dream forms mean that in a dreaming state of consciousness muscles are detached, logic is suspended, and movement, time, and space are distorted. Thus, I'm arguing that form and transformative content are two interrelated components of dreams and hallucinations needed to successfully interpret their meaning.

Learning to lucidly control dreams and hallucinations in a dual state of consciousness permits potential control over and enactment of whatever dream or hallucinatory content we choose[2,3,4]. Controlling dream and hallucinatory content sheds new light on the dynamic, bidirectional image transformations occurring in these states of consciousness[5,6]. And, lucidly controlling the contents of consciousness provides a new window of observation on the autonomy of self.

In the spirit of first-person phenomenal research, note that the virtual and psychogenic processes entertained can only be observed in dual states of consciousness. The hard sciences of physiology and cellular biology can document brain activity related to psychogenic processes, but basic science cannot yet determine what these processes subjectively mean to the individual who experiences them. Furthermore, explanations of the hard sciences, although fundamental and necessary, do not come to grips with how the critical variables of belief and suggestion influence image transformations.

Lucid, cross-state analysis of dreams, hallucinations, and other altered states provides a means by which to view neuronal associations generating transformative imagery. Thus, combining phenomenal and empirical methods to interpret image transformations across states of consciousness offers a psycho-neuro-phenomenal model of how self comes to mind[7].

Setting the Stage to Analyze Bidirectional Image Transformations

As we prepare to review bidirectional image transformations in dreams and hallucinations, specific aspects of the proposed psycho-neural-phenomenal model need to be made explicit.

1. Dreams are an altered state of consciousness where higher order logic and muscles get disconnected from waking consciousness and times and spaces can be mixed in endless combinations as these elements are drawn from memory. Dreams represent a consciousness state where most sensory input is from internal sources—most notably, memory. Nevertheless, dream content can be and is influenced by a combination of external and internal stimuli.

2. Being able to follow image transformations in dreams through the use of lucidity opens a new window of meaningful insight into these brain-mind processes. From a practical point of view, understanding how sensory images are transformed by the brain-mind opens the potential to control nightmares and daytime hallucinations[8,9].

3. Dreams are both windows to our minds and a major source of self-understanding. With a little effort, we can learn to control much of our dreaming, or even program entire pleasant dream substitutes for nightmares[5].

4. Image transformations at our secondary level of consciousness turn primary process emotions into feelings, as well as concretizing and personifying these feelings.

5. In contrast to dreams, hallucinations are a dual state of consciousness where sensory input is coming from both our external environment and memory, and logic and muscles remain operative. This dual state of hallucinatory sensory processing tricks our brains into believing we have entered another dimension or plane of reality.

6. Hallucinations are "normal" expressions of our wonderfully creative minds, and like programming entire dreams, hallucinations can be enacted on command. Once we learn how to enact narrative hallucinations, the mystical visions of human history are no longer mystical. We all have hallucinations to some degree: The hat rack mistaken for an intruder, shadows on a dark street that are ignited by

imagination, haunting voices in an empty house, and most frightening of all are the "spirits" that physically touch us. Once we come to understand these fundamental image transformations, we no longer need to be controlled or frightened by them.

7. A critical part of interpreting dreams and hallucinations is to understand how belief, suggestion, and mood affect image transformations. We do not live in an external world defined by physics and chemistry, but in an "imaginary" world, a phenomenal world, created in our brains through the transformation of visual, auditory, and tactile sensations. How we transform sensory input into perceived reality is of central importance to understanding self and consciousness.

Thomas Metzinger supports a psycho-neural-phenomenal model of consciousness that appears to be compatible with the basic model being proposed. Specifically, he addresses the historical neglect of consciousness by the brain sciences:

> "The fact that we can actively design the structure of our conscious minds has been neglected and will become increasingly obvious through the development of rational neuroanthropology"[10].

Metzinger's "rational neuroanthropology" resonates with the basic assumptions of the psycho-neuro-phenomenal model being proposed. The following quote from Metzinger emphasizes the importance of combining empirical and phenomenal research. "There is an enormous number of possible neural configurations in our brains and [a] vastness of different types of subjective experience. Most of us are completely unaware of the potential and depth of our experiential space. The amount of possible neurophenomenological configurations of an individual human brain is so large that you can explore only a tiny fraction of them in your lifetime"[10].

In the following pages, I will try to demonstrate that transformative imaging (TFI) of sensory experience is fundamental to understanding states of consciousness we call dreams, hallucinations, visions, and out-of-body experiences. What follows is a description of my 60-plus years of first-person experiments interpreted within contemporary neuroscience research.

Bidirectional image transformations covered in this book can only be observed lucidly in dreams and other altered states of consciousness. Critically, I consider bidirectional transformative imagery of sensory stimuli to be the mechanism that generates the phenomenal-self—a self that is aware that it is aware.

SOURCES: PART II: Plasticity of the Phenmenal-Self in Dreams and Hallucinations

1. Hobson, J. A., & McCarley, R. W. (1977) "The brain as a dream state generator: an activation-synthesis hypothesis of the dream process." Am. J. Psychiatry 134, 1335-1348.

2. Voss, U. (2010) Lucid dreaming: reflections on the role of introspection. International Journal Dream Research, 3: 52-53.

3. Voss, U., Holzmann, R., Tuin, I., & Hobson, J. A. (2009) Lucid Dreaming: a State of Consciousness with Features of both Waking and Non-Lucid Dreaming. Sleep, 32 (9), 1191-1200.

4. Hobson, J.A. (2009) The neurobiology of consciousness: Lucid dreaming wakes up, International Journal of Dream Research, 2 (2), pp. 41-44.

5. Just, G. A. (2009) Autobiography of a Ghost. Mankato, MN: Eagle Entertainment USA.

6. Just, Glen A. (2012) Dreams, Creativity & Mental Health. Mankato, MN: Eagle Entertainment USA.

7. Just, G. A. (2015) Convergence of Subjective and Objective Methodologies in Consciousness Research, in Advances in Psychology Research. Volume 103, Hauppauge, NY: Nova Science Publishers, Inc.
8. Ibid, Just, (2009).
9. Hobson, J. A., & Just, G.A. (2013) "Lucid Hallucinations." In Hallucinations, Causes, Management and Prognosis, Ed. Sofia Alvarez. Hauppage, NY: Nova Science Publications.
10. Metzinger, Thomas. (2009) The Ego Tunnel: The Science of the Mind and Myth of the Self. New York: Basic Books.

CHAPTER 4

❧

Dreaming: The Effects of Belief, Suggestion, and Mood on Image Transformations

Image Transformations Are Age Dependent

Fetal brains at birth show awareness of their mother's voice[1], music preferences[2,3], and tastes[4]. Infants are not born with a blank mind; they are born with a brain that is already proto-consciously learning about the world they are about to enter. It's a myth to believe that the mind at birth is a blank slate.

The fetus displays rapid eye movements (REM) by about 30 weeks of gestation. Rapid eye movements occur during our most active periods of dreaming. During this time, the brain is as busy as it is during our waking moments. REM brain activity does not necessarily mean that baby-in-tummy is dreaming. REM activity probably means that the fetus is gearing up brain functions associated with life-survival behaviors such as nursing and preparing the brain's architecture to process all of the sensory inputs that will soon be experienced from its total environment.

Without reportable dream imagery, infants and toddler's overwhelming feelings of dread are experienced as night terrors. A monster from TV, being scared by an older sibling, experiencing newly broken bones, or living in a battering family—all can precipitate night terrors, bad dreams, or nightmares. Dream imagery is commonly treated as subjective fact by pre-school children.

The cultural meaning of words and related emotions are built together[5]. My mother defined "ghosts" as real entities. She then attached meaning to these entities, telling me they were magic beings that could enter and take control of my body and mind. When mythical beings such as "ghosts," the "Devil" and other evil spirits are defined as supernatural beings with power and the ability to enter and possess our minds and bodies, great emotional trauma can be experienced by children, as well as adults. Myth conveyed to children as fact becomes part of their subjective reality. Most critical, however, subjective reality whether based on myth or real-world facts is turned into sensory image transformations across states of consciousness.

Response to our children's dreams becomes an integral part of how they perceive reality. As children, we not only believe the myths of our parents, but we also turn these myths into concrete dream and hallucinatory imagery. Even more devastating during our waking states of consciousness, once we accept definitions of "ghosts" and spirits as real entities these mythical creatures gain power over us. The subjective reality of mythical beings is the lesson we take from comparative world cultures.

Dream and altered state interpretations are as much a part of our emotional and physical development as is food. It is not psychiatric symptoms or the Diagnostic and Statistical Manual of Mental Disorders[6] (DSMs) that define reality for each of us it is our individual attributed meaning. In other words, it is the reality that resides in human subjectivity. It's marginalization to tell children that they must experience the world according to the historical subjectivity of DSMs, or as we adults do. Our brains and socio-cultural histories are much more complex than one-size-fits-all. Cultural context is critical to understanding children's physical, social, and emotional development.

To a considerable extent, at our secondary level of consciousness life experiences do not directly enter our waking or dreaming states, only our subjective interpretations do. What interpretation enters our dreams is the subjective meaning we give to our waking experiences.

For example, the overly indulged child tends to feel deprived by the same rewards that bring joy to a child of poverty. An eagerly awaited rag doll for a child of poverty has a different meaning to an affluent child who is expecting a $1,000.00 doll house.

Each of us possesses a mind supported by a unique brain. Dream imagery is a product of subjective interpretation, and the special way our brain through its developmental history makes associations. It's important to recognize that subjective meaning guides the child in both waking and dreaming states. And it's extremely important that we attempt to see the world through the eyes of our children[7].

Dream imagery varies from child to child because of the individual, subjective way our brains translate language and feelings into "pictures," auditory, and tactile sensory images.

Suggestion Influences Dream Imagery

Suggestion is just what the word implies. While awake, we can use suggestion to tell ourselves what we want to dream. For example, a child confronted by a dream monster over a number of nights might be coached this way, "Honey, when the monster appears, tell him that you're his friend." Or "Dream monsters are the Cookie Monster in disguise." Or "Give it a hug and you will be friends for life." Use the animals and imaginary characters in your child's life. Suggestion can be used by children or adults. At a more accomplished level, suggestion can be used to program entire dream scenarios[8].

Krakow and Neidhardt[9] discuss techniques related to "Guided Imagery" and cognitive-behavioral therapy. These therapists are a helpful source as how to use one's own beliefs to influence and shape cognitive-behavioral outcomes. Lucidity in dreams can be used to employ guided imagery to instantly create the desired image (s). However, instant transformations of dream characters or other elements usually occur at a nonconscious level.

Suggestion and guided imagery can be used at all age levels. However, all age groups require use of image suggestion at their own level of comprehension. Belief comes before objective facts. We need to set aside adult "objectivity" with children. Using "scientific facts," while ignoring adult beliefs, can be equally disastrous. The therapist's job is to help the afflicted turn dream monsters into friends or permanently subdue them. With extra effort, we can learn to auto-create whatever pleasant dream scenarios we desire. The phenomenal world of subjective image transformations is as plastic as is our neural networks.

Dream programming that substitutes pleasant scenarios for nightmare trauma can be used to control nightmares for decades[10]. However, complete substitution of dreams requires learned control over the automatic imaging that naturally occurs in a dream altered state of consciousness. Dream substitution also requires employing self as an active agent. Active involvement in dream control calls into question passive client roles common to traditional psychoanalytic talk therapy.

Suggestion turned into belief affects individuals of all ages. If adults appear to be possessed by the "Devil," the priest or shaman's role is that of exorcist. Quick historical reflection informs us that exorcism came before talk therapy or pharmaceuticals, and exorcism still works. The exorcist treats belief—subjective reality—as fact. In similar fashion, parents can help children overcome traumatic dreams by judiciously treating the child's subjective image transformations as fact.

The brain isn't constructed to deal with the objective world as a science-based entity. Brains image the world in a subjective manner that facilitates functional survival, not as the world actually exists.

Effects of Mood and Auto-Suggestion in Dreams

Emotional need—conscious or unconscious—transforms the images in our dreams and hallucinations. Modern day occultists use these transformative imaging mechanisms to create a civilization on another planet, even visit and watch it change, as well as have all kinds of exciting encounters. Individuals immersed in their own religious beliefs use some form of auto-suggestion to enjoy journeys to the spirit world, nirvana, or their special place in "Heaven." Thus, expectation and/or suggestion triggers these "movies" in our minds, and our brain's automatic, transformative imager provides the action.

Drugs and pharmaceuticals can modify neuronal connectivity in our brains at any age. We can be horrified, disgusted, or pleasantly titillated by these auto-created images and journeys. Critically, we recognize the central role of emotions, beliefs, and expectations in the type of story or vision that our brain's global dynamics automatically generate[11].

The contents of our dreams and hallucinations change when we change our feeling states. Change our beliefs, and we change both the meaning and content of our mind's automated imaging processes across states of consciousness. Controlling dream imagery, through any means, has major implications for quality sleep and our daytime emotional wellbeing.

At a global level of brain activity, we create dream and hallucinatory images and related themes through our expectations, and the automaticity of our imaging system provides relevant content. The automaticity of these brain processes makes the content totally convincing while the "movie" unfolds.

Creating new chapters in our dreams or narrative hallucinations, adds substance to the assumed veridicality of these altered state images. We believe there is another reality out there because we can repeatedly visit our imaginary worlds whenever we want. Hence, it is easy to believe that spirits are working through or trying to control us. If we expect the "Devil," he shows up. If we expect "Heaven," it appears. If we think our neighbor is manipulating our mind with his computer, we feel his control as automatically as we transform images in our dreams.

If you've never enjoyed or experienced any of these latent capacities of your own mind, don't laugh. Exciting dreams and other worldly hallucinations feel just as real as any waking experience. A really dramatic and vivid dream or hallucination can affect us for days. We can be terrified or feel ecstatic. The choice is ours when we learn to use suggestion, and master control of other states of consciousness.

Personal Case Study: Language creates imagery

Individually, we translate the cultural meanings conveyed by language into sensory images, and the images that emerge in our dreams and hallucinations generally depend on our language sophistication and developmental age. The following example is from my "Japanese Submarine Nightmare" at age five.

After being hospitalized as an infant of about 15- or16-months, I was able to fly out-of-body whenever I wanted. Years later in my Japanese nightmare, I suspended myself in the "hole" of their ship. "Hole" was my five- year- old subjective interpretation of the submarine's "hold." Nevertheless, my dream image generator created a hole in the submarine and I virtually suspended myself in it. Note that "hole" as a transformed object, combined with my dream ability to fly, provided a dream-logic escape route. This nightmare stayed with me into university years and the "hole-hold" imagery was consistent for decades.

Children's dreams become more elaborate by the time they enter school. The richness of school social life is reflected in their dreams. With expanding social contact comes increased dream narrative action and character development[12,13]. Younger preschool children have more concrete, static dream imagery. After entering school, dream imagery begins to take on movie-action quality. However, it would be an overgeneralization to say that preschooler's minds form pictures, and school-age minds make movies.

Dreaming as Adults

Dream content complexity parallels our waking brain's development and changes from infancy through our adult years. Dreaming is an altered state of consciousness that has both physical and emotional consequences: The healthy, in control person understands *The Twenty-Four Hour Mind*[14].

In a state of lucidity, we can watch the brain's transformation of emotions and moods into dream imagery[15]. To my knowledge, the automatic transference of feeling into imagery can only be observed in lucid dreams and hallucinations. Knowing how to change dreams or control hallucinations can make us better parents, it can make us healthier individuals, and it can make us more compassionate companions to the elderly.

Recalling Dreams and Hallucinatory Imagery as Adults

Personal Example: My first recall of altered state visual imagery was my toddler out-of-body, near-death experience at 15/16 months of age. These early images remain vivid life-long. I recall floating at shoulder height between my father and the nurse, looking down at my dead body, and journeying off to "Heaven." On the way, I met "angels" who were dressed like my aunts and uncles, and about the same age. I refused "Heaven," returned to bedside, decided I didn't want to be dead, and reentered my body. Calling attention to the language confusion that exists across disciplines, some would call this experience a vision, some would point out the similarity with dreams, and others would use the term hallucination.

Note the concrete specific appearance of visionary images as aunts and uncles. Note the attribution of meaning given to a typical near-death experience by a toddler. Note the ability of a newly forming self to act by refusing "Heaven" and deciding to reenter its body. Also, imagine the "Heaven" and "angel" discussion that was probably occurring over my newly announced dead body.

Lucidly moving across states of consciousness, from waking to dreaming, calls attention to common aspects of imagery in these various states[16]. Nevertheless, a major developmental difference between small children and adults is adult fluid image motion and character complexity during dreaming.

Helpful sources to understand children's dream recall are found in Cartwright and Lamberg (1992) and Foulkes (1999). For sources on infant memories see Doidge[17].

Personal Case Study: My hallucination at age 50

When I was in my late 50s, I had a vivid hallucination of being in a crib and being attacked by my mother. At the time the hallucination occurred, I was undergoing a form of specialized management training and seated on the floor in a yoga pose. Without warning, the room and trainer quickly faded from my consciousness to be replaced by the attack scene. I recall that the scene transition happened like a Hollywood movie, in which one scene fades as another replaces it[18].

Memories can be triggered by emotional situations, specific environments, physical posturing, or a combination of many different elements[19,20,21,22,23]. We associate some element in our immediate environment with an earlier memory. I suspect that the way I had been sitting in the dimly lit room of the adult training session led me to recall this memory of being attacked in infancy.

Recalling memories from physical posturing is a form of what used to be called "muscle" memory. Lucid dreaming reminds us that memory association, across all of our senses, mixes and matches times and places. However, as noted, these dream-forms also occur in spontaneous hallucinations.

The term muscle (proprioceptive) memory is being used in the sense of a nonconscious memory that is brought into conscious awareness[24]. In this crib attack example, sitting in a yoga position approximated my posture in the crib. Admittedly, the veridicality of this interpretation can be questioned due to my young age. Nevertheless, 50-years after the abuse, the subjective imagery remains and is extremely vivid.

Our brains bind and integrate complex memories from different sources—muscles, focus of attention, emotions, sight, or any combination of our senses[25]. Thus, the "memory residue" from one or more of our sense triggers recall of the total scene. For me, this meant activating non-conscious memories in a yoga position with dimed lighting. System biology[26,27] takes all of these elements into consideration and "system psychology" recognizes that functioning brain modules are dynamically interacting with each other and taking input from both memory and environment.

Early memories from infancy are rare. In that we adults have about 60 percent of a 3-year-old's brain's neurons, it seems reasonable that many of our early childhood memories should disappear as these surplus connections are pruned off because we don't use them[28]. And, this pruning process of "use it or lose it" continues throughout our lifetime.

Sleep and dreaming employs pruning, along with the formation of new neuronal connections, to shape and reform our memories over our lifetime. To help us update memories, the hippocampus produces a relatively small number of new brain cells daily, about 1,400[29]. The idea that the brain could generate new neurons was rejected through most of the 20th Century. Today, neurogenesis is gradually coming under the microscope of science[30,31,32,33].

Sources: Chapter 4: Dreaming: The Effects of Belief, Suggestion, and Mood on Image Transformations

1. DeCasper, A. J., & Fifer, W. P. (1980) Of human bonding: new-borns prefer their mothers' voices. Science, 208(4448), 1174-1176.
2. Kisilevsky, B. S., Hains, S. M., Lee, K., et al. (2003) Effects of experience on fetal voice recognition. Psychological Sciences, 14(3), 220-224.
3. Kisilevsky, B. S., Hains, S. M., Jacquet, A. Y., Granier-Deferre, C., & Lecanuet, P. P. (2004) Maturation of fetal responses to music. Developmental Science, 7(5), 550-559.
4. Baars, Bernard B. J. & Gage, Nicole M. (2010) Cognition, Brain, and Consciousness, 2nd Ed. New York: Elsevier, Academic Press: 476
5. Panksepp, J. (2008) The Power of the word may reside in the power of affect. Integrative Physiological and Behavioral Science, 42, 47-55.
6. Frances, Allen. (2013) Revised Ed. Essential of Psychiatric Diagnosis: Responding to the Challenge of DSM-5. New York: The Guilford Press.
7. Gold, Claudia M. (2011) Keeping Your Child in Mind: Overcoming Defiance, Tantrums, and Other Everyday Behavior Problems by Seeing the World through Your Child's Eyes. Cambridge, MA: A Merloyd Lawrence Book, Perseus Books Group.
8. Just, G. A. (2009) Autobiography of a Ghost. Mankato, MN: Eagle Entertainment USA.
9. Krakow, B. & Neidhardt, J. (1992. Conquering Bad Dreams & Nightmares: A Guide to Understanding, Interpretation, and Cure. New York: The Berkley Publishing Group.
10. Ibid, Just (2009).
11. Pace-Schott, Edward F. Dreaming as a story-telling instinct. Frontiers in Psychology, doi: 10.3389/fpsyg.2013.00159.

12. Foulkes, David. (1999) Children's Dreaming and the Development of Consciousness. Cambridge, MA: Harvard University Press.

13. Cartwright, Rosalind, & Lamberg, Lynn. (1992) Crisis Dreaming: Using Your Dreams to Solve Your Problems. London: Aquarian/Thorsons.

14. Cartwright, Rosalind. (2010) The Twenty-Four-Hour Mind. New York: Oxford.

15. Hobson, J. A. and Just, G. A. (2013) "Lucid Hallucinations," in Hallucinations, Causes, Management and Prognosis. Ed. Sofia Alvarez. Hauppauge, NY: Nova Science Pubs., Inc.

16. Ibid, Just (2009). Just (2012) Dreams, Creativity & Mental Health. Mankato, MN: Eagle Entertainment USA.

17. Doidge, N. (2007) The Brain that changes Itself: Stories of Personal Triumph from the Frontiers of Brain Science. New York: Viking: 237 & 381-382

18. Ibid, Just (2009)

19. Zhang, Jie (2004) Memory process and the function of sleep (6-6 ed.) Journal of Theoretics. Retrieved 2006-03-13.

20. Barrett, Deirdre. An Evolutionary Theory of Dreams and Problem-Solving in Barrett, D. L. & McNamara, P. (Eds.) The New Science of Dreaming, Vol. III: Cultural and Theoretical Perspectives on Dreaming, New York: Praeger/ Greenwood. 2007.

21. Revonsuo, A. (2000) "The reinterpretation of dreams: an evolutionary hypothesis of the function of dreaming". Behavioral Brain Science 23 (6):877. Doi:10.1017/ S0140525X00004015.

22. Crick, F., Mitchison, G. (1983) "The function of dream sleep". Nature 304 (5922): 111-114. Doi:10.1038/304111a0. PMID 6866101.

23. Stickgold, R., Hobson, J. A., Fosse, M., (Nov. 2001) "Sleep learning, and Dreams: Off-line Memory Processing". Science

294 (5544): 1052-1057. Doi:10.1126/science.1063530. PMID 11691983.

24. Stepper, S., & Strack, F. (1993) Proprioceptive determinism of emotional and non-emotional feelings. Personality and Social Psychology, 64, 211-220.

25. Girn, Manesh., Mills, Caitlin., et al. "Neural Dynamics of Spontaneous Thought: An Electroencephalographic Study". Chapter in Augmented Cognition, Neurorecognition and Machine Learning: 11th International Conference, AC 2017, Held as part of HCI International 2017, Vancouver, BC, Canada. DOI 10.1007/978-3-319-58628-1_3.

26. Shapiro, Lawrence. (2011) Embodied Cognition. New York: Routledge.

27. Kauffman, Stuart. (1993) The Origins of Order: Self-Organization and Selection in Evolution. New York: Oxford University Press.

28. Tononi, Giulio, & Chiara Cirelli. "Perchance to Prune." Scientific American; August, 2013.

29. Kheirbek, Mazen A., & Hen, Rene' "Add Neurons, Subtract Anxiety." Scientific American; July 2014.

30. Ericksson, P. S., Perfilieva, E., Bjork-Ericksson, T., et. al. (1998) Neurogenesis in the adult human hippocampus. Nature Medicine, 4, pp. 1313-13-17.

31. Gould, E., Beylin, A., Tanapat, P., Reeves, Al, & Shors, T. J. (1999) Learning enhances adult neurogenesis in the hippocampal formation. Naure Neuroscience, 2, pp. 260-265.

32. Boldrini, Maura. Human Hippocampal Neurogenesis Persists throughout Aging: Cell, Apr 5, 2018 ...https://www.cell.com/cell-stem-cell/abstract/S1934-5909(18)30121-8.

33. Costandi, Moheb. (2016) Neuroplasticity. Cambridge, MA: MIT Press.

CHAPTER 5

✿

Dream Types: A Personal Interpretation

There is no standard classification of dreams in the research literature. In fact, there are still researchers who think that dreams are just static in the brain. The following dream types are the author's own creation, drawn from 75 years of observed dream patterns.

My dream types are organized according to specific types of stimuli that influence their content. Dream content is emphasized because image transformations in dreams are influenced by secondary states of consciousness top-down (cognitive) as well as by primary states bottom-up (affective). Dream forms, such as character composites or logic distortions, are present in any of the dream types.

The functions of dreams are another matter[1,2,3,4,5,6,7,8]. Dream functions that are emphasized integrate and consolidate experience, process emotions, and support the maintenance of cellular and self-processes. Analyzing the uniqueness of image transformations in dreams is a journey of self-discovery.

We humans are one of a kind, both genetically and developmentally. We process and interpret experiences in our own unique, subjective way. Thus, my dream types should only be taken as generalizations and guides. Nevertheless, I believe the following first-person dream observations resonate well with contemporary dream research.

Observing image transformations across dream types contradict popular cultural interpretations. Dream books that suggest standardized meaning for dream content are misleading. Sigmund

Freud is included in both criticisms. There are dream guide books that will tell you the specific dream meaning of everything from acorns to zucchini. I reviewed a number of these books in *Dreams, Creativity & Mental* Health[9] and will not repeat them here. Instead, dream type reviews will demonstrate how subjective meaning influences experiential reality and image transformations. All examples are drawn from my personal dream records.

Typical Dreams

There are common dream images that most of us tend to have, such as being naked in public, or being unable to locate a toilet someplace. We are talking to our spouse, but he or she looks like someone else. We perform supernormal physical feats, like flying off planet, or being the ultimate Kung Fu expert. Typical transformations associated with types of dreams will be analyzed in order to gain a better understanding of associated imaging processes.

Personal Case Study: Dream nakedness and eating discomfort (Somatic types)

I typically sleep with a night shirt through the colder months, and often sleep naked in the hot summer. In winter dreams, I'm naked from the waist down, and I'm often totally naked in summer dreams. Seasonally, my sleeping brain incorporates being naked or semi-naked in my dreams. I've observed this pattern consistently on and off through the seasons and over the decades. I'm stuffed and uncomfortable if I've eaten an overly large meal late in the evening. Commonly, I'll get up in the middle of the night and have bathroom needs. My dreams, however, have me looking for a public toilet. I wander down streets, or through dream malls. Eventually finding a toilet, I sit on it naked from the waist down, and in public view—bodily needs have entered my dreams.

Even Aristotle and later Freud[10], and Freud's contemporaries made similar somatic dream observations. This is old stuff!

Personal Case Studies: Functional behaviors and skill development

Thirty years ago, I created a number of stained-glass art pieces. I resurrected the hobby when I retired in 2009. Skills get pretty rusty after 30-years as our brains stop maintaining fine neural connections that support precise cutting and drawing motions. I found myself engaged in dream drawing as if I was actually practicing my old craft. My focus was on drawing motions as the medium in my dreams was not glass, however. Note the dream emphasis on function—fine tuning neuronal connections can ignore the medium in dreams. Observing this functional distinction, I'm suggesting that previous research looking for a direct relationship between daytime activity and dream content was operating under false assumptions[11,12,13]. Cartwright has also noted these and other similar research attempts failed as well[14].

Examples of skills being reinforced in our dreams support the idea that our dreaming brains are busy integrating and consolidating all of our waking experiences[15]. In my later-in-life dream of drawing, my brain wasn't concerned with the stained glass itself. Cutting and drawing specific outlines for stained glass construction never occurred. My brain was busy creating new neural connections for fine drawing and cutting motions, which were associated with common memories from years gone by. Logically, I seemed to be building on historically dimmed neural outlines that needed hi-lighting. Note the implications of my pattern analysis for neuronal associations.

The most recent waking experiences from the previous day or

days might appear in one's dreams. The brain efficiently seems to be modifying existing associated memory images to fine-tune skills or consolidate related associations. Integrating memory content can mix associations from yesterday, last week, or 30-years-ago. Thus, memory associations seem to occur according to their functional relationships.

Routines that are reinforced daily do not show up in my dreams; for example, eating motions. In my dream of 27 May 2013, I ate pancakes slathered with fruit sauce. All the eating motions were left out of the dream, but not the tastes and textures. Individually, our own dream patterns appear to depend on personal history, emotional state, and specific brain imaging preferences, and our most common or uncommon existing neuronal associations.

As an aside, let me note the effects of daytime activity in a dual state of consciousness as I entered sleep on 7 September 2014. I had spent a good hour pruning fruit trees in my yard. I hurried to complete the task before dark, showered, ate dinner, and played video games for two hours before retiring. Imagery of branches being trimmed from three different perspectives totally dominated my transition into sleep. Clearly my brain was still busy with my daily activity. However, as had happened before, familiar routines did not directly enter my dreams as concrete, nor exactly the same imagery.

Skill maintenance doesn't have to mimic all of our waking behaviors—that would be a waste of neuronal energy. Thus, I'm suggesting that dreaming brains take the efficient route and only support re-acquiring lost drawing and glass cutting skills, or the taste of fruit sauce. In contrast to finer drawing and glass cutting skills, tree trimming as a gross motor activity was not concretized or personified by my dreaming brain.

The distinction between fine motor skills being reinforced in dreams, and gross motor skills being ignored was a helpful insight into why my dreams violate waking use of time and space. It appears that neuronal efficiency only needs to fine tune specific skills. Thus, skill acquisition and maintenance in our dreams does not require all the elements of context, and time and space can be violated in support of neuronal efficiency.

Memory Associations

The following examples connect preexisting memory associations with immediate sensory stimuli. I'm attempting to demonstrate with the following examples that the associative mechanisms of memory organize daily experiences around templates, or what might be described as neuronal maps, maps that I assume begin to form in the womb.

Cigarette smoking: I smoked cigarettes for a number of years as a young adult. My non-conscious brain permanently associates dry lungs and throat with dry winter air and smoking. It took me years to make this smoking and dry winter air connection in my dreams. Follow your dreams as a hobby, and you will find your own special associations. And be cautious with contrived psychoanalytic interpretations such as, "You have a disguised wish to smoke again." Balderdash! I hate the habit.

Spousal Imaging: Most of us marry or have long-term live-in relationships. Personal relationships inevitably show up in our dreams. My spouse doesn't appear like a photograph in my dreams. Her physical dream appearance is a composite of many different memory associations, not that of a picture. She looks like someone else, but I know it's Ruby from my emotional reactions. Affect[16], how we feel when we're dreaming, tends to take preference over what types of image transformations are being generated.

People tell me they never recognize family or friends in their dreams. I suspect that's because they expect dream characters to appear like photographs. Our eyes don't take photographs. Our brain uses over 30 different processing centers to create visual images. We only experience these composite creations as though they are photographs with immediate environmental feedback.

When dreaming or hallucinating, our image generator instantly and efficiently composes by integrating fragments from memory. And, it appears, we efficiently compose dream image on pre-existing templates. When lucidly observing in our dreams, we should remind ourselves that expectations and suggestions alter the dream imagery at both conscious and nonconscious levels.

Primary Image Transformations

Image transformations at our primary-level of consciousness are reimaged at our secondary-level of consciousness. In the following example, physical pain is transformed into dream torturers.

Personal Case Study: Image transformation of pain

Once the cast came off, any pressure on the ankle and foot was uncomfortable. At any age, but especially amongst us older folks, broken bones create great discomfort. I stopped using pain killers at the end of the third week, which exposed raw nerves to new adventures. I was subject to foul play in one of my broken ankle dreams. Dastardly types were abusing my ankle to the point of torture. I woke to discover that heavy blankets had bunched over my ankle, and the added weight had confined my foot to an uncomfortable and painful angle. Specifically, bottom-up image transformations from heavy blankets became dastardly types of secondary dream consciousness.

This is a straightforward example of how physical sensation is turned into what I call dream image metaphor. Note that pain in the brain's dynamic core is personified through transformative imagery at our secondary level of consciousness. Our automatic image generator personifies physical ankle pain into dream character bad guys. I assume that the self as author requires personification in order to engage in and take social roles in this dream aspect of secondary consciousness.

Image transformations observed by the self can be either top-down or bottom-up. With dream lucidity, the self can consciously learn to identify either top-down or bottom-up image transformations; even though these image transformations usually occur automatically at a nonconscious level.

Dreaming brains can be as active, or even more active, than our waking brains[17]. However, dream forms function according to their own logic. By dream logic, I mean the subjective way our brain processes sensory information in this altered state of consciousness. The lucid component of my dreaming brain often, but not always, expects an upon-waking cause and effect; however, causes and effects have a different meaning at the dynamic core level of primary consciousness that is automatically creating the imagery content. In contrast to waking cause and effect relationships, ankle pain was metaphorically present in my dream as torture, and for the self, personification of torture requires bad guys. Thus, the brain's dynamic core appears to make associations using related image transformations on its own unique terms. And, the self of secondary consciousness tries to impose waking logic that one finds in social roles.

Personification is a functional image transformation that the brain generates automatically. Historically, in lucid dreaming, or conscious waking analysis of our dreams, these automatic image transformations have resulted in a great deal of confusion. Nevertheless, I marvel at the creativity of my dreaming brain. Pain has so many transformative associations—so does sweat, or any other body sensation.

The weight of bedding on a half-healed ankle becomes an act of torture. And, our most uncomfortable winter lungs may get turned into dream smoking. Notice that these examples are all personal associational dream image transformations between the automaticity of the brain's dynamic core and higher cortical centers. Feelings are not just feelings in our dreams, feelings become concretized and personified image transformations. Dream personification generates a social narrative experienced as story-telling[18].

The dream-self appears to require personification for social involvement. From this perspective, the self is as much of a social construction from birth to death as it is a neuronal construction. Note how the above interpretation negates assumptions in "hard core" behaviorism that neuronal information is recorded in reflex fashion, or that self is an illusion. This line of thought also questions the assumption that emergent properties of secondary consciousness can be reduced to physics and biochemistry alone[19].

Recapping, the brain's automatic transformations of feelings into images create confusion when being viewed lucidly by the self. Being lucid in dreams means there is a waking component of secondary consciousness that remains active. Thus, in a dual state of consciousness we observe a process of image transformation that follows a logic that is unlike that of our waking moments. Transformative imaging appears to be a functional process in terms of efficient neuronal memory maintenance, but a process that seems strange to our higher order logic's waking expectations of cause and effect.

I'm suggesting that functional efficiency at the level of our brain's dynamic core is supported by dreams that produce distortions of time, place, and characters. But once we wake, the brain's dynamic core dream logic is illogical. For me, the confusion between the brain-mind's waking and dreaming logic disappears with the realization that each level of brain dynamics serves its own function (purpose).

Furthermore, network image transformations between our higher cognitive centers and dynamic core levels can be meta-cognitively observed by the self in dreams. The meta-cognitive ability of the self to observe across states of consciousness is supported by the circular and reentrant neural connections between brain modules and neural networks. Thus, I'm extrapolating from Paul Nunez's work that our brain's reentrant neuronal loops maintain dynamic integrated linkages across states of consciousness[20].

All kinds of stimuli enter my dreams: My spouse's gentle cuddling may evoke an erotic dream, night sweating may call up various kinds of water scenarios, and unusual noises can enter my dreams as gunshots or unwanted intrusions. I find it helpful when analyzing my dreams to remind myself that neuronal functions in dreams follow different rules than our waking consciousness does. Thus, it's apparent that the dream forms supporting physiological and neuronal needs of our brains during sleep and dream sequencing are not the same as the waking forms of logic required to cross the street.

I'm unusually sensitive to horror scenes in the mass media and avoid them. Personally, I retain super-sensitivity to experiences that I associate with childhood trauma. Our brains are not passive recipients of sensory neuronal inputs[21]. Percepts are translated into secondary working concepts that the self can manipulate. From infancy through adult years we learn that most of our social interaction is unconscious. Consequently, primary affect emotions become feelings at our higher cortical levels that are concretized and personified in our dreams[22].

Any observed cruelty to another human being can be incorporated into one of my uncomfortable dreams. Movie scenes do not directly replay in my dreams any more than actual photographs get recorded by my brain. But movie themes do get creatively transformed in a manner similar to the image transformations of my broken-ankle dream. Note that thematic manipulation of movie themes suggests an active role for an autonomous self. Thematic dream content manipulation takes us beyond the stimulus-response model of behaviorism.

Dream analysis has greatly increased my own sensitivity to horror media and how it disrupts a good night's sleep. Desensitizing ourselves to blood and gore in films works for some but has various levels of carryover for the rest of us. Our individual developmental histories matter. Nothing disturbs my dreams more than trauma movies; that is, unless it's oxycodone for a broken ankle. Analyzing dreams over time sensitizes us to the great variability and subjectivity of individual dream image transformations.

Fixed Action Pattern (FAP) Dreams

A fixed action pattern (FAP) is a series of memory elements that become integrated and automated[23]. When I began riding bike in 2009 after a 30-year hiatus, my waking balance was in need of fine-tuning. I was surprised when my dreaming brain took up bike riding; after a couple of weeks my dream biking exhibited supernormal performance[24]. Soon I was riding on dream mountain ledges and over rugged terrain that would have been impossible to navigate while awake.

FAPs automatize sequences that eventually occur without conscious thought. In the example of dream biking there was a direct and positive correlation between my supernormal dream biking and daytime ability. This is an example of how the integration and consolidation of FAPs have a direct correlation with virtual dream practice. Complex FAPs permit me to play a dream piano without actual practice. My memory duplicates the music while my dreaming brain has the illusion of connecting my fingers with the notes. This type of dream rehearsal is much like the mental rehearsal of an athlete before actual performance. A mental pattern of embedding a musical routine suggests that dream enactment is enhancing neuronal patterns that support waking performance. Further, I'm suggesting that this musical form of nonconscious learning is generally reflected in the automatic, transformative imaging that occurs across a broad range of dreams and hallucinations.

The marvel of dream skill mastery is acquisition without apparent effort: It is dream eroticism, mental music, mind-controlled flight, and physical acts that defy the imagination. These are mental accomplishments that can be had for the asking. And they can be ours regardless of age or physical limitations. They are free of financial obligation; a gift from the brain's transformative imager.

Dramatic skill mastery can often be demonstrated most fully in late-morning dreams. In waking-states we acquire skills with effort. In dreams, skills improve without waking effort. Dreams and particularly REM sleep enhances memory by facilitating change in neuronal plasticity[25,26]. As my bike-riding example illustrates, dreams reflect skill acquisition that parallels the timing of our waking experiences. After a couple of weeks of actual practice, my night dreams' bike riding skills increased to an amazing degree. Eventually, by the break of dawn, I was biking where no man had ever biked before. Star Trek in my own bedroom!

Once again, I note that lucid dreaming is the only state of consciousness where this neuronal functionality of FAP dreams can be observed.

Nonconscious (Hebbian) Learning, Dream (7 October 2013)

A series of the same dream over several weeks' time can provide an example of how nonconscious processes can break into consciousness. Initially, I was treating this particular dream as just another "potty" dream. In the dreams, I actually get up and use the bathroom only to find that I'm merely flatulent. The dream setting is in a school or on a military site. The stool is overflowing and dirty and I must flush it and clean the seat with toilet paper. I feel disgusted at people's behavior.

As I wake more fully, the phrase Hebbian learning pops into my head. I immediately think of Hebbian learning, which simply put: —neurons that fire together, wire together. I connect Hebbian learning with the mild discomfort I've been experiencing from gas. The following associations occur in rapid order as I return to bed.

(a) My brain's dynamic core is signaling that the dream is instigated by bloating.

(b) Creative imaging in this dream is turning a physical state, bloating, into a dream picture narrative.

(c) This image transformation explains how people can feel a medical condition that is impacting their bodies before a formal diagnosis.

(d) Hebbian learning exemplified in this dream occurs at a nonconscious level and explains what is often referred to as premonition.

(e) Sensitivity to dream imaging provided the key word, Hebbian, when I was transitioning awake in a dual state of consciousness.

It is fairly easy to identify this nonconscious process while dreaming lucidly, but maddeningly complex when awake. For psychotherapists, note that I've ignored Freud's reified notion of the preconscious in my Hebbian dream interpretation. Also, note that the mechanism of transformative imaging is substituted for Freud's latent and manifest dream content. Thus, I remain critical of too closely reinventing Freud[27,28,29]. For additional insight into Hebbian learning see Bernard Baars and Nicole Gage[30].

Dreams Induced by Our Own Brain's Chemicals

Adrenaline and testosterone dreams inform us differently as we age. For the past 10-15 years, if I drink coffee late night, the caffeine changes my sleep-dream sequence, and lighter sleep wakes me repeatedly. Repeated waking throughout the night disrupts both health-restoring sleep and REM dreaming. However, in the short run, repeated waking during the night enhances dream recall. As is generally accepted, health restoring rest does not equate with the number of hours we spend in bed. Coffee "highs," like pharmaceuticals and sleeping pills, alter our brain's chemical rhythms throughout the night[31].

Military strategists know the physical and emotional impact of disrupted sleep. Disrupting sleep and dream cycles is a form of torture. Being woken up from a sound sleep to take medications is annoying. Being woken up every two hours and moved in a military prison is extreme physical cruelty. Repeat this pattern for 30-days, and it is difficult to avoid one's breaking point. In similar fashion, hospital and nursing home routines that constantly disrupt sleep and REM-dream completion to administer drugs are unwarranted. The use of anti-psychotics in long-term care can further exacerbate the negative effects of nursing home routines[31]. Sleep deprivation adversely affects all age groups.

Waking while dreams are in progress reminds us that dreams are happening throughout the night. Although we have 25 or more dream scenarios nightly, we only remember a few. The dreamy state of drug and pharmaceutical-altered sleep cycles leaves us half awake and half asleep. Such an altered pattern disrupts deep sleep and normal REM and leaves us feeling tired and dragged-out. Enough sleep deprivation can cause waking hallucinations.

Adrenaline is much like caffeine. As a brain-manufactured chemical, its effects prolong the onset of sleep and fill our dreams with increased action intensity and feelings. If my mood is positive, adrenaline dream action is pleasant; if my mood is negative, the action is also. Be aware that mood is determining the specific effects of adrenaline on image transformations. This relationship suggests that we cannot explain states of consciousness by researching brain cells and bio-chemicals in isolation from system dynamics. Further, we are forced to question DSM-symptom interpretations when the same brain chemistry can create such opposite results. System analysis begs understanding of dynamic causation, neurological evidence that goes beyond clinical notations.

Adrenaline effects in dreams remind us that our psychological and physical states during the day carry over and affect dream moods as well. Mood plus adrenaline changes the transformative images generated by my dreaming brain. In both the negative and positive examples, our virtual image generator is equally online, but the dream content is changed. Thus, we more fully appreciate why analyzing dream content by itself is so unreliable.

Dream moods can also carryover from night into day. We sometimes get up feeling unusually grumpy. The common saying is that we've gotten up on the wrong side of the bed. If we search for a logical reason for our morning's negative mood, we are once again barking up the wrong tree. Brain chemicals drive our moods. This awareness is especially important as we cope with depression or anxiety brought about by sleep medications, alcohol, street drugs, bad habits, and pharmaceuticals

Clinical interpretations, especially when they're derived from DSM criteria that ignore the brain's chemical states can be misleading. In my opinion, a fuller understanding of how biochemistry affects sleep and dream cycles also challenges Freud's manifest and latent dream analyses.

The enjoyment we can get from using suggestion or dream programming is worth the effort. Read Krakow and Niedhardt's *Sound Sleep Sound Mind*[32], and Oliver Sacks' *Hallucinations* for additional advice[33]. A dreaming night of erotic fantasy, or day interludes of joyful hallucinations, can help us be more pleasant social companions.

Metaphor and Media- Influenced Dreams

I'm defining emotion as a bio-chemical state that is felt by the organism. Obviously, felt bio-chemical states become more complex as we move up the evolutionary ladder from bacteria to humans. But regardless of complexity, bio-chemical equilibrium at any level of evolutionary complexity is required for the organism's wellbeing.

Feelings derived from the bio-chemistry of emotion are fundamental to the self's origin and the body's physical survival[34]. We all wrestle with emotions during the day. When emotional tension crosses our personal thresh-hold of tolerance, we process tension in our dreams. As a five-year-old, fear of mother's physical attacks was metaphorically transformed, personified, in my Japanese nightmare. Interpersonal conflict, pain, and psychic pain of all kinds undergo image transformations in our dreams. And the personification of emotions, such as fear and anxiety, routinely produces monsters in our dreams as the personification of emotion produces "ghosts" and spirits in our waking hallucinations. It seems fairly obvious that the metaphorical image transformations and personifications occurring in dreams tend to mask the origin of stimuli that triggers dream imagery.

The terror of war, rape, and disasters of great emotional impact all influence our dreams. Movie mayhem inevitably generates trauma in my dreams. Consequently, I avoid the senseless dripping gore and horror of mass media. For some of us, post-traumatic stress reflects a supersensitive template of susceptible neurons that are easily set in motion by everyday environments. For a highly readable, authoritative review of PSTD trauma read Bessel van der Kolk[35].

Bad dreams and nightmares are the types of dreams we most often remember. Negative emotions are more common in childhood and tend to diminish as we grow older. This progression seems logical to me given dream image transformations. Imagine the powerful world a five-year-old child experiences—giant adults, mysterious forces, fierce animals, and all of nature's raw power. This vulnerability returns to me in adult moments of threat—what clinicians call regression. Negative dream content can emerge with any type of emotional or physical trauma, such as divorce or broken bones.

Theme Dreams

Dream scenarios are much like written stories; they become longer as the night wears on. I notice in late morning dreams that a cognitive or emotional theme has been repeated much of the night. For instance, a conflict theme repeats in the course of the night's dreams, even though the dream characters may be re-imaged in each dream segment. For example, in one dream scenario the conflict is with students, in another the conflict is with a teacher or some nondescript adult. Thematically, what is consistent is the emotion, such as anger, fear, irritability, or my anxious efforts writing this book. Dream analysis consistently reminds us that emotions trump cognition as our brain's attempt to regain homeostatic balance, and the self seeks emotional equilibrium.

An emotional theme appears when I'm caught up in an ongoing mood over many days. If I'm irritated at someone, angry about the last election, or happily caught up in the forthcoming marriage of a family member, accompanying moods are repeated in my dreams as emotional themes.

My brain has memory files that represent irritating and loving women, sexual and physical trauma, things associated with physical difficulties, and a myriad of other categories. Thus, much of my dream image associations are emotionally transformed and thematic—not literal. Both emotional and physical theme associations violate space and time. The way my brain operates, as I think most of our brains do, is through our personal, and familiar memory associations.

Dream characters are typically composites of more than one person. But notice the dream form twist—both feeling and cognitive memory content routinely violates time and space, as well as concretizing and personifying feeling and cognitive dream elements. Additionally, my memory associations are not organized by the clock or calendar, and I suspect yours aren't either. Memory associations are organized by neuronal efficiency, and they build and change throughout our lifetime. I view this process as neuronal plasticity at work.

I find it helpful to remember that feeling and cognitive elements are always combined in my dream characters with emotional content usually being more dominant in dreams than during my waking moments. However, my dream images can be true to life if I'm thoroughly familiar with the person or physical element. I don't have total recall; yet, as I dream, I can often read short sections of actual materials. For me, dream reading is more at a conceptual level, as the actual words will usually change with each viewing. In like fashion, I don't play and have never studied piano or violin; yet, I have played various pieces from memory in my dreams. Thus, there is dream image reconstruction for situational material and actual duplication for material that has been committed to memory.

My brain's memory files have two, distinct sources and related formats: waking memory files, and dreaming memory files. This distinction might sound a little strange if the reader is accustomed to thinking in terms of different types of waking memories, for instance, short- or long-term memories. Further on in this book, I'll elaborate understanding of dream memories (*de'ja vu*) as a separate memory process.

Personal Case Study: This book's theme dream (18 August 2013)

Remaining in bed, I have just reviewed a very clear thematic dream. I look at the clock and it is 3:45 a.m. The dream is exceptionally clear and a synopsis of this book. I make a special mental note that the book will be finished as soon as I add this dream material. (This is an example of dream waking logic). Freud might say, "A wish fulfilled." Actually, over the following weeks, I added over 150 pages to the original book (First draft, 2014).

I recall that in my dream, I review the main organization and themes I'd initially set forth for this book but decided to place a special emphasis on Freud. I got up to make notes on five 3 X 5 note sheets, and in doing so I recognized that a full-length critique of Freud's *Interpretation of Dreams* is warranted. I pulled out my copy of *The Basic Writings of Sigmund Freud* (Brill) and reviewed a few of his dream interpretations. Emotionally, I felt overwhelmed by how badly Freud had misinterpreted image transformations in all but the most common somatic dreams.

The Thematic Synopsis Dream of 18 August 2013

I wake in need of the bathroom, and am consciously aware of being in a lucid, dual state of dreaming for some time. As I reflect on the dream, the main themes and key conclusions start with Freud's disguise, censorship, and wish fulfillment concepts. I have a growing awareness that my interpretation of the metaphorical language of dreams directly confronts many of Freud's notions, and quite directly supports the conceptual use of metaphor as defined by Lakoff and Johnson[36]. Additionally, I think that my transformative image interpretation of dreams and hallucinations, if substantiated, negates a number of the specific mechanisms supporting Freud's theory and traditional psychoanalysis.

Other themes that emerge from this dream include: The importance of long-term altered state analysis by first-person, versus contrived third-person interpretations. As I reflect on the dreams content, I have a growing appreciation that first-person content analysis is as critical to understanding the meaning of dreams and hallucinations as is dream form of the Allan Hobson variety. As I finished making notes of my dream, I had the feeling that a new model of mental health was screaming for attention[37].

Note that cognitive and thematic dreams overlap to a high degree. The difference between the two types of dreams is that thematic types may contain mostly cognitive versus emotional content. However, my main point is that meta-cognitively the self is aware of the cognitive and emotional content differences in these dream examples. Let me further clarify how I'm using the term metacognition.

Metacognition is defined as the ability to know our own cognitive functions, and to be able to use that knowledge[38]. I experience the retrieval of information in lucid dreaming as a creative state of consciousness where we have greater simultaneous connectivity across the brain's modular structures, and parallel processes. In a lucid dreaming, dual state, we do not have to consciously attempt retrieval. It appears that our self as meta-organizer is always automatically attempting to integrate sensory input flowing across its various modular components in any state of consciousness[39,40,41]. This multi-sensory, meta-organization is how I experience dream creativity.

Cognitive Dreams

I classify some of my dreams as cognitive because they are instigated by long-term and intensive concentration on a particular subject. I'm compulsive about writing until I finish saying what I want to say about the subject. Overall, sensory stimulation from my compulsion to write enters my dreams as lectures, academic discussions, and a variety of educational scenes. Through memory associations, my dreams configure all of this cognitive activity in familiar thought sequencing, academic settings, and classrooms.

Personal Case Study: Cognitive dream (2 August 2013)

Note the amount of material encompassed by the following dream. In a waking state of consciousness, I would not normally

101

connect the numerous items that emerge. However, in the dream itself, I have a "felt" sense of the item interrelationships.

In my dream, I wake in a Seattle motel, look at the clock and believe it is 6:35 a.m. I'm taking a test and it has 25 questions. I've left a number blank and I'm concerned about doing well. I go back and answer a number of skipped questions, and I'm delighted at question number 25, "Define occult imaging." I note that this is an easy question as it is directly related to the book I'm currently writing. In the dream, I re-read the test question and it remains unchanged; thus, I note the question's veridical relationship to my current writing.

Still dreaming, I'm aware that the metaphorical form of dream material normally means that the content changes with each re-reading. The test question format of my dream flags a complex of emerging elements. I chastise myself for not memorizing the other questions that were giving me trouble. I'm aware while still dreaming that content is typically forgotten unless we make an extra effort to retain specific material for later recall. By dream memorization, I'm also aware that I'm placing specific dream content in working memory so the content will be accessible when I'm awake. (Lucid dreaming gives us this option).

I shift focus and let my mind free associate, and the following eight items are generated as I slowly wake up. Order of recall: 1) Definition of occult, 2) Comparisons with William James's *Varieties of Religious Experience*[42], 3) Barrett's Committee of Sleep[43], 4) Edelman's Neural Darwinism, and Lamarkianism[44], 5) Flanagan on the human spirit[45], 6) Pope/religionists and what the death of occultism means for them, 7) Re-birth of the human spirit and *coup de grass* of Enlightenment objectivity, 8) Reference Richard Dawkins[46] and the anti-spiritualist debate.

Associations that my dreaming brain pulls from memory swirl around this personal history. I've spent 20-years in the classroom and presented educational materials most of my adult years to employees, speeches at conferences and as a guest speaker/lecturer.

In my dreams, I'm in a classroom giving lectures, holding academic discussions, taking tests, going over charts and diagrams, reading books and articles and engaging in a broad range of educationally related activities. In waking-consciousness I'm writing this book. These cognitive dreams act as a "committee of sleep" providing additional direction and content for my daytime writings.

Creativity: Instigated by Cognitive Dream (23 August 2013)

Every time I write a book—this book included—a significant portion has been suggested by my dreams. Stephen LaBerge's section on "Creative Dreams" is about writers, artists, mathematicians, musicians, and many others who have tapped their creative minds through lucid dreams[47]. Lucid dreaming is not common but, it is also not unusual. For example, Ryan Hurd began offering lucidity training through his website at the beginning of 2016. If you've never learned to dream lucidly, you've missed this creative aspect of your own consciousness.

I have another technique to dredge up creative thoughts— dream content that seems to be pure metaphor. Dream image metaphor that I can't connect with waking thoughts often comes into focus as I transition, dual state-wise, from sleep to waking. By focusing on the dream's content, I'm able to translate the logic of the dream's metaphor. I observe that the self seems to have a subliminal awareness of dream image transformations that break through during free associations, after waking. But let me insert a note of caution.

If I try to logically connect dream content with waking consciousness, often nothing emerges. Accessing the meaning of dream content that has been metaphorically transformed in the dreaming process is similar to recalling a name that is on the tip of our tongue. The harder we think about forcing the name into consciousness, the less likely it is to appear. In these attempted recall-moments it is usually more effective to relax, or even think about something else and then the name or thought will appear. In effect, we need to let the self's meta-cognitive awareness find the missing item. Remember, metaphorical image transformations from nonconscious processes are not normally available to waking logic—a major problem for third-party analysts.

Readers familiar with clinical techniques will recognize a second note of caution in these efforts to access dream meaning. If I'm trying to help you, ---say as a client or patient---bring your feelings into focus, you are highly susceptible to suggestions at that specific moment. In similar fashion, if we try to force meaning from our dreams, we can easily distort what emerges. Nevertheless, if you are a non-lucid dreamer, try accessing dream meaning as you transition into waking consciousness by focusing on dream content without any attempt at translation.

Halfway awake, we are in a dual state of consciousness. I get about as much material for my books from this half-asleep/half-awake period as I do directly from the dreams themselves. If you have been anxious or stressed during the previous day (s), try focusing on your feelings during morning-awakening transitions. Post-sleep transitions are also a good time to practice being half-awake and half-asleep. Keep focus on whatever remnants of your dream remains. I immediately start analyzing the night's dream as I'm waking. Frequently, the meaning of the dream emerges as an "aha." I realize, "Aha!"—That was my spouse Ruby. Or, "Aha" I need to clarify my use of being spiritually possessed.

Our ability to control dreams, dream lucidly, or modify hallucinations is enhanced one small step at a time. We are all unique, but all of our brains experience dual states of consciousness. "Aha" experiences are enlightening. And the synergism of dual state "Aha" is there for the "finding."

Nighttime bathroom breaks have other options for me as well. If the dream does not continue during my bathroom break, I may pick it up where I left off after returning to sleep. Or I may repeat the dream totally or repeat the dream and change the ending when I return to bed. I've been a dream observer for most of my life, and these nighttime dream options came about naturally. Let your mind be open to possibilities and see what happens. Note, however, that autonomy of self-processes and meta-cognitive awareness must exist for the above dream options to be possible.

Automatic transformative imaging occurs with any state of consciousness. When I started regular dream analysis in the late-1950s, I never anticipated the extent to which dreams foster creativity, or the amount of control that is possible. My entire reading background on dreams consisted of Freud's *Interpretation of Dreams* with his contrived focus on thoughts and wishes. I became totally disenchanted with dream interpretations by psychiatrists and didn't reengage the dream literature until I finally retired in 2009.

Regardless of how much dream literature we encounter, once we begin to control our dreams and other altered states the "Aha" of discovery goes on and on. Each new discovery adds insight and appreciation for the range and vast content of consciousness states that are open to individual exploration. There's inspiration and ideas in the recesses of my brain that never comes out otherwise. My dreams suggest more books than I'll ever have time to write.

Creativity in dreams is facilitated by the mechanism that metaphorically transforms feeling into various kinds of sensory images. Following up on my earlier interpretation in *Dreams, Creativity & Mental Health,* creativity is enhanced by gaining lucid dream access to neuronal workspace at the dynamic core level[48,49,50]. And, at the same time, I'm also gaining conscious awareness of the transformative imaging that occurs automatically in dreams.

From my personal experience, I conclude that creativity for artists, writers, mathematicians, and engineers, would get a substantial boost by accessing enlarged neuronal workspace, its expanded neuronal connectivity, and the creativity of automatic image transformations. I made these notes, especially, to call attention to the creative aspect of our mind's metaphorical image transformations. Furthermore, it seems to me that non-conscious transformative imaging across different sensory channels replaces much of Freud's schemes of repression, disguise and censorship with my exposition of how transformative imaging is expressed across states of consciousness.

Since my interpretations of dreams in 2012, I have experienced a growing awareness that Freud's concept of the "unconscious" is both distorted and discredited. In this 21st year of the 21st Century, the nonconscious brain processes that Freud thought of as the "unconscious" are solidly grounded in empirical neuroscience. The complexity of therapeutic implications of transformative imagery for Freudian theory, I decide, goes well beyond the purpose of this book and warrants later development.

Nightmares

I have had two nightmares that were extremely debilitating and lasted decades—the Japanese submarine nightmare which started when I was 5-years old, and the sexual assault nightmare beginning at 14-years. Because of the significance of nightmares for mental health, let me address the importance of proper adult and parental guidance for these traumatic events.

The University of Warwick, UK, found that children reporting frequent nightmares before the age of 12 were 3.5 times more likely to suffer from psychotic episodes in early adolescence[51]. In essence, the more frequent nightmares are, and the longer they persist, the greater the elevated chance of psychosis. That study also holds a number of other variables constant; for instance, sleep insomnias do not elevate risk of psychoses. In that a majority of children younger than five years suffer nightmares and night terrors, and nightmares are indicators of later psychoses, parents should treat these episodes seriously.

By analyzing our dreams over decades, we become sensitive to accumulated dream histories, and how the self is expressed in these histories. Lucidly following our dreams over decades, we become aware that sleep-destroying nightmares can lay down permanent memory traces. In my personal examples, transformative content generated in nightmares becomes part of episodic memory alongside that of waking experiences. It seems warranted that how dream trauma memory gets mixed with everyday memory should be more fully researched now that an empirical relationship has been established with psychosis.

From personal experience, terrifying nightmares can break into consciousness even during the day. The nightmare mechanism of destabilizing emotional homeostasis can potentially help account for elevated risk in untreated children's nightmares. As a nightmare-wracked child, adolescent, and young adult, I can testify the degree to which emotional fragmentation of the self contributes to PTSD.

Recent research by Sam McKenzie and colleagues suggests that: The hippocampus may integrate overlapping memories into relational representations, or schemas that link directly related events and support flexible memory expression. Hippocampal networks develop hierarchical organizations of associated elements of related but separately acquired memories within a context, and distinct organizations for memories where the contexts differentiated object reward associations. These findings reveal neural mechanisms for the development and organization of relational representations[52].

It appears that what I tend to call mixing and matching of dream elements is a rather direct reflection of how neuronal organization is occurring in dreams. Associations in dreams, simply stated, reflect how memories are encoded by the brain's neurons. We know from the research of DeCasper, Kisilevsky, and others that memory traces are being laid down in the fetal brain. McKenzie and colleagues research provides evidence that relational representation is modifying neurons with every new instance of recall. Thus, I'm suggesting that psychoses may be furthered between childhood and adolescent years when trauma is repeatedly entered into memory with nightmares.

Summary of Dream Types

It is helpful for dream interpretation to recognize that all of my senses and body states—from highly noticed temperatures, touch sensations, sounds heard, even adrenaline and hormone changes, to variance in light—can influence and transform imagery in my dreams. Awareness that somatic sensations enter dreams is generally compatible with Freud's *The Somatic Sources of Dreams*[53]. Nevertheless, I've argued that Freud generally misinterprets the bidirectional image transformation dynamics between primary and secondary consciousness.

The dream samples presented contain typical image transformations that I've lucidly observed in thousands of dreams over the decades. They are typical dream examples that exemplify how somatic states, mood, suggestion, and daytime cogitations influence dream content. The uniqueness of our individual dream image transformations directly challenge standardized occult and later Freudian explanations of dream content.

Metacognition is self-awareness across states of consciousness. Meta-awareness in dreams means that the self observes across dream segments and is able to discern patterns, emotions content, abstractions, themes, and social role changes. Critically, as the dream examples demonstrate, the lucid-self can follow and analyze bidirectional image transformations in dreams. The two-way flow of image transformations between primary and secondary consciousness supports a discovery process. For instance, dream meta-awareness of organic discomfort may act as a premonition of an impending medical emergency. And, at our secondary level of consciousness we observe how primary sensations are being concretized and personified.

Cognitive dissonance appears to be transformed top-down into psychic pain that is felt throughout body and brain. Most critically, however, the self can enact very complex dual state content as we enter and exit sleep. Dual states can be enacted consciously, as well as occurring non-consciously, in both dreams and hallucinations once we learn to dream lucidly.

The dream types that I've proposed stress the uniqueness of our individual image transformations. Learning to dream lucidly, and analyzing the forms and contents of our dreams, sensitizes us to the combined sensory and cognitive communication occurring across states of consciousness and the effect of image transformations 24/7. Critically, we become aware as parents and members of the helping professions of the importance dreams have for our emotional wellbeing.

Do not take my classifications to be anything other than a beginning way to sort out your own dream experiences. My dream classifications can be organized in a number of different ways. The major point, however, is that any source of sensory input, internal (formal designation: interoceptive), bodily (labeled: proprioceptive), or external (called: exteroceptive), can stimulate a transformed image that, in turn, instigates a narrative dream scenario. Narrative dream scenarios can be guided, directed, and modified by the self's experiential history, expectations, and suggestion. Again, the automaticity of self-generating transformative imagery is most obvious when we lucidly analyze dream content over time.

I've associated much of the seemingly random images in my dreams with ordinary bodily activities. However, when I closely follow dream content over time, I connect associations with "day residue" events, my current emotional state, and the focused cognitive activities such as writing this book. Freud viewed much of the seemingly random images in ordinary dreams as "froth," or he imposed his own convoluted language interpretations. I've briefly criticized Freud because his interpretations of dreams have been widely incorporated in the popular culture. In contrast to Freudian interpretations of dreams, I've incorporated contemporary research that views dreams as neuronal fine-tuning, memory integration and consolidation, and emotional re-balancing.

Content analysis of bidirectional image transformations between primary and secondary levels of consciousness offers singular insight into dreaming, hallucinating, and related self-processes. Our individual socio-cultural histories generate an unimaginable variety of image transformations in dreams and hallucinations; thus, there can be no standard content analysis of dreams even though countless books make this claim. Dream forms and processes are consistently observed, but not content.

Differences in the structure of consciousness between waking and dreaming calls attention to dream logic and muscle disconnect, and how space, time, and characters are mixed and matched. We know these standard dream forms from extensive 20th Century research. What is less well known is how physical sensation and cognitive activity bidirectionally transforms imagery. The highly individualistic nature of image transformations in dreams and hallucinations has been an historical conundrum.

Sources: Chapter 5: Dream Types: A Personal Interpretation

1. Cartwright, R. D. (1977) Night Life. Englewood Cliffs, NJ: Prentice-Hall, Inc.
2. Diekelmann, S., and Born, J. The memory function of sleep. Nature Reviews Neuroscience 11, 114–126 (1 February 2010) | doi:10.1038/nrn2762.
3. Levin, Fred M. (2009) Emotion and the Psychodynamics of the Cerebellum: A Neuro-Psychoanalytic Analysis and Synthesis. London: Karnac Books, Ltd.: Chapters 1 & 2.
4. Zhang, Jie (2004) Memory process and the function of sleep (6-6ed.) Journal of Theoretics Retrieved 2006-03-13).

5. Barrett, Deirdre. An Evolutionary Theory of Dreams and Problem-Solving in Barrett, D. L. & McNamara, P. (Eds.) The New Science of Dreaming. Vol. III: Cultural and Theoretical Perspectives on Dreaming. New York: Praeger/Greenwood. 2007.

6. Revonsuo, A. (2000) "The reinterpretation of dreams: an evolutionary hypothesis of the function of dreaming". Behavioral Brain Sciences 23 (6):877. Doi:10.1017/S0140525X00004015.

7. Crick, F., & Mitchison, G. (1983) "The function of dream sleep". Nature 304 (5922): 111-114. Doi:10.1038/304111a0. PMID 6866101.

8. Stickgold, R., Hobson, J. A., Fosse, M. (Nov. 2001) "Sleep learning, and Dreams: Off-line Memory Processing". Science 294 (5544): 1052-1057. Doi:10.1126/science.1063530.PMID 11691983.

9. Just, G. A. (2012) Dreams, Creativity & Mental Health. Mankato, MN: Eagle Entertainment USA.

10. Brill, A. A. (1938) The Basic Writings of Sigmund Freud. Edited and Translated. New York: The Modern Library.

11. Hauri, P. The effects of evening activity on early night sleep. Psychophysiology, 1966, 4, 267-277.

12. Foulkes, D., & Rechtschaffen, A. Presleep determinants of dream content: Effects of two films. Perceptual and Motor Skills, 1964, 19, 983-1005.

13. Witkin, H., & Lewis, H. Presleep experiences and dreams. In H. Witkin & H. Lewis (Eds.) Experimental studies of dreaming. New York: Random House, 1967.

14. Cartwright, R. D. (1977) Night Life. Englewood Cliffs, NJ: Prentice-Hall, Inc.: 79-83.

15. Walker, M. P. (2009). The Role of Sleep in Cognition and Emotion. Annals of the New York Academy of Sciences, 1156: 168–197. doi: 10.1111/j.1749-6632.2009.04416.x.

16. Panksepp, Jaak & Biven, Lucy (2012) The Archaeology of Mind: Neuroevolutionary Origins of Human Emotions. NY: W. W. Norton & Company.
17. Hobson, J. A. (1988) The Dreaming Brain: How the Brain Creates both the Sense and the Nonsense of Dreams. NY: Basic Books.
18. Pace-Schott, Edward F. Dreaming as a story-telling instinct. Frontiers in Psychology, doi:10.3389/fpsyg.2013.00159.
19. Churchland, P. S. (2013). Touching a Nerve: The Self as Brain. New York: Norton.
20. Nunez, Paul L. (2010) Brain, Mind, and the Structure of Reality. New York: Oxford.
21. Melzack, R., Wall, P. (1965) Pain mechanisms: A new theory. Science, 150(3699): 971-79.
22. Damasio, A. R. (2010) Self Comes to Mind: Constructing the Conscious Brain. New York: Pantheon.
23. Restak, R. (1994) The Modular Brain: How New Discoveries in Neuroscience are Answering Age-old Questions about Memory, Free Will, Consciousness, and Personal Identity. New York: Scribners.
24. Barrett, D. (2010) Supernormal Stimuli: How Primal Urges Overran Their Evolutionary Purpose. New York: W. W. Norton & Company.
25. Marks, G. A., Shaffrey, J. P., Oksenberg, A., Speciale, S. G., and Roffwarg, H. P. (1995) A functional role for REM sleep in brain maturation. Behavioral Brain Research, 69:1-11.
26. Tononi, Giulio & Cirelli, Chiara. "Perchance to Prune." Scientific American", August, 2013.
27. Kaplan-Solms, Karen and Solms, Mark. (2000) Clinical Studies in Neuro-Psychoanalysis: Introduction to a Depth Neuropsycyology. New York: H. Karnac Books Ltd.
28. Solms, Mark & Turnbull, Oliver (2002) The Brain and The Inner World: An Introduction to neuroscience of subjective experience. New York: Other Press.

29. McGowan, K. The Second Coming of Sigmund Freud. Discover, April, 2014, 54-61.

30. Baars, Bernard B. J. & Gage, Nicole M. (2010) Cognition, Brain, and Consciousness, 2nd Ed. New York: Elsevier, Academic Press: 83-85.

31. Epstein-Lubow, G. & Rosenzweig, A. The Use of Antipsychotic Medication in Long-Term Care, Med Health R 193, no. 12 (2010).

32. Krakow, Barry. (2007) Sound Sleep Sound Mind: 7 Keys to Sleeping through the Night. Hoboken, NJ: John Wiley & Sons.

33. Sacks, Oliver. (2012) Hallucinations. New York: Alfred A Knoff.

34. Panksepp, J. (1998) The pernicious substrates of consciousness: Affective states and the evolutionary origins of the SELF. Journal of Consciousness Studies, 5, 566-582.

35. van der Kolk, Bessel. (2014) The Body Keeps the Score: Brain, Mind, and Body in the Healing of Trauma. New York: Viking.

36. Lakoff, G., & Johnson, M. (1999) Philosophy In The Flesh: The Embodied Mind And Its Challenge To Western Thought. New York: Basic Books.

37. Just, Glen A. (2016) Phenomenal Methodology: Toward an Egosyntonic Psyco-Neuro-Dynamic Model of Mental Health. In Advances in Psychology Research, Vol. 118. Nova Science Pubs. Huauppauge, NY.

38. Ibid, Baars, & Gage. (2010) 338.

39. Hong, C. C.-H., Harris, J. C., Pearlson, G. D., Kim, J.-S., Calhoun, V. D., Fallon, J. H., Pekar, J. J. (2009) fMRI evidence for multistory recruitment associated with rapid eye movements during sleep. Human Brain Mapping, 30, 1705-1722.

40. Hobson, J. A., & Friston, K. J. (2012) Waking and dreaming consciousness: Neurobiological and functional considerations. Progress in Neurobiology, 98(1), 82-98.
41. Rosenblum, L. D. "A Confederacy of Senses". Scientific American, Jan. 203, 73-75.
42. James, William. (1902) The varieties of religious experience; a study in human nature; being the Gifford lectures on natural religion delivered at Edinburgh in 1901—1902, by William James. New York: Longmans, Green.
43. Barrett, D. (2001) The Committee of Sleep. New York: Crown Publishers.
44. Edelman, Gerald M. (1987) Neural Darwinism: The Theory of Neuronal Group Selection. Basic Books.
45. Flanagan, Owen. (2009) The Really Hard Problem: Meaning in a Material World. MIT Press.
46. Dawkins, Richard (1995) River Out of Eden: A Darwinian View of Life. Basic Books.
47. LaBerge, S., & Rheingold, H. (1990) Exploring the World of Lucid Dreaming. New York: Ballantine Books: 166-172.
48. Beaty, R. E., Benedek, M., Kaufman, S. B. & Silvia, P. J. (2015) Creative Cognition and Brain Network Dynamics. Trends in Cognitive Sciences, xx, 1-9.
49. Brewer, J. A., et al. (2011) Meditation experience is associated with differences in default network activity and connectivity. Proceedings of the National Academy of Sciences of the United States of America, 1-6.
50. Christoff, K., Irving, Z. C., Fox, K. C. R., Spreng, R. N., & Andrews Hanna, J. R. (2016) Mind Wandering as spontaneous thought: a dynamic framework. Nature Publishing Group. Doi:10.1038/nrn.2016.113.
51. Fisher, Sebern F. (2014) Neurofeedback in the Treatment of Developmental Trauma: Calming the Fear-Driven Brain. New York: Norton.

52. McKenzie, S., Frank, A.J., Kinsky, N.R., Porter, B., Riviere, P.D., & Eichenbaum, H. Hippocampal Representation of Related and Opposing Memories Develop with Distinct, Hierarchically Organized Neural Schemas. DOI: http://dx.doi.org/10.1016/j.neuron.2014.05.019.

53. Ibid, Brill, A. A. (1938), 276.

CHAPTER 6

✿

Spontaneous and Controlled Hallucinations

Personal Case Study: Pre-sleep imagery

While visiting Allan Hobson in Brookline (July, 2012), I realized that I had paid little attention to pre-sleep (referred to as hypnagogic) imagery. I wondered if I could manipulate pre-sleep imagery the way I control dream content.

That night, the first pre-sleep image that appeared was a long-stemmed red flower. I focused on this single flower and thought of a bouquet. Pow! A bouquet was born. I then noted that there was no background environment. Pow! The bouquet was surrounded by a larger setting. I thought to myself, "Wow! This is fun." (This is an example of Kosslyn's backward imaging as it articulates with the model of transformative dynamic integrated systems)[1].

Tibetan Buddhists have a similar approach: they focus on an image and manipulate its size at will. Phenomenal image manipulation is not mystical; it's automatic image transformations that are intrinsic to how the brain functions when the self brings secondary imaging processes under its control. Playing with daydream images can be a form of relaxation that stops the buzzing in my brain. Playing with images in dual states of consciousness employs parallel steps toward mastery of dreams and hallucinations. By mastery, I mean enacting complete narrative scenarios, or sustaining modification of single images.

My lifelong focus has been on dream and post-dream

(hypnopompic) control. Maintaining dual morning states can be even more fun than pre-sleep image manipulation. Dual morning states give us more options. If you have never experimented with pre-sleep and daydreaming dual states, I suggest you do so before attempting the variety of post-sleep scenarios that follow.

Most of us recall only a limited number of our 25-plus nightly dream scenarios. My narrative dreams, as the night wears on, become more complex and longer. As an elderly person, I often use the bathroom in early morning. Thus, morning bathroom breaks are a good time for me to practice dual state control and manipulation. In contrast, younger folks can simply drink a lot of liquids before bedtime to prompt practicing dual states in the middle-of-the-night. Note that the first three options require that we return to sleep.

Option One: Before you get out of bed, pay close attention to detail in your dream. With practice, you can maintain dream imagery for longer and longer periods of time. I've had decades of practice as I want to remember and analyze my dreams.

Option Two: Try this option when you first get out of bed. I can sometimes keep the dream going at a muted level during the entire time I use the bathroom, and then resume the dream with heightened imagery when I return to bed.

Option Three: Try returning to bed and alternately changing your focus, from seeing the images to analyzing them. If I've had the right amount of sleep and am in the right mood, I might lie in bed indefinitely in a dual state; alternately changing focus on the dream imagery and my analytic thoughts.

Continuing dream imagery into my waking hours offers a special window into what function my brain is attending. Continuing dream imagery into waking states helps me understand that my dreams possess their own individualistic image transformations, and it's helpful for purposes of analysis for me to move in and out of, in essence across, these dual states.

Option four: You can also make mental or written notes of your dreams during breaks. However, if you make written notes or sound recordings of your dreams, my first three options will probably not be available. You will also miss out on the option of returning to sleep, re-engaging your dream, and/or changing its ending. A little reflection on the above dream options should help the reader more fully understand the limits of dream-lab analysis.

During waking periods in the middle of the night, I mentally note dream content, and often identify the image metaphors that highlight the dream's meaning and dream type. Regardless of which option I use, my last step is associating the dream with its function.

Antonio Damasio reminds us that feeling is always an integral part of the conscious state we call thinking[2,3]. For me, that's his way of saying that without feeling, consciousness doesn't exist. Emotional reactions are a reminder, however, that the notion that one can be totally objective is just that—a notion. Given this conclusion, it's amazing that subjectivity was mostly banished from objective brain-mind research throughout much of the 20th Century.

No, the objective study of human subjectivity is not an oxymoron.

The subjective mind transforms the rose as we slowly enter sleep.

Hallucinatory Voices

Personal Case Study: Hearing the voice of Moses

When I was a child, I didn't hear my Guardian Angel Moses' voice, I just heard his thoughts. When I was in my 50s, I recounted my experience with Moses to a psychologist friend. He asked if I had ever spoken to Moses, and when I said "No," he suggested that I try.

The next time I sensed Moses' presence as he sat on my bed, I said, "Moses is that you?" He replied in a strong clear voice with one word, "Yes." I was speechless. We should be prepared for dual state transformative imaging as we enter sleep or wake in the morning. If my dual state experiences can be generalized, I suggest that lucid dreaming increases our individual sensitivity to dual state experiences, as my Moses having talked back. Moses' voice, in this instance, is an example of dream image transformation occurring in a dual state of consciousness. I suggest that holding a dual state of consciousness as we enter sleep seems to approximate imaging processes of lucid dream image transformations.

If we are undergoing major stress for any reason, (in my case divorce) we can be easily shocked by the vividness of visual or auditory hallucinations. Western culture with its focus on dream pathology does not prepare us for these events. Yet, a number of unusual and situational states of consciousness occur to most of us over the course of our lifetime. As we slide into sleep, dual states of consciousness can bring vivid imagery or auditory dream-like voices to the forefront, and as in my case, freak us out.

Our brain's transformative imaging generator, which includes visual, auditory, and tactile sensations, transforms all of our sensory images when we dream or hallucinate. It's helpful to remember that in dreams and hallucinations our image-generator transforms emotion into pictures, sounds, and even a physical sense of being touched. My sense of self, wellbeing and self-control was enhanced every time I learned to control another state of consciousness. Nevertheless, vivid hallucinations with any of our senses still startle. Startle occurs when normally predicted images fail to occur. The greater the divergence between expected and actual imaged sensations, the stronger our reaction tends to be.

Ridding ourselves of the belief that our eyes take pictures, or our ears hear sound, or our body directly feels touch, shifts attention to the sensory imaging mechanisms in our brains. All sensory images are generated in our brains; thus, sensations can be as vividly generated and realistic in dreams and hallucinations as they are during our waking moments.

Dream and waking imagery feel different in that internally generated dream imagery is not cluttered with competing stimuli from our environment. Waking hallucinations differ from dreams because we are experiencing dual states of consciousness as we transition with half of our brain imaging our environment, and the other half generating images from internal memories. But note that the intensity and vividness of hallucinatory imagery can trump waking imagery with its intense emotional impact.

Hallucinatory imagery can be extremely bright, colorful, and exceedingly beautiful; while the waking half of our dual state of consciousness can be experiencing a dull overcast day. This effect enhances our sense of having entered another realm or reality plane—exactly as described in *The Visions of Hildegard*[4]. Composite effects during hallucinations enhance their reality and trick our minds into believing that all imagery is being formed from external sources.

Daytime hallucinations are even more attention-grabbing than dreams. Daytime hallucinations occur with full or dual state waking awareness when our waking logic is active and our brain is processing sensations from external sources in real time. And all of this imagery becomes associated with external sources.

Recapping: Brain modules below our higher cortical centers are dumb computer-like automatons. Nevertheless, as we note in lucid dreaming or hypnosis, core brain dynamics are subject to executive control by our higher cortical centers.

Brain modules do their processing work at each level of complexity. And at higher cortical levels in lucid dreams and hallucinations, our brains do not consciously distinguish between internally and externally generated sensory inputs. Thus, our higher cortical centers experience self-generated hallucinations as being veridical.

Personal Case Study: Hypnotic induction while dreaming (14 Nov. 2013)

I'm in a large classroom setting with a group of unspecified people discussing states of consciousness. The problem I'm confronted with is whether I can exit the classroom in a straight line. However, in order to do so requires me to pass through numerous rows of desks and chairs. I'm not permitted to consider moving over the tops of the chairs and desks. (Note that my dreaming self is meta-cognitively reflecting on this induction process).

As I am concentrating hard on the predicament, the desks and chairs begin to dissolve. A passage opens up, one that would enable me to walk in a straight line to the door. I can now move across the area that was full of furniture just moments before. I tell myself, "You are still able to control trance-like-imaging while dreaming."

I look at the clock, and it is 5:30 a.m. I've slept soundly though the night and feel relaxed. I contemplate the dream for 30 minutes, until 6:00 a.m. I realize that I've performed this "trance-like induction" many times in dreams but have never analyzed what it means. (As noted, I'm not unique as this appears to be a form of image control used by some Buddhist adepts).

The induction that is subjectively experienced while dreaming feels the same as it does when I'm awake. In that night's dream, I concentrated hard, and the classroom furniture gradually dissolved over a period of seconds—the desks and chairs slowly, but progressively disappeared. The sensations that I created in my dreaming brain generated a clear distinction between what feels like my mind and my physical skull. Experientially, I felt as though I could control every atom in my brain. This is an example of the sense of "total control" over dream content that I experience when I enact a trance state of consciousness. Obviously, continuous control over non-conscious brain imaging would be deleterious to everyday functioning.

A sense of power ensues, subsequently, and I'm able to control— at will—every aspect of my phenomenal-self. My skull feels like a metal container that encapsulates my mind. Thus, I have a strong sense of mind being distinct from brain tissue. It is this distinction between brain-mind and skull that so enhances my sense of control; and at the same time, my sense of a robust self.

Once this dream-trance state has been enacted, I can lucidly manipulate any of the visual content I choose. Thus, I dissolved chairs and desks and instantly moved in a straight line. I did not walk, directly to the exit door. Rather I "morphed" directly to the door by passing directly through the now-empty space previously occupied by desks and chairs.

Meta-consciously I was aware that my dreaming mind had an experiential sense of controlling matter. I connected the dots and recognized how easy it is for one who is in a dream, hallucination, or state of shamanic visioning to believe that mind can control, create, or dissolve our material world. I now conclude that the illusion of thought controlling or becoming matter lives in the biology of our brain's metaphorical imaging capacities. And that transformative imaging by the phenomenal-self makes religious and other worldly experience inevitable—at least for some of us.

The night preceding this dream, I had reviewed Thomas Metzinger's ideas about self and consciousness. (Incorporating Metzinger's review is a good example of how waking experiences are carried into cognitively focused dreams). Earlier dreams that I had that night are vague and over much of the night I felt as if I had been in a dual state of consciousness rather than just dreaming. After 6:00 a.m., I let my brain drift in a dual state of free association, and my brain began to connect many different thoughts with various states of consciousness.

I made no attempt to capture the details over the following 45-50 minutes. Nevertheless, I recall a re-occurring theme as to how non-conscious dreaming and dual state associations could predispose one to feel that mind can control matter. I think it is interesting that neuronal reconfigurations creating these images in my brain reflect the assumed, historical capacities of an "omnipotent God," or omnipotent cosmic force. Awake, we are reasonably certain that the actions of the brain-mind do not control matter. From a personal point of view, how do *you* interpret similar elements of your meta-cognitive dreams into waking?

Additionally, I realized that as an eight-year-old, I was perplexed by my ability to pass back-and-forth through my bedroom ceiling when I went out flying during the night. Comparing that flying experience through my bedroom ceiling with my desk and chair dissolving dream, I realized that in both scenarios, I was just manipulating—at will-- my phenomenal imaged space. As a child, I thought my body accompanied my mind when I passed back-and-forth through my bedroom ceiling. As an adult, I know I'm just manipulating phenomenal space.

Self-generated virtual spaces of the phenomenal-self are experienced as though they were behavioral spaces. This observation is compatible with Susan Blackmore's theory that in out-of-body episodes, the phenomenal-self experiences virtual space as behavioral space[5]. I suggest that this theory applies to phenomenal manipulations in any lucid state of consciousness.

Trance Enactment Interpretation in Dreams

Trance enactment in dreams brings home the realization that the mind is always creating a "phenomenal-self model (PSM)," as Thomas Metzinger calls it[6]. Thus, self-induced trance enactment permits control of both the "phenomenal-self model," as well as its environment. Dream observations support and resonate with rubber hands being subjectively perceived as part of one's body[7]. Or, a full-body virtual illusion created by Bigna Lenggenhager stroking Thomas Metzinger's back[6,8].

Cross-cultural awareness of shamans and shamanic-trance states sensitize us to these full-body illusions. Shamanic possession of a totem, such as a bear or eagle, poignantly emphasizes how the phenomenal-self model can be manipulated. We can learn these techniques of phenomenal-self manipulation, and following thousands of years of shamanic practices, enact similar subjective states as we sit in our living rooms or, in my case, student classrooms[9].

I'm using the term trance to refer to the brain's ability to enact, and act in, PSMs." Trance states recognize the brain's ability to hold PSM in memory while simultaneously, consciously or non-consciously, enacting the perceived presence of another entity. Of course, the characteristics of another entity are defined by the person's culture or a hypnotist. Does analysis of controlled shamanic states of consciousness suggest changes to the DSMs?

Personal Case Example: Movement in dreams and hallucinations (17 Nov. 2013).

Perhaps I can best elaborate on what I mean by movement in dreams by using an example derived from my use of what Deirdre Barrett calls *The Committee of Sleep*[10]. Upon waking, I reviewed this dream between 4:20 a.m. and 4:35 a.m.

In this dream, I was reviewing my movements in an out-of-body experience when I was approximately one-and-a-half-years old, as well as reviewing my flight to the moon and passing back-and-forth through my bedroom ceiling when I was 8-years old. I also recalled dream movement when I flew from hand-hold to hand-hold in barns and other large buildings, my Genesis Journey, and my dream of three days before this one in which I had mentally removed classroom desks and chairs before I directly moved in a straight line to the exit door. By having all these movements in one composite dream, my brain seemed to be integrating a lifetime of associated memories.

Just before I checked the clock at 4:35 a.m. as my dream was concluding, I noted visual imagery that was running in the background of my thought processes. I focused on an object and its configuration instantly transformed. I became aware that I've been dreaming and reviewing dream movement at the same time. I'm in a dual state of consciousness. This observation adds weight to my assertion that creativity in dreams occurs when the dreamer accesses both waking and dreaming neuronal workspace simultaneously.

Personal Case Study: OBE hallucination experience

First, I'm aware of standing between my father and a nurse as we three are all looking down at my dead body (15-16 months of age). This hallucination would typically be categorized as an Out-of-Body Experience (OBE). Years later when I analyze this imagery, I realize infants aren't tall enough to be standing between two adults; therefore, I must have been floating between dad and the nurse. Instant morphing occurs in this hospital hallucination, and the next image sequence is that of moving down a tunnel that has neither people nor objects in it. Twinkling lights appear in the tunnel at a distance, move closer, and eventually take on the physical characteristics of aunts and uncles. I think of these characters as angels who have come to take me to "Heaven." I refuse "Heaven" and instantly return to bedside and continue to view my dead body. Next, I decide not to be dead and reenter my body.

Susan Blackmore suggests that OBEs occur when our brains are cut off from external sensory input[10,11]. She further suggests that the viewing perspective in OBEs is from an upright position from which we are looking down. My infant OBE squares with Blackmore's observations. But, also note that in the case of an infant's perspective my view is from a perch, a "bird's eye view" as if I'm being carried by an adult.

I'm following Gerald Edelman's "The Out-Of-Body Experience" in this analysis[12]: "OBEs are a well-known class of states in which one undergoes the highly realistic illusion of leaving one's physical body, usually in the form of an etheric double, and moving outside of it". In Edelman's personal OBE experiences, he moves around his bedroom in "jumps." In "jumps," he simply goes from point A to point B without any awareness of transit. "Jumps" were my experience in the infant OBE. We have no need of sidewalks in phenomenal space.

"Jumps" occur in our dreams as noted; however, if I focus on walking or running in my dreams, I can duplicate the same movements that I make in my waking hours. In other words, the phenomenal expectation of movement determines how we move in our dreams. If our intent in a dream is to get solely from point A to point B, we move in "jumps." I referenced "jumping" movement in previous writings as "morphing." (Here I'm using Edelman's terminology).

As an eight-year-old, when I went out flying for the night, I repeatedly experimented with passing back and forth through my bedroom ceiling, but there was no sensation of touching anything during these passages. Later at the same age, however, I began to sense temperatures. I shuddered at the cold of inter-planetary space on my 8-year-old trip to the moon.

In the Genesis trip, I enjoyed the physical warmth of my living room as I traveled out-of-body to the beginning of the universe. However, this time, I physically hit the plasma wall at the beginning of time. In my Genesis Journey movement was accomplished at mind-blowing astronomical speeds. Nevertheless, I observed successive stages of the universe's evolution. In a single "jump" I returned from the beginning of the universe. Expectation triggers the phenomenal sensation and related images.

Edelman says, "[In] the OBE state—namely, that the body model does not move as the physical body would, but that often merely thinking about a target location gets you there on a continuous trajectory[12]." Note that movement is just as subject to instant transformative imaging as objects are.

In another OBE, Edelman observes that his vision was poor and sensations of cold and warmth were lacking[12]. He associates most OBEs with night when vision is poor. I don't find this interpretation to be compatible with my own experiences. Focused attention, day or night, can intensify imagery, and imagery can take on aspects of intensified color and light depending on one's expectations. For me, it is expectation and my personal orientation that determines how I experience imagery in both dreams and hallucinations: A point of significance for psychotherapists.

As an encouragement to read Edelman, and give your phenomenal-self permission to experience OBEs and other paranormal episodes, I quote Edelman one more time:

Various studies show that between 8 and 15 percent of people in the general population have had at least one OBE. There are much higher incidences in certain groups of people, such as students (25 percent), paranormal believers (49 percent), and schizophrenics (42 percent); there are also OBEs of neurological origin, as in epileptics[12].

Note how easily DSMs lump these different groups of people into one metric. The above analysis and resources make us painfully aware of how Freud and Western cultures pathologized common dreaming and dream-like experiences.

Learning how to influence dream content with suggestion was my first step toward mastery over nightmares. I used pre-sleep self-hypnotic suggestion to intervene whenever a nightmare emerged. After a few weeks of using this form of suggestion to substitute erotic dreams for nightmares, my phenomenal-self automatically intervened in the process—meaning that erotic dream partners were changed while the dream was still unfolding. My self actively controlled nightmares and traumatic dream content for 20 years. I then consciously discontinued these self-hypnotic controls at 42-years of age.

Theory Rejection at Mid-Century

When I started self-experiments in the late 1950s, behaviorism debunked phenomenal methods of the type I was practicing. The mind was treated as being nothing more than a repository for learned reflexes. My executive control over altered states of consciousness did not square well with the determinism of behavioral theory. Ignoring mainstream psychology, I enjoyed my emerging abilities and quietly went about conquering one state of consciousness after another. And in this conquest, as my phenomenal-self became more focused, my social world and professional productivity continued to improve.

Psychiatry was dominated by Freudian theory at mid-century. Direct intervention in and control of consciousness states with hypnosis was out, and Freud's black box was in. As an undergraduate, every area of study I engaged, psychology, sociology, and anthropology, taught the Freudian model. Freud's dream observations, as I note throughout this book, didn't resonate with my experiments any more than the "Biblical" truths of behaviorism. Freud too was set aside.

Without Freudianism or Behaviorism, I was free to explore the content, patterns, forms, and processes of altered states. When we move across altered states, it becomes impossible not to observe image constructions and transformations. The questions became how, why, and what. Note that during the two decades from the later 1950s to 1970s there was no enlightening neuroscience to guide or interpret the phenomenal self-manipulations that I experimented with. Nevertheless, I found it necessary to skirt both Behaviorism and Freudianism during these years.

By lucidly observing and intervening in dreams over a period of months and years, I gradually discovered that I could control any number of altered states of consciousness at will. Thus, began lifelong experiments enacting and observing the effects of control and suggestion across states of consciousness.

Part III further dissects the subjectivity of image transformations. The subjective-complexity and global quality of image transformations in hallucinations and trance parallels that of dream image transformations. Therefore, the subjective, transformative content of these altered state forms will be analyzed from the perspective of phenomenal presence, movement, prediction, and metaphor.

Sources: Chapter 6: Spontaneous and Controlled Hallucinations

1. Kosslyn, S. (1994) Image and Brain. Cambridge, MA: MIT
2. Damasio, A. R. (1999) The Feeling of What Happens. Orlando: Houghton Mifflin Harcourt Publishing.
3. Damasio, A. R. (2010) Self Comes to Mind: Constructing the Conscious Brain. New York: Pantheon.
4. Hildegard von Bingen's Mythical Visions: Translated from Scivias. Bruce Hozeski (1986) Santa Fe, NM: Bear & Co.
5. Blackmore, Susan J. (1982) Beyond the Body: An Investigation of Out-of-Body Experiences. London: Granada.
6. Metzinger, Thomas. (2009) The Ego Tunnel: The Science of the Mind and the Myth of the Self. New York: Basic Books: 98-101.
7. Botvinick, M., & Cohen, J. "Rubber hands 'feel' touch that eyes see." 1998, Nature 391:756.
8. Ibid, Metzinger (2009).
9. Just, G. A. (2009) Autobiography of a Ghost. Eagle Entertainment USA.
10. Barrett, D. (2001) The Committee of Sleep. New York: Crown Publishers.
11. Ibid, Blackmore (1982).
12. Edelman, Gerald. (2009) The Ego Tunnel: The Science of the Mind and the Myth of the Self. New York: Perseus: 82-98.

PART III

Transformations Of The Phenomenal Self

I argue throughout this book that the phenomenal-self emerges and is made possible by the bidirectional image transformations that occur between primary and secondary levels of consciousness. Recall that earlier, I emphasized the role of neuronal plasticity and dynamic connectivity that underlies the brain's ability to transform imagery, as well as the effects of belief and culture on these processes. And that by maintaining lucidity in dreams and hallucinations we can observe image transformations between these levels of consciousness.

In the following chapters, I'll explain the phenomena of faith healing as a form of phenomenal-self-content manipulation. Presence and possession, in turn, are unraveled from personal experience. I'll also briefly examine shamans and shamanism, and how our human ancestors, ages ago, discovered how to manipulate the phenomenal-self. Locking the idea of the phenomenal-self in a mystic Freudian box was a bad idea. As an undergraduate student, cross-cultural studies of shamanism offered more insight into my personal psychic world than volumes of Freudian psychoanalytic musings, or objective experiments by behaviorists.

I'll also take time to focus on illusion, the de'ja vu self, and call attention to dreams in which imaging processes get carried into wakefulness. When I entered the University of Minnesota (1957), behaviorism denied the autonomy of the self; and Freudianism placed it in another black box. In the 1950s, this same line of thought was the objectivity of Western Science, which in my personal experience failed to explain the real world of subjective reality that I was playing with. I discovered that in order to follow Freudian or Behavioral assumptions, it was necessary to mystify my own subjective experiments and deny the autonomy of self. Thus, I came to reject both models as being incomplete.

Conceptual Overview

The following section discusses our human sense of self as an emergent property of the biological brain and argues that a functional process called self emerges along with secondary consciousness. I arrive at this conceptualization by integrating theoretical material from Gerald Edelman, Thomas Metzinger, Allan Hobson, and a multitude of self-experiments I conducted over a number of decades across various states of consciousness.

First, let me distinguish between neural correlates of consciousness (which I associate with primary and primitive forms of consciousness), and secondary forms of consciousness (which make image transformations of the phenomenal-self possible). Following David Chalmers ASSC definition, neural correlates of consciousness are a ". . . specific system in the brain whose activity correlates directly with states of conscious experience[1]." Following this interpretation, we are conscious if at least part of the neural system is active.

I use the expression "phenomenal correlates of consciousness" to refer to the neuronal process of image transformations at the human-level of secondary consciousness. In contrast with the neural correlates of consciousness, which explain the neuronal substrates of sensory image formation, the phenomenal correlates of consciousness identify processes associated with image formation in dreams, hallucinations, body size, out-of-body experiences, and other spontaneous and self-controlled image transformations. The phenomenal correlates of consciousness are "pseudosensory" images by definition.

Various phenomenal properties of the subject are simply different neural configurations present in the nervous system. Therefore, any notion, religious, supernatural, or philosophical, that suggests that dreams, visions, out-of-body experiences, etc., are other than natural phenomena can be rejected.

I distinguish between neural correlates of consciousness and those of phenomenal, self-engendered semantic correlates. Further, I argue that traditional mechanistic and deterministic attempts to explain image transformations of the phenomenal-self fail.

Thomas Metzinger's "The Subjectivity of Subjective Experience: A Representationalist Analysis of the First-Person Perspective[2]" is further developed in his subsequent writings. Following Metzinger's 2000 interpretation, ". . . no such things as selves exist in the world." And, "The self-model is an episodically active representational entity, the content of which is formed solely by properties of the system itself[2]". In agreement with his "things" interpretation, the organism's nervous system and brain alone account for the emergence of a human-level sense of agency.

Metzinger goes on to say that In our own case the phenomenal self-model is a plastic, multimodal structure that is plausibly based on an innate and 'hardwired' model of the spatial properties of the system (e.g.), a 'long-term body image . . . while being functionally rooted in elementary bioregulatory processes . . . [Ibid]. I follow Metzinger's conceptual model with reference to the self as a dispersed set of multimodal neurons and biochemical processes that functionally acts as agency at our secondary level of consciousness. I will continue to demonstrate ways that the phenomenal-self transforms sensory images across various states of consciousness and rely on some of his other works to further consolidate this interpretation.

The self-model that I'm proposing adds another research heuristic to the analysis of borderline cases associated with mental illnesses, such as schizophrenia. Hearing voices, seeing things that do not exist in the real world, feeling presence of others or things that are not there, experiencing taste without having anything in the mouth or experiencing smells from nowhere—these are "pseudosensory" images by definition.

Heuristically, I argue that analysis across states of consciousness furthers our understanding of the phenomenal-self model, as well as its origin, maintenance, and image transformations, as is the case with hallucinations$_4$. All arguments are compatible with my analysis in "Convergence of Objective and Subjective Methodologies in Consciousness Research"[3].

In the following chapter, the self is conceptualized as an emergent phenomenal entity. The phenomenal-self is functional and a dynamic dispersed process that emerges and is maintained across the brain's global biological systems. The term phenomenal-self is used rather than "self" alone to emphasize that it is never a specific brain part or non-material entity.

SOURCES: PART III: Transformations of the Phenomenal =-Self

1. Chalmers, David (1996) The Conscious Mind: In Search of a Fundamental Theory. New York: Oxford University Press: 17-18.
2. Metzinger, Thomas, Ed. (2000) Neural Correlates of Consciousness: Empirical and Conceptual Questions. Cambridge, MA: The MIT Press: 285-306.
3. Just, Glen A. (2015) Convergence of Subjective and Objective Methodologies in Consciousness Research, in Advances in Psychology Research. Volume 103, Hauppauge, NY: Nova Science Publishers, Inc.

CHAPTER 7

※

The Phenomenal-Self as Transformative Virtual-Self

The phenomenal-self appears to emerge proto-consciously in the fetus, develops from infancy-on as interaction with its environment occurs, and matures according to subsequently acquired social roles and beliefs. In the overall development of the phenomenal-self any kind of physical and/or emotional trauma appears to play a critical role in the phenomenal-self's overall development and expression.

There is dynamic interplay between the brain's hierarchical levels and modular architecture. It is of critical importance to acknowledge that how genes are expressed depends upon a multitude of biological, social, and environmental factors[1,2]. Central to how the phenomenal-self sees itself is the automaticity of transformative imagery. Let me start this review by considering the relationship between core brain dynamics and self as the phenomenal-self.

Antonio Damasio refers to the complex, integrative core dynamics of the brain as core-self[3,4]. I use Damasio's terminology as a reference to the brain's core dynamic processes that give mammals and humans primary consciousness. A more complete understanding of how consciousness arises can be found in Edelman's *Wider than the Sky*[5]. Also, try Hobson and *Voss's A Mind to Go Out of*[6], which covers differences between primary and secondary consciousness. Panksepp and Biven are succinct and insightful and highly recommended regarding primary-process feelings[7], as is Mesulam's discussion of how sensation becomes cognition[8].

We sense our brain's dynamic core processes as core-self, and our higher-order brain functions as phenomenal-self. Core-self represents all the sensations of flesh and blood. Thus, core-self is an organizing concept representing all the activities of the brain's core-processor, so to speak. As in dreams, our higher-order phenomenal-self personifies complex sensations; hence, core-self is experienced as a separate entity. The model being proposed views the phenomenal-self as a virtual creation from flesh and blood—it is epigenetic and develops in interaction with the individual's total environment.

The phenomenal-self is a virtual process intimately entwined (co-occurring) with secondary consciousness. According to this analysis, the self as a phenomenal entity is dependent on bidirectional transformative imagery at both the primary and secondary levels. The self as process is not even a single complex of neurons. We can lose vision or any single sensory channel but, higher-order consciousness still persists[9]. Thus, it is helpful to think of the self as a process that exists across the brain's global workspace.

Self-processes spread across the brain's global workspace can grow stronger with interpersonal support, or the self can gradually be weakened and dimmed until it totally winks out and ceases to be, as with conditions such as dementia. I conceive the dispersed neural network that is the self as being strengthened with the integration of neuronal process across the brain's global circuits[9].

Phenomenal-Self Plasticity and Pathology

Anxiety, depression, neuronal damage, or trauma of any kind runs counter to and can decrease the brain's neuronal integration[10,11,12]. When we study multiple personalities, it becomes clearer that the self is a virtual process that can be affected by physical damage to the brain, as is the case with dementia. Similarly, multiple personalities demonstrate the subjective nature of how sensory input appears to be manipulated. Similar to how we humans assume various social roles, the brain can create more than one virtual self. Using a very questionable example from psychiatry, as virtual creations selves can become as prolific as the potential roles we play across complex societies, reaching the absurd and improbable psychiatric number of 162[13].

As a virtual creation, the self can become a shamanic bear or the "Other[14,15]." Much of the mystery of possession, shamanic states, and psychogenic illness fades away once we conceptualize the self as a phenomenal entity created by the brain's neurons. This phenomenal entity also depends on sleep and social-environmental support to keep the brain's biochemistry in balance[16].

According to Edelman, evolution has created the self as a virtual process of neuronal activity. As we come to appreciate how the self is generated and changed throughout our lifetime, we gain insight into how this generative process can go wrong. The self as a co-emergent of secondary consciousness gives meaning to all of our experiences by filtering sensory input through the lenses of belief and cultural definitions. However, our subjective reality based on belief and culture can be thrown into chaos with trauma and/or brain damage. I've found Oliver Sacks' books to be especially helpful in sensitizing me to self-sensory distortions from multiple sources of brain trauma.

My example of becoming possessed by a "ghost" exemplifies how the self can use auto-generated sensations created in the brain's dynamic core to create a sense of being possessed by a spirit[14]. Simply, the brain can create as many and different kinds of virtual selves as it chooses. World ethnographic studies attest to this great variety of virtual selves. Re-conceptualizing how this virtual process of self-creation unfolds and is expressed from womb to tomb, we gain insight into self-inflation and deflation, its strength, or its sense of being nothing, and even into self-attributions we call anorexia.

The anorexic experiences the physical-self as fat, even to the point of death. The accident or war victim still experiences a severed limb as part of his or her body. Panic can become strong enough for individuals to stop their own hearts and experience death[17]. In dreams, the virtual-self can perform any manner of superhuman feats, from flying to breathing under water. In hallucinations, the virtual self can project an entire alternate reality. Thus, virtual elements generated in various states of consciousness, altered or not, partial or total, are understood as creations of our brain's imaging generator and our world modeling ability[18].

Brains can be altered through accident, drugs, pharmaceuticals, or ageing. Brains can be split in half with surgery. Each half of a surgically split brain can act as a separate self. Half of our brain can generate a separate reality in visions, while the other half experiences the here and now. And dreams can create *de'ja vu* memories that are later associated with our waking world. Let me tease these phenomena apart.

The Mind is a Mansion with Many Rooms

The mind is a mansion with many rooms is dictionary metaphor for our many different states of consciousness.

Examples of "rooms" of consciousness

In a dual state of consciousness, such as lucid dreaming, I'm in the kitchen and the den at the same time. My core-self is in the kitchen but my phenomenal-self is in the den observing. When I hallucinated being smothered by my mother, my waking state began to fade in the living room as my memory pulled files from the archives in the basement. Eventually, my waking state was replaced by total immersion in the archives of memory.

In a bipolar state, we go from manic activity in the kitchen to the depressed immobility of being locked in a small closet.

In schizophrenia, we frantically move from one room of consciousness to another without control.

When I consciously engage a narrative hallucination, such as my

Genesis Journey, I go into the mansion's multi-media room and turn on the projector. When my mind was cluttered with myth, such as stalking "ghosts" and hallucinated spirits, then at those times the aura of feeling crazy I resided in a locked room pounding on the door to be let out. The mind experiences whatever states of consciousness it inherits, or is being pressed into by environmental demands, or as in my own case, has learned to control. Controlled exploration of altered states has greatly enriched my life. It takes a high degree of control over focused consciousness to enter, direct, and leave a state of consciousness such as my state of shamanic possession. The more states of consciousness I learned to control, the greater my sense of wellbeing and self-fulfillment. Extrapolating from the assumptions of Metzinger and Edelman, it is health-promoting to control these various states of consciousness. To counteract nightmares, hallucinations, anxiety, depression, addictions, and mental health challenges such as OCD, we individually need to achieve partial or near-total control over different states of consciousness[19].

The Reality of Dual Brain States

Science has greatly modified traditional beliefs about the brain. Dual brain states—both night and day-- are a common part of human experience. The brain doesn't shut down when we sleep but is busy processing the day's activities. In parallel fashion, daydreaming reflects our ability to float between waking consciousness and the edge of dreaming[20,21,22]. Daydreaming is a time when the brain is free of task orientations; a time when creative ways to re-image the world emerge[23]. Paying attention to the self moving from one state of consciousness to another also sensitizes us to how the "wandering mind" engages meta-awareness[24]. We can open and close the doors in the mansion of our minds in endless combinations across 24/7.

Realizing that we create reality in our minds changes how we see ourselves, how we learn to enjoy our various brain states with new-found controls, and how we develop the ability to counteract the anxiety of false beliefs. New knowledge from the brain sciences permits year-to-year bootstrapping where knowledge enhances personal control, and personal control leads to new insights. We have a growing recognition from science that a genetically given architecture supports the development of the self. The self is a virtual creation, adaptable and malleable according to the social, cultural, and physical environment in which it develops. The brain's plasticity at the level of the phenomenal-self creates culture and all its wonders. It permits us to dominate the beasts, and it permits us to modify our physical planet.

A Quick Tour of Injured and Subsequently Altered Brains

The overwhelming position of the neurosciences is that mind and brain are one[25,26,27,28]. Without the brain's neurons there is no mind. Alter our brain cells by killing some with stroke or accident, and we have a different person. Hearing the statement, "Jane was not herself after her last stroke," brings us to the realization that the mind is always connected to its supporting tissue. Run a piece of metal through our frontal lobes in the right place, and our morality and conscience are out the window—as noted in the famous medical history of Phineas P. Gage[29]. I like the term brain-mind because it emphasizes the fact that brain and mind are always one entity and need to be analyzed as a global system.

A quick tour of physical changes to our brains offers insight into different ways our consciousness comes to be altered when brain sections have been lost or modified. Oliver Sacks *Hallucinations, Awakenings,* as well as *The Man Who Mistook His Wife for a Hat,* are excellent sources, and great readings, for exploring how physical and chemical changes to our brains alter consciousness[30].

Ramachandran's therapy with phantom limbs helps clarify how our virtual-reality generator works, and how illusory reality is turned into fact in the recesses of our brain's core dynamics. His phantom limb therapy works by manipulating the subjective reality of transformative images in our brain. With phantom limbs, stimulation from the stump limb elicits a memory image of the entire limb, and the brain continues to experience pain or discomfort[31].

Note that with phantom limbs, there is a nonconscious relationship between the automaticity of core-self dynamics and the brain's higher cortical centers. That is: a template of the entire limb still exists as a neuronal set in the brain, and partial limb sensation activates the entire limb imagery in the brain. Virtual limb creation can be viewed as a type of neuronal "chunking." Basically, in terms of severed limbs, "chunking" means that part of the limb is activating a neuronal template that has an image of the entire limb.

Automatic linkages operate between the self and our brain's core dynamics in any given state of consciousness—when the self feels possessed, when it possesses a totem, when it experiences paranoia, or when it enacts other forms of "multiple" personalities.

Lack of conscious awareness between higher brain and core centers parallels the effects of the two selves of brain bisection. With bisection, one self is unaware of the other. Thus, interpreting and supporting "multiple selves" modifications become a complex therapeutic issue. Symptoms are not just symptoms. Experiential reality in all these different states of consciousness involves active interpretation by the phenomenal-self. Neither brain imaging nor neuroscience's careful biochemical analyses, explains these phenomena well enough to establish protocol for therapeutic intervention. The brain is not simply a collection of bio-chemicals and cells[32,33].

Combining lucidity across states of consciousness and dual brain imaging research suggests causal distinctions between types of virtual "self-other" disorders. Attribution of cause by our higher cortical centers makes the difference between feeling being possessed by a spirit manipulating our brains and behavior or being paranoid that a neighbor is manipulating our brains with his computer.

Brain States that Alter Perception

We do not experience the world directly. Individually, we create a virtual model of the world, our physical self, along with our phenomenal-self. How we fit these models to our external social and physical worlds is critical for our mental health.

The world as we experience it is a selective sensory construction that is put together in the brain-mind. For example, we only experience a small range of electromagnetic waves. Bats, dolphins, and birds have abilities to sense electromagnetic waves beyond the human range. Bats use echolocation, birds detect the earth's magnetic lines, and dolphins have a type of radar. Living organisms process the forces and energies of physics according to their individually evolved ability to survive in their respective environments.

If the brain-mind is capable of a virtual orgasm that feels like the real thing, it surely is capable of phenomenally duplicating any of its other senses. We have numerous examples of virtual senses of sight, sound, and smell emerging and replacing our actual lost senses[34]. As in dreams and hallucinations, internally created sensations feel just as real as sensory experiences stimulated externally.

Neuroscience recognizes that neurons and brain modules alone are "dumb" information processors[35,36,37]. Neuroscience increasingly recognizes that processes in our higher cortical centers have the job of interpreting and attaching meaning to the sensory data forwarded from brain modules that only act as "dumb" information processors.

Controlled dreams and hallucinations inform us of the brain's virtual transformative imaging capacities; thus, controlling dreams and hallucinations provides insight into many other virtual experiences. Dreams also remind us of the monism of brain-mind interdependency. If my brain is physically altered by any means, so are my dreams and hallucinations, and so is my identity and personality[38]. With severe physical damage to our brains, we stop dreaming altogether and we stop being the same person[39,40].

Sensory imaging with Dual States of Consciousness

Let me further explore semi-waking image generation with dual states of consciousness. I'm drifting off to sleep and feel my Guardian Angel Moses sit on my bed. I talk to him, he answers, and I freak out. Decades ago, if I had been more informed about pre-sleep imagery, I would have realized that I was entering a dual state of consciousness—half-asleep, half-awake. However today, the brain sciences are gradually removing the barriers to our understanding of dual states[41].

We can be daydreaming, entering sleep, or waking up from a dream, and play with various dual state images. If we are under stress, loaded with pharmaceuticals, or experiencing sufficient pain from broken bones or surgery, our brain can flip in-and–out of dual states on its own. According to the Minnesota Multiple Personality Inventories (MMPIs) and the Diagnostic and Statistical Manual of Mental Disorders (DSMs), if we're sensitive to enough dual state images, we're "crazy." In my experience, DSM set points on the Bell Curve of *Homo sapiens* phenomenal states of consciousness are way too narrow.

When we thought that sleep was a time when the brain shuts down and imaging stops, pre-and post-sleep images were considered abnormal and referred to as trance or interpreted such that anxiety was elevated. If a person—on his or her own, in person—wants to explore lucid dreams and hallucinations, learning about our personal myths, and how these myths affect brain imaging, is essential.

We resist the experiential effects of dual states of consciousness if we think related imagery is strange, or if we are startled. Yet, when we follow our dreams over time, or create hallucinations on demand, we know that the brain's core dynamics instantly transforms sensory images. My pre-sleep imaging of a flower morphing into a bouquet is an example of instant transformative imaging. Programming my dreams to instantly substitute an erotic partner for nightmare images is another example.

Failure to understand sensory transformation of the brain's subjective imaging processes can elevate emotional tension and panic—panic that can lead to hysteria. For example, in my nightmares, primary images such as pain became bad guys. Daytime stress and biochemical changes in our brains can be transformed into waking hallucinations. Learning to control dreams with suggestion or lucidity can be a dramatic eye-opening experience. Most importantly, lucid observations in dreams and other altered states permits potential manipulation and control of transformative imaging that naturally (unconsciously) occurs in our brains.

Prediction and the Startle Effect of Transformative Imagery

The human brain is designed to predict our ongoing relationship with the environment[42,43,44,45]. When the brain fails to accurately predict the next anticipated change between core-self and the phenomenal-self and environment, we are startled. Unexpected occurrences in dreams are accepted without conscious reflection while we are dreaming. During waking or hallucinatory states of consciousness, we can be overwhelmed by the unexpected.

The startle effect during hallucinations shifts focus to our emotions. But notice that a startle effect--for whatever reason can trigger dramatic transformative imagery, especially for sensitive individuals. Transformation of sensory imagery that naturally occurs in our dreams breaks through into waking consciousness when we hallucinate. Nevertheless, we are aware that to possess consciousness at any level the brain is always transforming sensation.

A state of panic does not encourage logical analysis, as logic gets "disconnected" when we are overwhelmed by the automaticity of the biochemistry of emotion. Once we understand how our automatic image generator works, a wide range of guided imagery options opens up. Guided imagery in dream-work or therapy is fairly well understood[46]. Applying guided imagery in other states of consciousness is a new experience for most people. Nevertheless, controlled practice over states of consciousness can preempt unwanted transformative imagery, as I've demonstrated with dream programming, and controlled hallucinations.

Why is it so shocking when a Moses-like-figure appears and speaks for the first time, or a visual image of demons appears where none have ever appeared before? Part of the answer lies with our ability to momentarily predict what is happening. Regardless of our age, we've become accustomed to predicting daily routines in real time. We are easily startled when anticipated scenarios in real time don't happen. Note that prediction is an automatic neuronal process interlinked with transformative imagery in a circular loop. Thus, I've added transformative imagery to J. M. Fuster's treatment of circular causation in the prefrontal cortex[47].

Our brains process sensations differently in altered states. Knowing that dreams are an altered state in which brain modules, altered or not, follow their own rules is helpful. As Allan Hobson and colleagues have demonstrated, in dreams waking logic is suspended, our muscles are disconnected, and the normal sequencing of space and time is violated. Thus, as we enter sleep in a dual state, we should not be surprised that our image generator is creating what the waking half of our brain logically interprets as bizarre. Again, this observation recognizes a common, transformative imager across states of consciousness.

When Half of Our Brain Hallucinates

I was lucky to have had an out-of-body experience as an infant. I recall flying out-of-body routinely by the time I was three. All I had to conquer was my fear of heights, and the virtual universe was mine. If you've never had an out-of-body experience, as your first step, learn how to dream lucidly. Edelman's "Out of the Body and into the Mind: Body Image, Out-of-Body Experiences, and the Virtual Self," provides specific examples of how to enact these illusions[48].

Mastering altered states not only gives us a whole new universe to explore, but also creatively connects parts of the brain that are normally shut off from each other during waking consciousness. At least this has been my experience.

In his book, *Hallucinations*, Oliver Sacks uses the expression "Bisected Hallucinations in the Half-Field." One of his patients, Ellen O had "a vascular malformation in her right occipital lobe[49]. Initially she'd hallucinate an object, such as a flower, in the affected eye that was taken from her real environment. The hallucination would last for days. Later, real images from her environment were replaced by hallucinated creations from memory, such as the fictional character Kermit the Frog. These images were superimposed on her field of vision. They changed over time in terms of size, thereby, allowing a determination of how much of her visual field had been occupied. Her images were particularly disconcerting as they could be grotesque with dismembered faces and deformed eyes. Ellen O could not associate these images with any of her moods. Sacks does not explore the combined effects of expectation, auto-suggestion and anxiety on Ellen O's automatic imaging processes. Nor does he appear to use guided imagery to see if Ellen O could control and/or change unwanted visuals. However, in my opinion bidirectional image transformations between primary and secondary consciousness can potentially explain Ellen O's hallucinated images, for example, my broken ankle image transformations.

Our visual pathways in the temporal lobes process figures and faces; Sacks speculates that this process was the source of Ellen O's "neurological" images. However, note that pre- and post-sleep images are a product of the brain's intact image generator. Even though images are automatically generated in different states of consciousness, as is the case with nightmares, we may be able to manipulate the content even if we cannot totally stop the imaging. In other words, all the underlying neurology is not adequately understood. Nevertheless, selective, automatic imaging can occur at the same time that we interact with and normally experience the rest of our environment—a partial visual field hallucination like Ellen O's, or a full-blown narrative hallucination such as my Genesis Journey.

In contrast to Ellen O, I recall another of his case studies that involved Gerti C who had an ageing, deteriorating brain that spontaneously generated an erotic friend. She was able to control the narrative imaging process well enough to meet him every afternoon about the same time. Thus, it appears that we can manipulate automatically generated imagery with deteriorating sets of neurons—at least some of the time.

What does this conclusion mean for the use of suggestion with people like Ellen O? In my experience, the effects of emotional priming, across degrees of neurological deterioration, needs greater evaluation, especially for therapeutic intervention. As I demonstrate from personal example, the self as a meta-conscious entity is active across our various states of consciousness.

Now let me make some comparisons with commonalities between dreams and hallucinations that I've previously mentioned. Ellen O's images are like still photographs of the young child, or similar to still images that many people tend to hallucinate when overly tired or stressed. The commonality of imaging forms suggests limited, selective, and partial malfunction across related imaging circuits.

The beauty of experimenting with pre- and post-sleep imagery, as well as lucid dream manipulation, is twofold: We become comfortable with imaging that is not part of our normal waking visual experience, and we can learn degrees of control over these images. The fact that Ellen O's later images morphed from pleasant to grotesque, suggests the possibility of self-modification through anxiety-induced auto-suggestion.

A complex, combined neuropsychological effect appears to be involved with patients such as Ellen O. Top-down psychological effects on brain imaging are clearly involved in my controlled dreams and hallucinations. The experience I felt—of being possessed or controlled by outside forces in a state approaching paranoia—is attribution of meaning by my higher cortical centers. For example, when I was eight-years old, I struggled nightly with a "ghost" attempting to possess me as I went upstairs to bed.

Positive or negative moods alter what we image in dreams and hallucinations. Random images from our environments, including mass media images, enter our dreams. And as I've demonstrated with my "ghost" example, automatic transformative imaging fostered by cultural myths occurs in our dreams as well as in our hallucinations. Without controlling mood, our pre- and post-sleep imagery, dream imagery, and hallucinations can become whatever images our anxious brains automatically conjure up. The brain's image generator transforms feelings of pain, fear, and anxiety into specific visuals (bad guys), sounds (Moses voice), and touch (the "ghost's" presence) that we experience as being real.

Controlling positive emotional states acts as a form of suggestion, which can produce whatever pleasant imagery we choose. Hence, when third-person observers try to associate pre-sleep and dream imagery, which is first-person subjective experience, with waking associations, the third-person observer explanation often doesn't work. How do third-person observers gain an understanding of image transformations when they always observe from the outside? It appears that clinical and philosophical focus on language alone is not up to the task.

Empirically oriented philosophers are charting new directions[50].

In my dreams and hallucinations, the automaticity of my brain's image generator does not depend on waking associations. Clarifying this point, image generation in both dreams and hallucinations draws on memory, and what images emerge depend on how memory is transformed by the brain's core dynamics in interaction with our higher cognitive centers[51].

Having recently experienced surgery on a broken ankle and the effects of pain medications, I know that sensory stimulation from pain gets "metaphorically" transformed in my dreams. My mood after surgery was positive. My dream history for the past decade has been unusually free of negative dream images. Nevertheless, my ankle pain induced unwanted dream image transformations into bad guys and torture.

Constructions of the Phenomenal-Self

Sensations, internal or external to our bodies, affect the brain's transformative imaging processes. Practice with pre- and post-sleep imagery reminds us that various degrees of control over these images are possible. Hallucinating persons with deteriorating brains, such as Gerti C and Ellen O, remind us that control can be executed consciously or non-consciously. Genesis Journeys of my variety, and visions of shamanic scope, remind us that complex hallucinations can take on all the qualities of complex, narrative dream movies, and still remain under our control.

Half of the brain can dream while the other half watches. Half can hallucinate while the other half watches. One half can lucidly observe in alternating sequence with a dream within a dream.

We come full circle to the realization that our virtual selves can be whatever we chose them to be. The brain's ability to simultaneously hold multiple images is physiologically limited. Thus, the most that we seem capable of is one self actively watching another at any given moment—a global awareness by the self is the tri-partite element of this dual relationship—meta-consciousness. Nevertheless, we can store as many selves in memory as we choose to. In similar fashion, we can store as many social roles as we can learn. From my perspective, both selves and social roles are neuronal constructions generated in social and environmental interaction, and they have much in common.

We have a different understanding of multiple personalities once we accept the self as a created artifact of the physical brain. I can have a dream within a dream and, alternately, be watching both lucidly. By lucidly observing a dream within a dream, I become aware that I'm sequentially creating and holding two parallel imaging processes, but only lucidly observing one at a time. I am also controlling two parallel imaging processes in a half-awake, hypnopompic, dream scenario. I'm controlling select aspects of my virtual visual field when I enact a trance within a dream.

Post-hypnotic suggestion can mask behaviors that seem to come out of nowhere for the hypnotized person[52]; thus, I note that hypnotic suggestion has created a temporary neuronal set that is held in memory and behaviorally expressed and "chunked," without direct oversight by the phenomenal-self. The self's ability to actualize behaviors stored at a nonconscious level is not mysterious if we reflect on the automaticity of bike riding or walking fixed-action-patterns (FAPs). More specifically, the self routinely does not pay attention to millions of neuronal actions occurring in the brain's dynamic core moment-to-moment. It would be behaviorally dysfunctional to do so.

The self, as noted, is not a brain part. The self "winks" on and off from deep sleep to waking states, and it can be actively directed in various states of consciousness. If my phenomenal-self can observe and move across various states of consciousness on command, what does this mean for the self as an illusion? Self is a virtual creation of our brain's neuronal processes. Virtual self is a functional entity—virtual self is not a synonym for illusion.

The Logic of Phantom Limbs: The Reality of Belief

Case Study Example: V. S. Ramachandran's "cure"

The well-known neuroscientist V. S. Ramachandran originated a cure for phantom limbs by using a mirror. He positioned a mirror in a simple cardboard box. His patient inserted his attached limb in the box across from the mirror. The resulting mirror view created the impression of two good working limbs. This illusion tricked the patient's brain into believing that he could manipulate his phantom limb. Note the automatic, nonconscious linkage between the self and the brain's dynamic core. It is this normally nonconscious linkage that becomes accessible with self-hypnosis.

When I'm manipulating with self-hypnosis, I'm consciously taking control of an automatic core-brain relationship. Access to non-conscious brain processes permits me to create narrative hallucinations/visions on demand. What results is a controlled automatic link between hierarchical neuronal structures that enable experiences, such as Zen-driving.

Mirror therapy for severed limbs could have been practiced by the ancient Egyptians or Romans. Of course, they couldn't do Zen-driving in a car. Military personnel on long, forced marches also understand how the brain's automatic core dynamics take over when the self experiences the body as being totally exhausted. Fatigue alters brain functions—another physiological state in which to research transformative imagery. Also, note that there is a reduced expenditure of energy when the brain's core dynamics act without the self's direct involvement, e.g., Zen driving or automatic writing.

The critical point is recognizing that external world reality is of secondary importance to our brains. Ramachandran's phantom limb therapy views the brain's subjective beliefs as the critical elements. This concept is a stark reminder that you and I are not objective beings. We live in our own subjectively constructed world. Our brain's subjective reality is so fundamental to perception that it overrides directly, observable, objective elements in our perceived environment. The phenomenal-self is an entity unto itself.

Personal Case Study: Visual trickery to fly

I mastered flying above the clouds through the Rocky Mountains with my own form of visual trickery when I was seven. I didn't use Ramachandran's mirror; I merely positioned myself by the car window such that I obscured the body of the car, and then created the perception of zooming over the clouds. Individual subjective perception means there are endless ways to create illusions that our brains interpret as reality.

There is a critical piece that accompanies visual trickery in the above example, that is, if one wishes to get the full effect of flying. For me, it was important to subjectively experience my body being fused with the car. Fusing with the car means that I am subjectively incorporating the car into my physical space model phenomenally. In "being one with the car," I was able to float effortlessly as the car merged with my physical body; hence, my initial experience of a form of Zen-driving. Botvinick and Cohen's "rubber hands that feel" phenomenal experiment helps clarify the subjectivity of this body-object fusing process[53]. At the same-time I was fusing with the car, visual processing was still coordinating with my brain's core dynamics. In this altered state, my phenomenal-self was free of contact with the car while I experienced a sense of flying over mountains, clouds, and valleys. Fun without mystery! Flying without wings!

A quick insight to understanding the kind of sensation I had—I believe it parallels that of a blind person feeling the sidewalk through his or her walking cane, or the entire body[54,55]. My flying was much like the enraptured state of a teenager fused with his muscle car. In each of the above examples, the cane, mannequin, or car becomes part of the extended phenomenal body. Identity is our phenomenal self-model living in perceived behavioral space.

I used self-hypnosis to gain control over autonomic body functions such as pain. As an eight-year-old, I practiced flying back and forth through the roof of my bedroom—I believed my body went with me on these excursions. My physical body passing through the ceiling of my bedroom violated my waking-self's understanding of cause and effect. Being bewildered does not make one crazy. Controlling the contents within states of consciousness is not only active imagination, or a piece of "crazy" putty between the ears. It is an experienced subjective reality.

I took my first interstellar flight at eight years of age. I did so in fear after my father attempted to cut off my brother's head with an axe. For safety, I decided to go sit on the moon. I flew halfway to the moon, stopped, and shuddered in the cold of interstellar space, and then—fearful of getting lost— quickly returned to bed through my bedroom's ceiling. Much like learning to control a phantom limb, I had forever breached the subjective boundaries of my phenomenal world.

Our sense of being in direct contact with the outside world becomes dominant as we pass from infancy into childhood. In one sense, this shift is unfortunate. The subjective reality that energizes imaginary childhood playmates fades with Santa Claus and the Tooth Fairy—we forget all reality is subjective. Children's dreaming seems to reach a mature adult form somewhere between eleven and thirteen years of age. This period of dream maturity is probably a good age to research transformative imagery. In fact, transformative dream imagery appears to undergo changes during our individual stages of brain maturation around entrance to school, puberty, and again in our later teens.

We can employ ritual, self-hypnosis, or rhythmic routines to change and control states of consciousness. Our brains can also learn to remain in two states of consciousness at the same time. Tibetan Buddhists have been practicing dual state techniques across states of consciousness for centuries[56]. Controlling states of consciousness is not new. Controlling states of consciousness has been an integral part of religions, large and small, at least since we started remembering or recording these practices.

Belief Undergirds Phenomenal Perception

There is a group of occultists who practice these virtual journeys under various names: astral travel, remote viewing, or visitations to other planets and civilizations. Those individuals with a more religious bent might visit what they term "Heaven" or be confronted by "Hell."

My caution to you is to be careful about what you read. Popular occult literature is titillating while failing to inform. Ancient Egyptian, Hebrew, Greek, Roman, Persian, and East Asian literature contains numerous accounts of occult interpretations that are still widely believed today. Throughout history, people of all these different cultures created virtual realities from their most fundamental beliefs. We should not scoff at this great variety of mythical creatures and places, as our believing minds perform the same transformative magic in this 21st Century. We should however strive harder to understand how we misuse myth to kill and abuse each other. A contemporary understanding of dreams and hallucinations puts these experiences in perspective. A contemporary understanding of these altered states of consciousness also permits us to lucidly play with the effects while we are experiencing them.

Our cultural and religious orientations underlie the sense of reality that we all subjectively create. Belief and suggestion are twins that can undergird any of the altered transformative imagery generated by our brains. Selective perception guides what we pay attention to and sculpts the subjective inner world that is our reality. Belief acts to focus perception's subjective mirror. Thus, belief can direct image formation in dreams and hallucinations. Waking stereotypical images also distort perception as our minds struggle to overcome the contents of our own primary neuronal templates. *Selective perception fueled by belief forms the basis of the only reality we are privileged to know.* When we hallucinate, the brain's virtual reality generator creates real time images as it does in our dreams. The popular cultural idea, found in such examples as *The Visions of Hildegard*, that dreaming or hallucinating can collapse long-time segments into minutes or seconds must be false. The brain's neurons can only fire so fast—and that's in real bio-electro-chemical time.

We don't have to imagine content for a planned narrative dream or hallucination. As I've previously noted, content is an automatic, transformative imaging creation that takes place in any state of consciousness. (As the book progresses, continue to bear in mind the differences between primary and secondary image transformations). During our waking moments, our brains attempt to sequence narrative continuity; and the same real-time mechanism appears to be operating in other states of consciousness. However, waking continuity of time and space is lost across dream scenarios as Allan Hobson has noted[45,57].

Because our virtual reality generator provides dreams and hallucinations with automatic content, we receive subjective validation of being in another world or experiencing another dimension. I'm suggesting that automatic imaging is a product of the brain attempting to literally predict the moment's next event during wakefulness. In dreams or hallucinations, suggestion and expectations replace waking predictions.

All states of consciousness appear dependent on our brain's binding internal and/or external sensory input into virtual imagery. When I programmed erotic dreams as a young man, I initially selected my companion before sleeping and let my virtual dream generator create the scenario. My brain, like yours, operates with subjective meaning, not dictionary definitions, and not DSM classifications; especially when DSM classifications strongly reflect historical, non-empirical classifications by authoritative figures such as Bleuler, Freud, and Kraepelin[59].

Physical and Virtual Size through the Lifecycle

Individuals experimenting with hallucinogens or other psychoactive drugs will sometimes report radical changes in physical size—seeing their physical selves as being dwarfs or giants. Subjective perception of our physical size is a virtual creation along with all of our other sensory image transformations. Nevertheless, dramatic and momentary changes to our perceived physical sizes are startling.

If my history is relevant, continuous emotional battering and physical threats by authoritarian and neglecting parents affects perception of physical size, as well as one's emotional wellbeing. Analysis of dreams and hallucinations informs me that my self is continuously updating feelings of self-acceptance or rejection. Stated differently, the brain and self-processes maintain a real-time, functional relationship with the environment.

Support for positive self-concept has been incorporated into America's educational system and has become part of our popular culture. What is not part of popular culture is being informed by parallel psychological processes that affect perception of our physical size and body image. Consider self-perception on the part of my core-self's automatized, non-conscious, virtual image creations. My dynamic core unconsciously feeds and can neurologically distort information to my higher cortical centers. I might think I'm smart when I'm not; I might think I'm fat when I'm not; or I might feel like a dwarf or a giant when I'm not. Attempting to treat anorexia with logic is illogical. Nonconscious processes don't understand higher order logic; especially when non-consciously generated communications from the brain's core dynamics have been transformed at higher cortical levels and has been given a veridical interpretation.

Logic does not correct subjective perceptions. Subjective re-interpretation by the affected individual is necessary to correct life-threatening images of obesity or anorexia, as is the case with phantom limbs, or with "ghosts." Objectively treating either condition solely as a problem of nutrition or bad habits is illogical. In parallel with Ramachandran's virtual limbs, our entire virtual body image has become distorted. Where is modern medicine's equivalent of the anorexic's mirror box?

I already have an equivalent "mirror box" for "ghosts," and "spirit possession." My "mirror box" resides in understanding the transformative imagery that creates the "ghost" illusion. Entities that we feel possessing us disappear once the self subjectively understands how the mind creates them[14,19]. Throughout the remainder of my life, I might still experience the conditioned presence of the "ghost" I've felt earlier in life, but the sensation has now lost its power and impact. In my experience, how the phenomenal-self is created and maintained is often poorly communicated to clients by therapists.

Feelings of the moment, as generated by our emotional states, are not an add-on feature of consciousness. Consciousness exists as a component of how our brain continuously transforms sensation into imagery. At the primary perceptual level light waves become colors that we experience, sound waves become something we hear, and at higher cortical levels, secondary consciousness imaging becomes how we see ourselves, perhaps as example, as being fat or thin. Consciousness ceases when transformative processes stop. We gain or lose weight when we modify transformative processes at the secondary level. We grow or shrink in a similar phenomenal fashion.

If you had asked me when I was fourteen-years old how tall I was the answer would have been 5'4." On a good day, I would have said that. If it had been a bad day, I might have said 3'0," or 4'6." Cultural expectations accepted by the phenomenal-self provide the objective 5'4" answer. The raw feeling component of our core-self is usually left out of this discussion. However, the subjectivity of core-self must be considered and nurtured for optimum mental health.

Changing phenomenal self-images of core-self is likely the basis for the recovery of a real-life body image. This has been my experience. A common example of feeling small in size occurs when we are belittled or humiliated repeatedly. The child who is treated as a "nothing" comes to feel as if he or she is nothing. As nothing children, we often experience a sense of being physically small, as well as being of little personal or social value. The cowed child before a threatening authoritarian parent senses helplessness, as does a battered spouse. This interpretation applies to social and cultural discrimination as well. Emotionally and physically battered adults can develop a similar perception of a shrinking self. Thus, virtual size changes can have either or both emotional or physical causes.

Grandin and Panek[60] do a superb job of discussing what Grandin calls the "acting self" and the "thinking self". These are her terms for the dual selves that I call core-self and phenomenal-self. When professional people talk about zombies as disconnected brain modules of human-reflexive behavior, or when people become perceived of as just composites of symptoms, our humanity goes out the window. Subjective "being" is the essence of who we are.

We also create our relationship to our environment and to other people through the same virtual mechanism. The room we're in can subjectively enlarge or shrink. If we don't shrink with the room, the panic of being squeezed to death might occur. If we shrink, but the room stays the same, we might experience a sense of insignificance. These are effects that drug, pharmaceutical users, as well as abused children and adults know well. I'm emphasizing the point that in various states of consciousness we can mix and match our virtual physical images in both weird and wondrous combinations. Lucid dreaming or lucid hallucinations help sensitize us to these change processes.

Repeated experiences of felt helplessness can have lifelong impact. Crossing the line between a temporary sense of helplessness, and a lifetime of damaged self, is critical to our mental health. Unfortunately, related depression and anxiety often becomes habituated before health-restoring interventions occur. Habituation becomes a challenge to our innate ability to change. The longer we retain a habit, the more difficult it is to exercise the innate neuronal plasticity we are all born with[61].

Personal Case Study: Three examples of changes of size

My first time to experience a radical, virtual size change occurred during the time of my first divorce. A later incident occurred while I was at my university where I went from a subjective size of 3' to a full 6'2" inches. The most recent and virtual size change happened after I had broken my ankle. During surgery while in a dream/drug-induced state, I subjectively shrunk. After surgery on days that my ankle pained me, I "felt" as if I were a foot shorter. The non-conscious transformative imaging of self in waking states can parallel that of the brain's subjective imaging in dreams and hallucinations. Once I was able to walk and could put weight on both feet, my physical size returned to normal. I suspect that my abusive childhood makes me more receptive to physical size changes than individuals who grow up in emotionally supportive families.

Modifications of phenomenal-size are an automatic process under control of the brain's transformative image generator. Speaking developmentally, phenomenal image transformations across the lifespan are partially dependent on our early childhood experiences. In that child neglect and abuse is so rampant in American society, there are probably millions of people who feel variations of perceived physical size throughout parts of their lifetime. Comments such as, "I'm feeling small and insignificant" can represent virtual, day-to-day experiential realities.

The dramatic effect of size change can be immediate, much like dream imagery that shifts and morphs instantly. Again, this is a reminder that all image transformations at the level of core-self and phenomenal-self are virtual creations. I'm arguing that our virtual reality generator is a functional automaton in all states of consciousness. Thus, the self can feel the size of a giant, or be our former infant crib size. In my experience, physical perception of size can change across all states of consciousness, and across all age groups.

Small changes in how we feel our physical or virtual size changing are warnings to examine dysfunctional stress in our lives. I pay attention to sudden increases in the frequency of negative dream imagery. Repeated, daytime hallucinations about size changes might well indicate a trip to see the mental health doctor. Note, I'm stating rather directly that I do not consider radical modifications of perceived-size and body images to equate with a person being labeled crazy. Each one of us possesses a personal history of behavioral conditioning.

The third example of dramatic size change occurred in an adult therapy session. My therapist was aware that I had left my "soul" in outer space as an eight-year-old during my abbreviated trip to the moon. Unable to concentrate and fly out of body while talking with the therapist, I felt as if I were growing to astronomical proportions. My phenomenal size extended from Earth halfway to the moon. Like any good hallucination, these dramatic subjective perceptions are mind-blowing.

Now before you scoff, consider what you might know of anorexia. Anorexics view themselves as being fat as they gradually waste away, and sometimes literally waste themselves right into the grave. Body images of the phenomenal-self create the illusion of being fat or thin, infants or giants. Our only reality is virtual reality, and it can take us to these extremes.

As we age or have been forced to embrace live-saving pharmaceuticals—at least two options are open. We can lament the loss of our historical, comfortable states of consciousness, or we can explore the multitude of consciousness states in the waiting wings of our minds. I suggest we try to enjoy the various states of consciousness that nature or the pharmaceutical companies offer. Positive attitude can create positive images. I know from personal experience that anxiety or physical damage to my body makes me a waking, grumpy old man. I also know that my dreams follow suit. Be mentally prepared and when hallucinations appear. Try to relax. Focus on maintaining a positive mood by employing suggestion.

An excellent and up-to-date review of the effect of childhood trauma on adolescent and adult mental illness and physical health can be found in Bessel van der Kolk's *The Hidden Epidemic*[62]. I'm in compete agreement with him, as I've spent most of my working life teaching, conducting research, or involved in direct contact with individuals passing through correctional, mental health, social service and educational institutions. I used to tell my university students, "Any cruelty you can imagine being done to a child, you will experience first-hand if you work long enough in the Criminal Justice System."

Transformative Imaging: Dual State and Birth Deficient Constructions

I question the concept of pre-sleep hallucination as commonly used in sleep-related research. Pre-sleep imagery is a dual state of consciousness wherein the individual is half asleep and half awake. As one slides into sleep, emerging dream imagery mixes with waking awareness. Dream-like images often emerge when the brain transitions from one state to another. In effect, the terms pre- and post-sleep hallucinations confers a pathological meaning. What advantage is there in labeling a normal brain state transition as a hallucination? Being in dual states of consciousness as we fall asleep or wake up is as normal as it gets.

Some people who have lost their sight due to neurological accidents or the ageing process insist that they can still see things. Some who have lost their hearing for similar reasons insist that they can still hear. Some people hear music where there is none. Some people still feel pain and discomfort in their severed limbs. Such is the trickery of our brain's auto-creative imaging. The transformative virtual generator that creates all of our imagery represents trickery when our brain modules fail to communicate according to our everyday expectations. The above illusions of seeing and hearing poignantly remind us that transformative imaging doesn't only occur in the middle of the night.

We virtually generate sensory images in dreams and hallucinations by pulling sensory elements from memory. What especially makes us ask, "How is this possible?" is when those who've been blind-from-birth speak as if they see in their dreams, or the deaf-from-birth say they hear. Understanding such visual and auditory experiences presents and intriguing problem and suggests that the brain has some innate neuronal mechanism that supports primary imaging starting before birth. Such experiences offer strong support to Hobson's protoconsciousness theory[63]. There are other situations that also offer support for primary imaging theory; for example, if from birth an infant shares preferences for tastes and sounds of its mother.

Other evidence suggests that blind-from-birth individuals who see images inside their heads might be creating everything *de novo*. Or perhaps, the phenomenon is a kind of synesthesia of visual imagery that builds from cross-sensory, neuronal connections. Synesthesia is a neuronal state where information processing has been mixed up. For example, numbers might appear as colors, such as the number five as red.

Much more research needs to be done on how images are transformed at both primary and secondary processing levels. How, for example, does a primary image such as pain transform into secondary dream-images of "bad guys?" When dreaming, how is it possible that sensations—such as pain, vibrations, and objects with which the body makes contact—can be heard, or felt, or seen?

Lawrence Rosenblum is a professor of psychology at the University of Riverside in California. He states, "[Multisensory] . . . perception is a much more prevalent aspect of the brain's neural architecture than reseachers realized, suggesting that the brain evolved to encourage such sensory cross talk"[64]. Once sensory information reaches the brain, the information is functionally integrated to enhance and facilitate our total relationship to the environment.

Research by Paul Bach y Rita demonstrated that vision can be tactile[65]. Sensors placed on a person's back or on the tongue can enable a blind person to see well enough to discern and move about his or her environment. Neural plasticity means that one part of the brain that normally controls vision, for example, can be taken over by another part that normally processes touch. This is the case with blind Braille readers[66].

Realizing that image transformation is part of how the brain processes sensory input in any state of consciousness suggests that sensory cross talk should be researched from a meta-modal perspective. In my analysis, some hallucinations can be interpreted as a form of sensory cross talk.

Case Study: The woman who "can leave her body at will"

Let me close this chapter by emphasizing the plasticity of self-imaging. In this example, the subject's physical body is experienced as moving upward from where she knows it to be. This is also a good example of using brain imaging to interpret an actual phenomenal experience. And in parallel fashion to sensory cross talk, the subject's whole-body image is experienced as a veridical entity. Note the subject's meta-cognitive awareness of this process.

This research was conducted at the University of Ottawa, Canada by Andra Smith and Claude Messier. Functional magnetic resonance imaging (fMRI) was used to examine the extra corporeal experience (ECE). The researchers discovered a "strong deactivation of the visual cortex," and "increased activity in the middle and superior orbitofrontal gyri (A, B, D) the supramarginal gyrus (B) and inferior temporal gyrus (D)." The subject is a 24-year-old psychology graduate.

The subject's report:

"I feel myself moving, or, more accurately, can make myself feel as if I am moving. I know perfectly well that I am not actually moving. There is no duality of body and mind when this happens, not really. In fact, I am hyper-sensitive to my body at that point, because I am concentrating so hard on the sensation of moving. I am the one moving—me—my body. Rather, my whole body has moved up. I feel it as being above where I know it actually is. I usually also picture myself as moving up in my mind's eye, but the mind is not substantive. It does not move unless the body does".

The subject started performing this phenomenal maneuver when bored with "sleep time" at preschool. She continued activating this experience into her university years and was surprised to learn that everyone could not experience it. The experimenters speculated that ". . . the ability might be present in infancy but is lost without regular practice."

Over the years, student and client contacts have taught me that real stories are only told when individuals form a trusting relationship. With trust, and only with trust, do we hear the actual stories that underlie the realities of the phenomenal-self.

Sources: Chapter 7: The Transformative Virtual-Self

1. Levin, Fred M. (2009) Emotion and the Psychodynamics of the Cerebellum: A Neuro-Psychoanalytic Analysis and Synthesis. London: Karnac Books, Ltd.

2. Tyssowski, Kelsey M., et al. Different Neuronal Activity Patterns Induce Different Gene Expression. *Cell Press*, DOI: https://doi/10.1016/j.neuron.2018.04.001.

3. Damasio, A. R. (1999) The Feeling of What Happens. Orlando: Houghton Mifflin Harcourt Publishing.

4. Damasio, A. R. (2010a) Self Comes to Mind: Constructing the Conscious Brain. New York: Pantheon.

5. Edelman, Gerald. (2004) Wider than the Sky: The Phenomenal Gift of Consciousness. New Haven: Yale University Press: See Chapter 7.

6. Hobson, J. A., & Voss, U. (2011) A Mind to go out of: reflections on primary and secondary consciousness. Consciousness and Cognition, 20(4): 993-997.

7. Panksepp, Jaak & Biven, Lucy. (2012) The Archaeology of Mind: Neuroevolutionary Origins of Human Emotions. New York: W. W. Norton & Company: See Chapter 11.

8. Mesulam, M.M. (1998) From sensation to cognition. Brain, 121: 1013-1052.

9. Baars, B. J., & McGovern, K. A. (1999) Consciousness cannot be limited to sensory qualities: Some empirical counterexamples. Neuro-Psychoanalysis, 2: 11-13.

10. Anacker, C. et al. "A role for the kinase SGK1 in stress, depression and glucocorticoid effects on hippocampal neurogenesis" in Proceedings of the National Academy of Sciences, (May 2013). www.pnas.org/cgi/d... S.1300886110.

11. Pariante, Carmine. "Stress Effects on New Brain Cells and Depression" in Neuroscience Research from King's College London, May 6, 2013.

12. Siskova, Zuzana., et al. Dendritic Structural Degeneration Is Functionally Linked to Cellular Hyperexcitability in a Mouse Model of Alzheimer's Disease." DOI: http://dx.doi.org/10.1016/j.neuron.2014.10.024.

13. Frances, Allen. (2013) Saving Normal. New York: Harper Collins.

14. Just, G. A. (2009) Autobiography of a Ghost and (2012) Dreams, Creativity & Mental Health. Mankato, MN: Eagle Entertainment USA.

15. Berns, Gregory S., Blaine, Kristina., Prietula, Michael J., Pye, Brandon E. (9 Dec. 2013) Short-and Long-Term Effects of a Novel on Connectivity in the Brain. Brain Connectivity Vol. 3, No. 6. https://doi.org/10.1089/brain.2013.0166.

16. Nedergaard, Maiken, & Goldman, Steven A. Brain Drain. Scientific American. (Jan. 2016), 45-49.

17. Hinton, et al, 2005 Hinton, D.E., Pich, V., Chhean, D. & Pollack, M. H. The ghost pushes you down: sleep paralysis-type panic attacks in a Khmer refugee population. Transcultural Psychiatry. Mar. 2005; 42(1):46-77.

18. Hobson, J. A., Hong, Charles C.-H., Friston, K. J. Virtual reality and consciousness inference in dreaming. Frontiers in Psychology, Oct. 9, 2014. Doi: 10-3389/fpsyg.2014.01133.

19. Just, G. A. (2016) "Phenomenal Methodology: Toward an Egosyntonic Psycho-Neuro-Dynamic Model of Mental Health" in Advances in Psychology Research, Vol. 118, Ed. A. M. Columbus.

20. Barth, 1997 Barth, F. D. (1997) Daydreaming: Unlock the Creative Power of Your Mind. New York: Viking Penguin.

21. Occhionero, Miranda., & Cicogna, Piercarla. Phenomenal consciousness in dreams and in mind wandering, Philosophical Psychology, Vol 29, 2016, Issue 7.

22. Christoff, K., Gordon, A. M., Smallwood, J., Smith, R., Schooler, J. W. (2009) Experience sampling during fMRI reveals default network and executive system contributions to mind wandering. Proceedings of the National Academy of Sciences, 106 (21), 8719-8724. Christoff, K., Keramatian, K., Alan, G.M., Smith, R., Maedler, B. (2009) Representational topography in lateral prefrontal cortex according to levels of abstraction. Brain Research, 1286, 94-105. Christoff K., Gordon, A., & Smith, R. (in press). The role of spontaneous

thought in human cognition. In: Neuroscience of Decision Making. (Eds: O. Vartanian and D. R. Mandel) Psychology Press.

23. Baird, B., Smallwood, J., Mrazek, M.D., Kam, J.W.Y., Franklin, M.S., & Schooler, J.W. (2012) Inspired by distraction: Mindwandering facilitates creative incubation. Psychological Science, 23, pp. 1117-1122.

24. Schooler, J.W., Smallwood, J.K.C., Handy, T.C., Reichle, E.D. & Sayette, M.A. (2011) Meta-awareness, perceptual decoupling and the wandering mind. Trends in Cognitive Science, 15, pp. 319-326.

25. Baars, Bernard B. J. & Gage, Nicole M. (2010) Cognition, Brain, and Consciousness, 2nd Ed. New York: Elsevier, Academic Press.

26. Panksepp, Jaak & Biven, Lucy. (2012) The Archaeology of Mind: Neuroevolutionary Origins of Human Emotions. New York: W. W. Norton & Company.

27. Hobson, J. A. (2014) Ego Damage and Repair: Toward a Psychodynamic Neurology. London: Karnac Books; Hobson, J.A. (2014) Psychodynamic Neurology. UK: Taylor & Francis.

28. Hobson, J. A. (2016) forthcoming) Dreaming as Virtual Reality: A New Theory of the Brain-Mind. Clarendon: Oxford University Press.

29. Harlow, J. (1868) Recovery from passage of an iron bar through the head. Massachusetts Medical Society Pub. 2:327-347.

30. Oliver Sacks Hallucinations (2012), Awakenings (1990), or The Man Who Mistook His Wife for a Hat (1985).

31. Ramachandran, V.S., & Blakeslee, Sandra. (1998) Phantoms in the Brain: Probing the Mysteries of the Human Mind. New York: Harper Perennial.

32. Noe, Alva. (2009) Out of Our Heads: Why You Are Not Your Brain, and Other Lessons from the Biology of Consciousness. New York: Hill & Wang.

33. Ibid, Panksepp and Biven, 2012.

34. Ibid, Sacks, 1985.

35. Restak, R. (1994) The Modular Brain: How New Discoveries in Neuroscience are Answering Age-old Questions about Memory, Free Will, Consciousness, and Personal Identity. New York: Scribners.

36. LeDoux, J. (2003) Synaptic Self: How Our Brains Become Who We Are. New York: Penguin.

37. Baars and Gage, 2010.

38. Solms, Mark. (1997) The Neuropsychology of Dreams. Mahwah, NJ: Lawrence Earlbaum Associates.

39. Kaplan-Solms, Karen & Solms, Mark. (2002) Clinical Studies in Neuro-Psychoanalysis: Introduction to a Depth Neuropsycyology. New York: H. Karnac Books Ltd.

40. Bischof, Mathias & Bassetti, Claudio. Total dream loss: A distinct neuropsychological dysfunction after bilateral PCA stroke. Annals of Neurology, Oct. 2004, vol. 56 (4) 583-586.

41. Dresler, M. et al. Neural correlates of dream lucidity obtained from contrasting lucid versus non-lucid REM sleep: a combined EEG/fMRI case study. Sleep, 2012 Jul 1;35(7):1017-20. Doi: 10.5665/sleep. 1974.

42. Friston, K., Mattout, J. & Kilner, J. (2011) Action understanding and active inference. Biological Cybernetics. 104, pp137-160.

43. Adams, R.A., Shipp, S. & Friston, K.J. (2012) Predictions and commands: Active inference in the motor system. Brain Structure and Function, Epub ahead of print.

44. Clark, Andy (2013) Whatever next? Predictive brains, situated agents, and the future of cognitive science. Behavioral and Brain Sciences, 36 (3), pp. 181-204.

45. Hobson, J. A., Hong, Charles C.-H., & Friston, K. Virtual reality and conscious inference in dreaming. Frontiers in Psychology, 9 Oct. 2014. Doi: 10-3389/fpsyg.2014.01133.

46. Krakow, B. & Neidhardt, J. (1992) Conquering Bad Dreams & Nightmares: A Guide to Understanding, Interpretation, and Cure. New York: The Berkley Publishing Group.

47. Fuster, J.M. (2001) The prefrontal cortex—an update: Time is of the essence, Neuron, 30, pp. 319-333.

48. Edelman, Gerald. (2009) The Ego Tunnel: The Science of the Mind and the Myth of the Self. New York: Perseus.

49. Sacks, Oliver. (2012) Hallucinations. Toronto: Random House of Canada Limited: 165-169.

50. Metzinger, Thomas. Why are dreams interesting for philosophers? The example of minimal phenomenal selfhood, plus an agenda for future research. Frontiers in Psychology, 31 Oct. 2013. (https://doi.org/10.3389/fpsyg.2013.00746).

51. Poupart, Julie. New research shows memory is a dynamic and interactive process. EurekaAlert, Canadian Association for Neuroscience, 28 May 2014.

52. Barnier, A. J., et al. Developing hypnotic analogues of clinical delusions: mirrored-self misidentification. Cognitive Neuropsychiatry, 2008 Sept: 13(5):406-30. Doi: 10.1080/13546800802355666.

53. Botvinick, M., & Cohen, J. "Rubber hands 'feel' touch that eyes see." 1998, Nature 391:756.

54. Metzinger, Thomas. (2009) The Ego Tunnel: The Science of the Mind and the Myth of the Self. New York: Basic Books: 75-114.

55. Metzinger, T. (2013) Being No One: The Self-Model Theory of Subjectivity. Cambridge, MA: MIT Press.

56. Thompson, Evan. (2015) Waking, Dreaming, Being. New York: Columbia University Press.

57. Hobson, J, A. (1999) Dreaming as Delirium, Cambridge: The MIT Press.

58. Whitney, David, & Fischer, Jason, et al. (posted online April 7, 2014). 'Brain's 15-second delay' shields us from hallucinogenic experience. Reuters/Eddie Keogh.

59. Panksepp and Biven, 2012, 441.

60. Grandin, T. & Panek, R. (2013) The Autistic Brain: Thinking Across the Spectrum. New York: Houghton Mifflin: See Chapter 4.

61. Doidge, N. (2007) The Brain that changes Itself: Stories of Personal Triumph from the Frontiers of Brain Science. New York: Viking: 298.

62. van der Kolk, Bessel. (2014) The Body Keeps the Score: Brain, Mind, and Body in the Healing of Trauma. New York: Viking: 143-147.

63. Hobson, J. A. (2009) REM sleep and dreaming: towards a theory of protoconsciousness. Nature Reviews Neuroscience 10 (11), 803-813.

64. Rosenblum, L. D. "A Confederacy of Senses." Scientific American, Jan. 2013, 73-75.

65. Bach y Rita, Paul (1972) Brain mechanisms and sensory substitution. New York Academic Press.

66. Pascaul-Leone, A., Hamilton, R., Tormos, M., Keenan, J.P., and Catala, M.D. (1999) Neuroplasticity in the adjustment to blindness. In J. Grafman and Y. Christen, eds., Neuronal plasticity: Building a bridge from the laboratory to the clinic. New York: Springer-Verlag, 94-108.

67. Griffiths, Sarah. 12 March 2014. http://www.dailymail. co.uk/sciencetech/article-2575550/The-woman-leave-body-Student-sheds-light-strange-brain-activity-involved-body-experiences.html; Smith, Andra M. & Messier, Claude. "Voluntary out-of-body experience: an fMRI study. Front. Hum. Neurosci., 10 Feb. 2014. https://doi.org/10.3389/fnhum.2014.00070.

CHAPTER 8

🐝

Shamans and Shamanism

I define the shaman as: "Any individual who practices altered states of consciousness within a cultural worldview that assumes the existence of a supernatural plane of reality. Shamanism is the systematic use of altered states of consciousness to make sense of the world and community inhabited by the practitioner and that use contributes to the development and maintenance of social order within the practitioner's community"[1].

The emergence of our higher-order self in the course of human evolution demands explanation. The human's essential, virtually created self is an entity that feels—in a sense—similar to how we feel an emotion when we feel the color of a sunset, or when we feel we are in love. Failure to objectively explain how our virtual self is able to "feel," has been a historical problem for science. The human spirit has not changed with contemporary neuroscience, but our ability to understand how the human spirit feels has.

Shamanic Possession

I want to flip-over the coin of consciousness, which has my phenomenal-self on one side of the coin and my physical-self on the other. In this act of possessing the bear as a shaman, I will replace my phenomenal-self with the persona of the bear. As the phenomenal-bear, I will assume its feelings and physical power.

Remember, the higher, cortical centers experience and interpret as real events hallucinations that have been self-induced by a shaman, or by my-self sitting in an easy chair at home. The brain only knows self-generated images, virtual reality[2,3,4,5,6]. We can feel subjective states generated from external or internal input in the brain—consciousness requires felt-sensations. Remember, what we are feeling at any moment of consciousness is a specific bio-chemical neuronal configuration; we never directly experience the external world. So, stay with me as we take a further step together.

When we practice controlling various states of consciousness with self-hypnosis or any other technique, we know what it feels like to have our bodies act on their own volition[7]. For example, Zen-driving or letting our skis manage moguls automatically. Controlling automatic sensory input in any state of consciousness means that we can control single sensations such as pain, or if desired, substitute entire "Other's" feelings for our virtual self[8]. Thus, I'm acknowledging two hierarchical levels of brain function that normally act on their own (automatically) but are functions that can be controlled separately[9]. I'm also calling attention to the hierarchical relationship between the brain's core dynamics and higher-order consciousness as brain functions that can be differentially mixed and matched, so to speak.

For example, I can dissolve the sense of pain and make it disappear. Or I can enter my dreams and "mentally" dissolve chairs and desks to create a passage through the classroom to the exit door. Stated differently, my phenomenal-self is a virtual creation and, as a virtual creation, I can learn to control its content as well as its relationship to body and environment. Nothing new at this point, shamans have been performing these feats for millennia. What I've added is observing the process lucidly in a dual state of consciousness.

The brain can automatically create a phenomenal-self, or a virtual (phantom) limb, or an entire virtual double[2,5,6]. However, this ongoing, automatic process of creating virtual "things" can be modified or turned off. Consciousness consists of all our body sensations simultaneously keeping millions of neurons active.

Transforming images on the part of our higher-order consciousness is an automatic, invisible process. However, as demonstrated with self-hypnosis, dream scripting or meditation, we can learn to manipulate and control content that is normally a nonconscious part of the phenomenal-self.

What I find pleasing about lucidity developed through self-hypnosis, and the controls it offers over core brain dynamics, is the ability to move across states of consciousness. What I mean is that sensory input—internal or external—can be reconfigured on demand. The self can become a single, atom-like point and then disappear, or the self can be expanded to encompass the universe[1]. As a single point, the self "dissolves" and is no longer experienced. As an expanded entity that fills the universe, the self experiences kinship with the cosmos and everything in it. These phenomenal aspects of self are also observed in Buddhist and Hindu religions[10].

There is a very distinct, existential commonality that emerges between my sense of being an infinitesimal point and sensing that I have become an expanded cosmic entity. Both exercises strengthen my phenomenal-self because I've increased control over the contents of another state of consciousness.

Personal Case Study: An example of cosmic self-expansion

In the initial phase of my Genesis Journey to the beginning of time, I had to change my attention to focus on the dot that was my newly forming universe in order to stop my virtual essence from moving out into 360 degrees of behavioral space. When I was in my 50s and retrieved my 8-year-old "soul" from interplanetary space, my physical-self grew halfway to the moon. In the following two examples, note how my higher-cortical centers were able to enact and manipulate both my phenomenal-self and virtual images of my physical self[11].

Inducing a self-hypnotic state of altered consciousness (also referred to as trance) can activate virtual movement without the conscious exercise of will by our higher cortical centers. For example, when you're first learning self-hypnosis, movement without the conscious exercise of will is the practiced effect of letting your leg rise without direct conscious commands. From a behaviorist or neurologist's point of view, learning leg movement without conscious willing is a practiced process of "behavioral sensitization."

Example of activating movement without conscious exercise of will

Using no conscious effort to move your leg, think to yourself, "My left leg is rising; it is rising on its own. I'm exerting no conscious attempt to have it move, but it's moving." You might have witnessed this effect if you've ever watched the planchette move on an *Ouija* board.

Ouija is a game common to my childhood and a number of generations before my time. The Oxford American Dictionary[12] defines planchette as "a small board on casters with a vertical pencil said to trace marks on paper at spiritualist seances without conscious effort by hand." Simply interpreted, players have no conscious sense of moving the planchette, but in effect do so at a nonconscious level.

My interpretation: the self has deferred conscious control of our limbs to the automaticity of our brain's core dynamics. Some people defer this control to a hypnotist. The automaticity of the brain's core dynamics is the "will" that operates in any perfected skill such as bike riding or skiing. And with practice, movement just seems to happen. The automaticity[13] of the brain's core dynamics also comes into play with the long-term acquisition of social roles such as being a teacher or parent, as well as behaviors such as walking, and many of our speech expressions such as "please" and "thank you."

In the example of walking, thought alone seems to be activating sets of relevant neurons as our legs move. But note, as I activate movement with my thoughts, I'm consciously giving core brain dynamics control. Professional and lay people alike have historically called automatized behaviors that appear detached from higher cortical center control as trances. However, thought in these examples is perceived by the self as exerting force. I'm suggesting that the idea of thought becoming substance has a neuronal base[8].

Let me take the idea of "thought" alone controlling my leg movements during a trance state and combine "thought" moving my leg with transformative imaging. Top-down, my subjective, 5-year-old, transformative imager created a "hole" in the Japanese dream submarine. Image transformations are "invisible" to our waking consciousness, a process that is true of image transformations generally. Suspending conscious effort as I enter trance, my brain's core dynamics moves my leg. Thus, I acknowledge that my modular, parallel processing brain has two loci that can initiate movement. Throughout human history, "automatic" movement initiated by the brain's core dynamics has been deemed mysterious— "spirits" at work.

The Automaticity of Role-Taking

How is hypnosis possible? In hypnosis, I defer control of my phenomenal-self to the hypnotist. We all have extensive practice deferring to others as we play our relative roles in life—deferring to the authority of parents, work superiors, teachers, and others in societal relationships. Role transference ability is acquired by children by the time they enter school. In the course of social development, we learn role transference that is immediately executed without conscious thought. A common practice in therapy is to focus on role transference.

I find it helpful to focus on self-talk and the automaticity of role-taking. In self-talk, I'm the one introducing alternately the

"Other" into my consciousness, and holding it in an active state, while also conducting social intercourse. (The reader might compare this example of social role taking with lucid observations in dreams). Following is a personal dream example of self-other relationships in one of my dreams on 27 May 2018.

Snake-Connectome Dream

This dream was entered into memory the night of the 27th, however, I recorded it on the 29th. I had forgotten to record it but was reminded of its uniqueness while writing on this latter date. I am standing in my current office on the second floor of my home observing a snake emerge from a pile of books and then quickly reentering the pile and disappearing. I remark to a "nondescript" person observing with me that there is a snake in that pile of books. The snake's tail briefly appears and then disappears for the remainder of this dream segment. As I contemplate the dream in a half-awake state the term "connectome" pops into my head. I wake up and use the bathroom and note three items to remember: snake, connectome, and sense of self.

Snake-connectome is a vague abstraction and I struggled with its associational history and meaning. Hence, my desire to document and interpret the dream. My half-awake/half-asleep brain automatically generated the term "connectome". A term that I had been mulling over recently as I made final corrections to another book's references. The associative meaning is not clear but seems related to the snake being metaphor for something hidden that needs to be made explicit in another new book. The pile of books in my office, along with 100 or so articles spread across the floor, are sources that I have been evaluating.

The nondescript person in this dream is a type of social foil. Nondescription of dream persons is much like self-talk when self is the role player. I view this nondescript other in my dreams as a bilocated other[11]. It is self-representation that permits cognitive reflection, logical discourse with another person, and yet emphasizes the subjectivity of dreams and thought. In "The bilocated mind" Furlanetto, Bertone, and Becchio discuss ". . . different components of self-representation: self-localization in two different places at the same time, self-identification with another body, reduplication of first-person perspective." In this dream, bilocation of self is the social other.

Bi-location of self as a social other, as I'm describing it, is a common "nondescript" entity in many of my dreams. It is concretizing a social other for mental discourse. It is metaphor of self when self needs another entity for reflection and as a place holder for thoughts being digested and reflected. Readers will recognize this self-other effect through common everyday self-talk. Note that the automaticity of image creations at our higher cognitive level resonates with the automaticity of learned social roles. Our higher-order, automatic image generator creates either a non-physical or physical dream "other" as appropriate for the unfolding dream narrative.

Most importantly, in my various examples of automatized behavior, we recognize that the self as a phenomenally enacted, virtual, entity can be Its-self or it can be the "Other[14]." Awareness that the self is a virtually generated entity that is created according to cultural expectations and belief sets the stage for us to explore the shaman's phenomenal-self.

Shamans and the Phenomenal-Self

For millennia, traditional cultures have identified themselves with totem animals. As a child and then young teenager, I spent endless hours in the woods of NW Wisconsin observing animals and nature. By the age of 14, I stopped hunting because I felt the pain of the hunted as though it were my own. In this way, I came to appreciate the bond that we humans naturally develop with our fellow creatures. We love our dogs and cats.

Pet owners and zoo keepers come to love their animals and identify with them. Mirror neurons and empathy circuits in our brains seem to dictate this emotional transference, which enhances our "mirror" identification with other life forms. Soon after television became a part of my life as an adult, I learned to substitute "movies on the silver screen" for real-life woods experiences[7]. Movies and films of all kinds can be used for these fun exercises. First, a reminder as to what the brain can do as we learn to control content in these other states of consciousness.

We can make bodily sensations concrete and then attribute these sensations to imagined entities. We can feel the "ghost" possess us, and that belief makes the experience terrifying. Our mind's mirror neurons and virtual imaging ability can make all things we believe feel concrete. Manifest examples of these processes can be found in my accounts of dream programming (scripting) and controlled waking-narrative hallucinations[7]. As with role taking, in dream programming we create a virtual "Other," holding it in consciousness in much the same way that we hold social roles, and then we fully experience attributed sensations to these other objects. Subjective reality is existential reality.

World ethnographies of pre-literate people are full of shamanic ritual. Shamans were probably humankind's first clinicians; they were the keepers of spiritual, physical, and medicinal remedies. Those who scoff at superstitious beliefs fail to appreciate the central role belief plays in our everyday transformative imaging constructions of reality. After all, the brain can only create virtual reality components that become part of our phenomenal-self model in any state of consciousness. Scientific explanations of the brain's biochemical and neuronal processes might be closer to objective truth; nevertheless, belief systems guide human behavior not objective scientific truth.

A more sophisticated, and highly recommended, neuroscience explanation of our "phenomenal self-model" is found in Metzinger's

The Ego Tunnel[15] and *Being No One*[16]. I you are not familiar with Metzinger and would like a comprehensive, technical view, try reading *Being No One*.

Shamanism as a biochemical process has been relegated to the realm of mystery along with exorcism. What does it feel like to be in a shamanic state of consciousness? And what does it mean to project into another persona, say the bear? In my interpretation, it's the flip-side of being possessed by a "demon". When we feel a "demon" beginning to possess us, we experience the phenomenal "Other" as a real entity. And similar to the phenomenal sense that we experience in hypnotic trance, personal control is transferred to the "Other." The "Other" as "demon"—that entity that takes control of our phenomenal-self—can be our addiction or, perhaps, the controlling entity that causes us to kill our in-laws in our sleep[17].

When we possess a totem such as the bear, we feel the phenomenal bear as a real entity. Viewing the virtually created self as a phenomenal entity helps remove the mystery of historical shamanic practices. As I compare myself taking on the persona of a totemic bear with my ability to assume complex social roles, the difference is more a matter of degree. By degree I mean role assumption that approximates that of an accomplished actor who assumes a role so completely that it takes months to return to being the actor's former self.

If major world religions can cast out demons, I should be permitted to take virtual possession of bears. Or at least, I suggest, we should stop being smug and degrading about a shaman who substitutes totem animals for self. Similar to the theatrical actor, the shaman becomes subsumed by the role itself. In any case, my personal experience says that shamanic possession of a totem is a complex phenomenal process. Critics of shamanism should learn how to enact this state of consciousness in order to appreciate its complexity. Nevertheless, phenomenal shamanic possession of a totem loses its mystery when the process is being interpreted naturally.

I have yet to hear of a priest or church leader being forced into therapy for practicing "witchcraft" because of using religious ceremony to cast-out demons. And most assuredly, we do not castigate any Christian Biblical figures for doing so. I also don't know of any priests forced into asylums for these practices. Priests get a free pass from psychiatry. Understanding "demon possession" trumps ignorance. And although shamans and clergy are faster and cheaper than psychoanalysts, my personal experience says that clergy and psychoanalysts are not necessary once we understand the natural process of how our brains create "demons," or how we become possessed.

The Veridical Nature of Human Consciousness

I hope my observations have helped sensitize the reader to self-induced sensations of the "ghost" and the state of consciousness we call possession. The key point is that self-generated sensations are experienced by the phenomenal-self as being real. Belief makes it so. This capacity to virtually image a phenomenal-self is an integral part of our genetic makeup. This capacity is a biological-phase change that makes self-emergence with secondary consciousness possible. Nature's biology is responsible for all of our subjective reality. The nature of human subjectivity is to experience sensation across states of consciousness as being veridical[18].

We are not being objective when we dismiss scientific exploration of subjectivity. "The existence of subjectivity in the brain also means that we cannot simply approach the study of brain functions with the traditional third-person tools of science[19]". Careful observation of human nature has been an integral part of philosophy and psychology for generations: Descartes, Hume, Locke, Kant, William James, Charles H. Cooley, and George H. Mead being good examples. And careful Eastern philosophical observations go back at least to the Upanishads 6th and 7th centuries B.C.E.[10]. My bias in the exploration of the self and consciousness is to hone careful observation with control of consciousness states while holding our observations to the mirror of science. The brain is our master sensory processor. We experience what our brains are selectively paying attention to and processing. Brains are always converting the objective elements in our environment into subjective experience. Light rays become colors, jiggling air molecules become sounds, and pressure on skin becomes felt-sensations. Critically, improving our understanding of how the brain-mind transforms emotion into images and felt-sensations suggests new multi-modal approaches for improved cognitive-behavioral and affective therapies[20].

Is it possible to imagine that the human mind is just meat and nothing more? I am baldly stating that human consciousness and the virtual self must be treated as real artifacts of biological evolution if the narrow focus of 20th Century "talk-therapy" and mysticism are to be permanently put to rest. Simply stated, keeping image transformation of sensory experience within limited metrics is fundamental to the treatment and maintenance of positive mental health. And in my experience, studying and experimenting with shamanism has deepened my understanding of how the human brain transforms sensation bottom-up and top-down.

Subjectivity, the felt essence of consciousness, emerges with networks of complex cells turning bio-chemical signals into sensations (qualia) that we experience, such as color, sound, and touch. You will note that color, sound, and touch are first-person qualitative experiences. These sensory experiences are not something that exists, third person-wise in the external, objective universe. Third-person "objectivity" (as I contend was the case with Freud) offers endless interpretations. Possession or shamanic incorporation of the "Other" are not fully understood until we gain first-hand experience. Fortunately, first-hand experience can be gained through lucid dreaming or lucid hallucinations[21].

Add mirror neurons to our understanding of first-person, subjective experiences and we realize that biology has given each one of us a physical basis that we can and do use to share each other's subjective states of consciousness[22,23,24,25,26]. In this sense of biologically shared subjective states, we are all mind-readers, and we are never alone. We can only feel alone in the universe by ignoring our own biology—by denying our innate human capacity to share emotions and create a multitude of phenomenal states.

Introduce lucidity[27,28,29,30] where the normal hierarchical relationship between higher-order cerebral centers and the brain's core dynamics becomes a side-by-side relationship and presence, possession, and other shamanic states begin to reveal their essence. We can learn to create the contents of any consciousness state and lucidly observe phenomenal-selves in these various states once they have been entered as content in our own minds. Perhaps the true mystic is the person who insists on mystifying brain-mind states that have been so commonly enacted across world cultures and history.

When my brain shifts over to processing mostly internal sensory stimuli, I dream, hallucinate, or enter what is called trance. Learning to control internal brain-mind processing, various states of consciousness can make me a shaman, a "priest," a mystic, or an interesting neighbor. For me, it's a personal loss to mystify and obscure any of the wondrous processes of which my brain is capable.

As I assume the persona of the bear, I am subjectively duplicating and substituting its size and power for my usual felt, physical sensations that are being processed in my brain's dynamic core. I am entering a separate virtual creation into the content of my consciousness. I am doing no more and no less than A. Damasio proposes in his explanation of how self comes to mind[31]. Meta-cognitively, my phenomenal-self experiences these virtual creations as its actual physical-self. A mental health point of view might say that I can also experience the self as the "Other". As a virtual construction, the "Other" can be constructed in part or in whole; thus, we come to realize that paranoia can occur in degrees.

With totemic-possession such as the bear, the phenomenal-self attributes auto-created sensations to the bear and, at the same time, feels self-generated sensations attributed to the bear as mirror-like reflections of its own mind. Be aware that transformative imaging is the mechanism that enables shamanic trance, such as the bear example. As my experience implies, the self can observe these shamanic creations in a dual state of consciousness that is similar to lucid dreaming.

The marvel of our higher- order consciousness is this dual ability of the phenomenal-self to reflect back upon the physical-self or to hold in memory the contents of the physical-self as it reflects back upon the phenomenal-self. Note the meta-cognitive awareness in these dual abilities; a meta-cognitive awareness that permits the self to transcend any one state of consciousness. These dual-state reflections can and do involve all of our senses. We can become the bear, or we can reverse the felt-origin of totems and become possessed by spirits. In various psycho-pathogenic illnesses, the self fails to distinguish felt sensations as virtual, auto-created entities. In my experience, meta-cognition through lucidity can overcome the illusions of pathogenesis.

The Significance of First-Person Observations

Lack of common definitions across disciplines has added confusion to terms such as trance, possession, hallucinations, and visions. I'm trying to cut through this confusion of terms by focusing on imaging processes in our brain's basic dynamic states or forms of consciousness that are involved. Like all subjective states of consciousness, each state must be experienced from a first-person point of view for its full appreciation. We do not understand the self of consciousness by defining it as illusion. We understand possession by employing it. We understand the self's phenomenal capacities through engagement. Third-person-wise, we observe Plato's wall shadows of dual states of consciousness through imaging technology.

Ursula Voss's and colleagues' imaging research documents dual brain centers being active in lucid dreaming. Neuroscience has a great set of growing imaging tools that can take the phenomena of presence and possession out of the hands of mystics.

SOURCES: CHAPTER 8: Shamans and Shamanism

1. Just, G. A. (2011) Mind of the Mystic. Eagle Entertainment USA: Mankato, MN: 139.
2. Botvinick, M., & Cohen, J. (1998) Rubber hands "feel" touch that eyes see. Nature 391:756. doi: 10.1038/35784.
3. Ehrsson, H. H., et al. (2007) Threatening a rubber hand that you feel is yours elicits a cortical anxiety response. Proc. National Academy of Sciences U.S.A. 104, 9828-9833. doi: 10.1073/pnas.0610011104.
4. Blanke, O., & Metzinger, T. (2009) Full-body illusions and minimal phenomenal selfhood. Trends Cogn. Sci. 13, 7-13. doi: 10.1016/j.tics.2008.10.003.
5. Petkova, V. I., Bjornsdotter, M., Gentile, G., Jonsson, T., Li, T. Q., & Ehrsson, H. H. (2011) From part-to-whole-body ownership in the multisensory brain. Curr. Biol. 21, 1118-1122. doi: 10.1016/j.cub.2011.05.022.
6. Tsakiris, M. (2010) My body in the brain: a neurocognitive model of body-ownership. Neurospychologia 48, 703-712. doi: 10-1016/j.neurospychologia.2009.90.034.
7. Just, G. A. (2009) Autobiography of a Ghost. Mankato, MN: Eagle Entertainment U.S.A.
8. Just. G. A. (2011) Mind of the Mystic. Mankato, MN: Eagle Entertainment U.S. A.
9. Just, G. A. (2017) "Clinical Advantages of Self-Hypnosis," in Advances in Psychology Research, Vol. 128 (Ed.) A. M. Columbus. Hauppauge, NY: Nova Sci. Pubs.
10. Thompson, Evan. (2015) Waking, Dreaming, Being. New York: Columbia University Press: p. xxxiii.

11. Furlanetto, Tiziano., Bertone, Cesare., & Becchio, Cristine. Front. Hum. Neurosci., 08 March 2013. https://doi. org/10.3389/fnhum.2013.00071.
12. Oxford American Dictionary (1980)
13. Hari, R., Henriksson, L., Malinen, S., & Parkkonen, L. Neuron. 2015; 88: 181-193.
14. Metzinger, Thomas. Why are dreams interesting for philosophers? The example of minimal phenomenal selfhood, plus an agenda for future research. Frontiers in Psychology, 31 Oct. 2013. (https://doi.org/10.3389/fpsyg.2013.00746).
15. Metzinger, Thomas. (2009) The Ego Tunnel: The Science of the Mind and the Myth of the Self. New York: Basic Books.
16. Metzinger, Thomas. (2001) Being No One: The Self-Model Theory of Subjectivity. Boston: MIT Press.
17. Cartwright, R. D. (2010) The Twenty-Four-Hour Mind: The Role of Sleep and Dreams in our Emotional Lives. London: Oxford University Press.
18. Panksepp, Jaak & Biven, Lucy. (2012) The Archaeology of Mind: Neuroevolutionary Origins of Human Emotions. New York: W. W. Norton & Company.
19. Ibid, 422-423.
20. Just, G. A. (2016) "Phenomenal Methodology: Toward an Egosyntonic Psycho-Neuro-Dynamic Model of Mental Health. In Advances in Psychology Research, Vol. 118 (Ed.) A. M. Columbus.
21. Hobson, J. A., & Just, G. A. (2013) "Lucid Hallucinations." In Hallucinations, Causes, Management and Prognosis, Ed. Sofia Alvarez. Hauppauge, NY: Nova Science Publications.
22. Iacoboni, Marco. (2009) Mirroring People: The Science of Empathy and How We Connect with Others. NY: Picador.

23. Hickok, Gregory. (2014) The Myth of Mirror Neurons: The Real Neuroscience of Communication and Cognition. NY: W. W. Norton & Co.

24. Rizzolatti, G., & Arbib, M. A. "Language Within Our Grasp," Trends in Neuroscience 21 (1998):188-94.

25. Gallese, V., & Lakoff, G. "The Brain's Concepts: The Role of the Sensory-Motor System in Conceptual Knowledge," Cognitive Neuropsychology 22 (2005):455-79.

26. Zahavi, D. "Beyond Empathy: Phenomenological Approaches to Intersubjectivity," J. of Consciousness Studies 8 (2001): 151-67.

27. Hobson, J. A., Hong, Charles C.-H., & Friston, K. Virtual reality and conscious inference in dreaming. Frontiers in Psychology, 9 Oct. 2014. Doi: 10-3389/fpsyg.2014.01133.

28. Dresler, M. et al. Neural correlates of dream lucidity obtained from contrasting lucid versus non-lucid REM sleep: a combined EEG/fMRI case study. Sleep, 2012 Jul 1;35(7):1017-20. Doi: 10.5665/sleep. 1974.

29. Hobson, J. A. (2009) The neurobiology of consciousness: Lucid dreaming wakes up, International Journal of Dream Research, 2 (2), pp. 41-44.

30. Voss, U., Holzmann, R., Tin, I., & Hobson, J. A. (2009) Lucid Dreaming: A State of Consciousness with Features of both Waking and Non-Lucid Dreaming. Sleep, 32(9).

31. Damasio, A. R. (1999) The Feeling of What Happens. Orlando: Houghton Mifflin Harcourt Publishing. Self Comes to Mind: Constructing the Conscious Brain. (2010). New York: Random House.

CHAPTER 9

Dream Illusion and the De'ja Vu-Self

Our sense of self changes over time. We are most aware of these changes when we make infant, child, adolescent, adult, and elderly comparisons. Decades of lucid dreaming sensitizes me to parallel processes of self-development between waking and dreaming states of consciousness.

I call the content of this dream progression—dream memories—and the dream-self the *de'ja vu-self.* Further, I suggest that there is carryover across states of consciousness in our 24-hour mind[1] that has implications for our mental health. Specifically, the relationship between *de'ja vu-self,* that is dream-generated versions of the self, and multiple-selves. In the following discussion, I'm in agreement with Rosalind Cartwright that a balanced relationship between waking and dreaming is necessary for quality mental health[2].

The Parallel World of Dream Histories

I find little mention in the professional literature of the dreaming brain's practice of creating virtual, imaginary worlds and evolving them over decades. However, the occult literature is full of examples where the individual in dreams or hallucinations returns to the same imagined world repeatedly. Historically, long-term virtual-world interpretations have generally been left at the mystic level. My discussion of dream histories places emphasis on their natural origin and general neglect in Western cultures.

In personal discussions with noted dream researcher Allan Hobson, we each have a dream farm. His dream farm also has an actual basis, and it exists in East Burke, Vermont. My dream farm is a take-off from one I lived on when I was 12-to-14-years old. Each of our dream farms evolve over time. Both farms are dream utopias. Let me tie this phenomenon of creating dream histories together with multiple selves and the virtual creation of these selves.

The concept of utopia is inevitable with evolving dream memories.

Personal Case Study: My utopian farm dream

One of the happiest times of my young life was on this farm. When I last actually visited in the 1980s, the farm had lost all its building except the house. I spent endless hours in the woods that totally surrounded the farm. I observed flying squirrels and rutting deer. It was heaven on earth, and the wonders of nature came to hold treasured personal memories.

If we follow our dreams over decades, we have an ongoing awareness of parallel self-integration between waking and dreaming states. My subsequent dream farm is a special fantasy as I played out-of-body there with Northern Lights and stellar constellations. I'm acutely aware that my dream-self is a virtual creation. My dream-self has an active history and evolves as my waking-self does. I would become a multiple personality if I were to explicitly bring my dream-self into waking hours.

When I drive into the Cumberland, Wisconsin Area and experience the beauty of its forests, lakes, and mostly unspoiled pristine landscapes, my mind and body relax; a sense of calm envelops my total being, and I'm home. In similar fashion, my dreaming brain goes back repeatedly to my heaven on earth. The dream buildings change, the landscape changes, the people change, but emotionally heaven remains. Note—hallucinations can be generated by evolving dream histories as well as waking experiences, as the two have much in common—they share the same neural networks[3,4,5]. Elderly persons experiencing multiple pharmaceuticals and interrupted sleep can be confused by this hallucinatory mechanism[6].

I want to repeat a point that I made earlier—the effects of *de'ja vu occur* between waking and dreaming states. Lucidly following my dreams over decades allows me to clearly separate *de'ja vu* elements of the night from my waking generated images. As noted, I would be totally unaware of these dreaming-waking parallel universes if I hadn't followed my dreams over decades. The parallel development of dream and waking histories is a graduate research project in waiting. What is the difference between the *de'ja vu* dream-self and the self in psychotic hallucinations? Is the difference one of perception and meta-cognition?

Dream Memories

Many people never analyze their dreams nor do they dream lucidly. However, observing and manipulating dreams over decades provides a window into brain processes that I would not be aware of otherwise. In this sense, dreams really are a window into non-conscious brain processes.

I have hundreds of dream memories that evolve in a fashion similar to how my dream farm changes over time. I generally pay attention to a thousand or more dreams annually. However, comprehensive daily documentation is tedious. For example, on 26 July 2013, I made notes of seven dream scenarios in a long, 90-minute afternoon nap. Nevertheless, day-to-day, I review the non-conscious nature of dream memory continuity and its dynamic interplay with waking consciousness.

Dream memory continuity, along with pre- and post-sleep dual state imagery, suggests that our virtual image generators are always on and form an essential part of meta-consciousness. Our brain's image generator must always be on in order to generate predictive imagery before the next visual can be actually imaged. Applying this awareness to dream consciousness helps explain how suggestion can so easily control dream content. Further, meta-awareness across states of consciousness suggests that we treat self as a functional mechanism and recognize the self's active role in image prediction.

The interesting part of dream memory construction is its ongoing integration and consolidation. Over time, dream memories parallel the waking changes in my life. They evolve together. This literally gives new meaning to the concept of parallel universes in physics[7,8]. The imagery that breaks through during pre-sleep or daydreams reflects this image evolution as well. Historical figures like Joan of Arc, and little-known shamans report the evolution of their visions/ hallucinations in similar fashion. The brain is a dynamic, virtual imaging machine that plays across multiple states of consciousness.

During waking moments, I encounter people, environmental settings, or emotionally triggered events that "flash back" (also known as *de'ja vu*) to dream memories. I know these are dream creations, but the emotional impact is such that I feel I've been to this place before, or I've met this person before. You can imagine the fun—and added income potential—a Freudian-oriented psychoanalyst has who believes all of these core dynamic brain constructions are attempts to disguise and censor imagery that is trying to break out of the "unconscious" into consciousness. My *de'ja vu* world has evolved over decades along with my emotional and cognitive maturation.

In my experience, metaphorical, transformative imaging in the brain's dynamic core represents functional brain processes that are integrating and consolidating memory[9,10,11]. I'm also guessing that lucid dreaming adds additional memory continuity to these non-conscious, historical memories. Following this logic, individuals sensitive to multiple daytime hallucinations, for whatever reason, have historically been considered visionaries and mystics.

Morris Moscovitch's research at the Rotman Research Institute, University of Toronto, focuses on the dynamic interplay between memories encoded in the hippocampus (episodic memory) and neocortex (semantic memory). Famous patients like Henry Molaison (patient HM) and Kent Cochrane (patient KC) have lost ability to form new memories, but are able to retrieve old memories. Moscovitch "multiple trace/transformation theory" explains why:

"According to multiple/transformation theory, each time an episodic memory is retrieved, it is automatically re-encoded by the hippocampus along with the new context in which retrieval occurs. Over time, and with every retrieval, multiple memory traces accumulate; the neocortex extracts similarities from these traces to form a generalized memory, the semantic memory. By this process, the memory is transformed over time, from a mostly hippocampus dependent, context-rich memory, to a more general memory, a recording of the essential elements of the memory, that captures the gist of the initial episodic memory."

Moscovitch's research can account for *de'ja vu* memory recall in my examples. His research shows that these ". . . same processes apply to memory about personal episodes and the environment, and become schematic memories that can be retrieved without the involvement of the hippocampus[12]".

The *De'Ja Vu-Self*

Let me tie subjective phenomena together with multiple selves and with the virtual creation of these selves. I interpret my experience of *de'ja vu* moments during waking hours as dream-generated, visual associations. What does this mean to the person who is frightened or startled by similar vivid images, or interprets these images as coming from the "spirit" world?

I maintain that I have a *de'ja vu-self* along with my real waking, everyday-self. Similarly, I have a *de'ja vu* environment, and a real, waking, everyday environment. Eighty years of dream awareness draws a clean line between the two. What happens to the person who doesn't follow his or her dreams over a lifetime? What happens to the person who starts mixing the *de'ja vu-self* with waking moments? How do therapists handle this difference?

The interface between uncontrolled hallucinations and dream imagery is what I believe needs greater scrutiny. Playing with and controlling pre- and post-sleep-imagery, and becoming a lucid dreamer strengthens the self. Self-strengthening helps maintain clear boundaries between these dual states. A series of experiments with patients like Oliver Sacks' Ellen O seems warranted. I maintain that playing with dual state imagery does not court craziness but rather supports maintaining clear self-boundaries. When a *de'ja vu* dream-element appears during waking moments, I generally know or explore its origin and simply compare the element with my recalled waking memories.

In a damaged brain, what is the range of imagery that can be brought under conscious control? Why do we frequently just report Ellen O-type hallucinations as titillating stories? Learning to dream lucidly acknowledges ability to intervene and exert control over dream content. Learning to self-induce waking hallucinations without drugs offers endless options to explore consciousness. Basically, anything the brain-mind can imagine, it can visualize. I'm suggesting that neuroscience should identify and study an adequate sample of individuals such as Sarah Griffith's report on "the woman who can leave her body at will[13]." Technologically imaged samples of individuals able to control states of consciousness can potentially help integrate phenomenal research with hard science.

Personal Case Study: My child image transformation in a nightmare

Recall the "Japanese Submarine Dream" I described earlier in this book. I was five-years-old and dreaming I was captured by Japanese and taken onto their submarine. Each time this nightmare occurred the Japanese would start drilling a hole in the middle of my back. At the point where I felt my spin would snap, I would manage to get free, and fly to a "hole" in the middle of their ship.

As I fell into the "hole" (that in my adult years I would realize was the hold of the submarine), I would concentrate hard and suspend myself out of desperation, as my mother said that if I ever hit bottom I would die. I believed mother as my subjective reality at such a young age did not separate my dreaming and waking worlds. My ability to "fly" saved me from the fear of Japanese invaders. I believe my self's flying response in this nightmare is an act of psychological resilience. Transformative imaging in this nightmare created a phenomenal "hole" in the submarine. Note that even at five-years-of-age, the word "hole" was transformed by my brain into an actual dream object. (For resources on infant semantic contextual knowledge, see Baars and Gage[14]). From my personal experience, this is top-down dream transformative image manipulation by the self.

Note the interplay of bottom-up primary consciousness and top-down secondary consciousness image transformations. The dynamic interplay between the brain's core dynamics and higher cortical centers suggests that affect can be generated at either level. Nevertheless, top-down/bottom-up observation of affect generation does not challenge affect as being primarily a bottom-up phenomenon.

I attribute my mother's attempts to use smothering as a form of behavior modification to cause my brain's transformative imager to metaphorically concretize into the Japanese submarine nightmare. Contrary to Freud, this type of image transformation is not disguise and censorship; it is transformative image personification of mother's physical attacks, which then became associated with a child's fear of Japanese invasion. The magnitude of war hysteria strengthened the nightmare's effect into decades-long trauma. Critically, a child's fear can directly affect how the brain transforms dream and nightmare images.

Functionally, the nightmare permitted me to live with an abusive mother. My personal experience suggests transformative imaging is a ubiquitous mechanism across states of consciousness. In cases of trauma, such as my mother's smothering attacks, transformative imaging in dreams and hallucinations can act as a form of psychological resiliency and defense. Do some psychoanalysts understand this mechanism as the dream censor at work?

As an older adult, I still associate "shadow" memories with other physical and smothering attacks that occurred even before the age of three. Neurons in the adult brain are severely pruned compared with those of a three-year-old. What does neuronal pruning mean for adult recall when the incident occurred before the age of three? As noted, prenatal memory is still controversial; nevertheless, research documents the initial formation of fetal memory that is associated with the mother's tastes, music preferences, and speech sounds as previously noted.

Early memories at such young ages are infrequent, unreliable, but documented. James L. McGaugh and colleagues at the University of California, Irvine have an active program studying hyperthymesia[15]. They are also documenting cases of memory recall that are comparable to my recall. Interestingly, hyperthymesic individuals have nine documented structural brain differences from those individuals with normal memories. One size doesn't fit all brain-minds.

SOURCES: Chapter 9: Dream Illusion and the De'Ja Vu Self

1. Wamsley, Erin J. Dreaming, waking conscious experiences, and the resting brain: report of subjective experience as a tool in the cognitive neurosciences. Frontiers in Psychology, 2013; 4: 637. doi: 10.3389/fpsyg.2013.00637.

2. Cartwright, R. D. (2010) The Twenty-Four Hour Mind: The Role of Sleep and Dreams in our Emotional Lives. London: Oxford University Press.

3. Wamsley, E. J., & Stickgold, R. (2010) Dreaming and offline memory processing. Curr. Biol. 20, R1010-R1013 10.1016/j.cub.2010.10.045 [PMC free article] [PubMed] Cross Ref].

4. Domhoff, W. (2011) The neural substrate for dreaming: is it a subsystem of the default network? Conscious. Cogn. 20, 1163-1174 10.1016/j.concog.2011 [PubMed] [Cross Ref].

5. Horikawa, T., Tamak, M., Miyawaki, Y., & Kamitani, Y. (2013). Neural decoding of visual imagery during sleep. Science 340, 639-642 10.1126/science.1234330 [PubMed' [Cross Ref].

6. Frances, Allen (2013) Saving Normal. New York: Harper Collins

7. Tegmark, Max (2013) Our Mathematical Universe. New York: Knopf Doubleday Publishing Group.

8. Kaku, M. (1995) Hyperspace: A scientific odyssey through parallel universes, time warps and the tenth dimension. New York: Anchor.

9. Born, J., & Wilhelm, I. (2012) System consolidation of memory during sleep. Psychol. Res. 76, 192-203. doi: 10.1007/s00426-011.0335.6.

10. Walker, M. P., & Stickgold, R. (2006) Sleep, memory, and plasticity. Annu. Rev. Psychol. 57, 139-166. doi: 10.1146/ annurev.psych.56. 091103.070307.

11. Walker, M. P., & Stickgold, R. (2010) Overnight alchemy: sleep-dependent memory evolution. Nat. Rev. Neuroscience. 11:218. doi: 10.1038/nrn2762-cl.

12. Morris Moscovitch's multiple trace theory. Rotman Research Institute, University of Toronto, Canada.

13. Griffiths, Sarah. 12 March 2014. http://www.dailymail. co.uk/sciencetech/article-2575550/The-woman-leave-body-Student-sheds-light-strange-brain-activity-involved-body-experiences.html; Smith, Andra M. & Messier, Claude. "Voluntary out-of-body experience: an fMRI study. Front.

Hum. Neurosci., 10 Feb. 2014. https://doi.org/10.3389/fnhum.2014.00070.

14. Baars, Bernard B. J. & Gage, Nicole M. (2010) Cognition, Brain, and Consciousness, 2nd Ed. New York: Elsevier, Academic Press.

15. James L. McGaugh and colleagues at the University of California, Irvine, hyperthymesia studies.

PART IV

Integrating Method, Theory, And Philosophy

In this section, I further detail self as an autonomous emergent of secondary consciousness. Qualia are viewed as primary sensory image transformations of core brain dynamics. Free will is discussed as a byproduct of secondary consciousness that represents our ability to manipulate and reconfigure primary sensory transformations. As previously noted, secondary sensory transformations are not simple neuronal correlates of consciousness. Secondary image transformations can be viewed, for example, as synesthesia-type transformation where pain, for example, is personified as dream "bad guys."

The phenomenal-self as active agent, both at a conscious and non-conscious level, uses belief and suggestion to transform primary sensory images. I treat these bidirectional image transformations, which are influenced and/or controlled by the self, as a type of biological structural realism. By biological structural realism I mean that neuronal and biochemical interactions across the brain's global workspace create emergent entities that are both transformative and representative of something that transcends the reality of cellular and biochemical biology itself.

"Transformative Imaging, Virtual Entities, and Free Will" emphasizes the dual nature of the brain's autonomous and automatic-levels of hierarchy. The brain's neuronal plasticity permits endless creations of virtual entities at our secondary-level of consciousness—including the self itself.

The chapter on self-hypnotic trance exemplifies manipulation of automatic brain processes. Our lucid, autonomous-self can learn to control cellular and biochemical actions with self-hypnosis. Trance is not a mysterious process. Trance represents a series of specific steps that one can use to control brain process and the contents of consciousness across states of consciousness. Of most significance is the realization that the contents of secondary consciousness are virtual creations, and this includes both virtual and physical self-models.

Protoconsciousness theory addresses research that supports the initial proto-formation of sensory processes and self—self-development in the latter stages of fetal maturation. I subsume protoconsciousness theory within my Transformative Dynamic Integrated Systems Model (TDIS) by extending second-order image transformations as the key element of secondary consciousness and self.

The final chapter on "Philosophical Reflections" reviews the major contributions of key writers and researchers who form the core research and philosophy of *Image Transformations of the Brain-Mind*.

CHAPTER 10

※

Self, Qualia, and Free Will

Neuronal integration and consolidation of daytime behaviors in dreams appears to approximate mental skill practice by athletes prior to competition. Observing fictive reenactment of bike riding in my dreams represents a fairly direct correlation of skill acquisition with daytime bike riding. I surmise this non-conscious dream function by correlating dream content with daytime activities.

Useful behavioral repertoires support how you and I engage our environments. To be useful, neuronal sets must reflect an active organism (you and me) moving through physical and social space. Real-life behavioral routines are correlated with fictive dream reenactments. Thus, the triangulation of dream scenarios, such as biking, with daytime behaviors provides additional support for dreams integrating and consolidating related skills in memory.

The use of suggestion to modify dreams presupposes the ability of the phenomenal-self to control secondary consciousness, as well as to manipulate primary sensory images. When I use self as free agent to initiate behavior called Zen-driving—driving that is under the automatic control of my brain's core dynamics—I'm quite sure my neuronal capacities have evolved past that of my neighbor's dog. This interpretation has not been acceptable to "hard-core" behaviorists, nor to those who deny the reality level of the self as active agent.

I've been arguing that to fully understand dream processes one must view the phenomenal-self and core-self brain dynamics—two, normally hierarchical levels of evolutionary neural development as co-occurring brain network processes. Brains are organized both in terms of modular and distributed structures that can act in parallel[1].

Neuroscience, especially neuroimaging, gets credit for the empirical evidence supporting this reasoning. Lucid dream analysis gets credit for identifying non-conscious processes of transformative imaging. Additionally, I'm arguing that combining subjective (first-person) and objective (third-person) methodologies are necessary for a more complete picture of consciousness, self, will, and free will. It is this emerging conception of how to engage and control automatic processes across primary and secondary consciousness that supports newer, direct intervention mental health treatment strategies, such as Kay Tye's discussion of optogenetic tools, and transcranial magnetic stimulation[2].

Subjectively, dream imaging is given meaning at two different levels. At the core-dynamic level, higher-order logic and motion is disconnected and the most fantastic images, such as flying, are experienced as real acts by the self. Lucidity on the part of our higher-order consciousness interprets these acts as being veridical while we are dreaming. After waking, flying and other superhero exploits seem fantastic. The critical piece is that our higher-order logic, in its "now" state, experiences dynamic core sensations as being real.

Awake, we know fantastic dream feats are virtual and not real. When these same processes occur while we are awake, we call them hallucinations or visions and, if they persist, we are classified as being mentally ill by the DSMs, or a mystic. H. R. Irwin in "The Disembodied Self," noted that being out-of-body is not necessarily pathological[3]. (I've noted that it's actually a lot of fun.) Thomas Metzinger's work inducing OBEs empirically supports Irwin's position.

Individual sensitivity to enacting altered states, especially controlling altered states, can be interpreted as an "outlier" on the normal curve of human phenomenal-selves. But perhaps I'm too conservative viewing enactment of altered states as outliers on the normal curve. Thousands of people play with remote viewing, astral travel, shamanic possession, being possessed ourselves, and doing automatic writing—can we all be "outliers?"—Ask the MMPIs and DSMs.

Analysis of dreams, hallucinations, speaking-in-tongues, possessing a totem, or being possessed ourselves, informs us about the relationship between secondary (higher-order) consciousness, and the primary consciousness of our dynamic core. Transformative imaging between primary and secondary consciousness is a simple but startling demarcation from standard models of psychotherapy as to how these two different levels of human subjectivity are experienced[4].

The subjective image transformations at the dynamic core level can and do act independently of our self as executive agent. Transformative imaging at the dynamic core usually remains invisible to the self. However, transformative processes that are usually invisible to the self-awareness of secondary consciousness remain subject to the influences of suggestion and cultural belief. Nevertheless, as I've demonstrated, we can learn to lucidly observe and manipulate these processes across states of consciousness.

Higher logic and motor connections get disconnected when we dream. Thus, research has determined that change in our brain's biochemistry alters the relationship between core brain dynamics and the self. In 2012, I proposed reimaging of primary sensation at our higher cortical levels as a component of "Dynamic Integrated Systems". Now, I'm extending this interpretation by stating that reimaging at our secondary level of consciousness also permits a dual state of consciousness to exist. Thus, with lucidity, a dual state of consciousness permits the self to act as executive agent over non-conscious dynamic core processes.

My personal case studies discussing my totem possession, "ghosts," and mind controlling sidewalk cracks addresses the two-way interaction between core dynamics and higher-order self-levels. This dynamic interpretation of the relationship between the self and the brain's core dynamics also follows the logic of Metzinger[5], and Edelman[6].

If I'm correct, rapid shifts in our dreams supports core brain dynamics rapidly morphing times and places to more efficiently integrate and consolidate associative memories. Simply, memory associations are not logged in our neuronal networks according to some contrived set of waking clock times or waking logic. I might go from fictive visuals as a dream bike rider in one dream scenario, to giving a lecture in another. Twenty-five or more nightly dream scenarios support a busy multi-tasking dream-works. Try comparing this analysis with Freud's "dream works."

Associations in our dream-works support neuronal networks being modified across our entire history. Stated differently—associative memory integration and consolidation appear to rewrite the chapters of memory, not just add new pages. Therefore, I assume that changes in brain chemistry during the course of a night underlie our dream multi-tasking functions: integrating and consolidating memory, emotional rebalancing, eliminating cell byproducts from metabolism[7], and re-balancing cell biochemistry.

Virtual imaging in dreams reflects functional processes occurring in our brain's core dynamics. It seems logical that the "now" of the phenomenal-self should experience dream and hallucinatory content as being veridical if self is a supervening dispersed set of global neuronal processes in our brains. Transformative imaging processes supporting consciousness remain invisible to the self as these processes create and sustain the sensory underpinnings of consciousness itself. The invisibility of transformative sensory imaging at higher cortical levels leads the self to assume that self-attributed sensations are "ghosts" and spirits. In a contemporary psychological sense, self-generated sensations can also be interpreted as paranoia and experienced as OCD.

My transformative, bidirectional image interpretation acknowledges that the brain can and does experience internal imaging transformations as being just as real as input coming from outside. In other words, consciousness is a subjective biochemical phenomenon that only knows the products of its own neuronal constructions. Therefore:

Transformative imaging at the primary and secondary levels is the essence of human consciousness and self-awareness.

Analyzing the transformative imaging capacities of my multi-tasking brain in dreams is a window into non-conscious processes. Lucidly observing transformative imaging across states of consciousness supports the work of neuroscientists by integrating subjective brain-mind processes with observable physiological and cellular processes. Following this interpretation of sensory image transformations, there are three levels of reality we humans must contend with: the realities experienced at (1) the phenomenal-self and (2) core-self levels, and (3) the objective (real) world that science seeks to explain.

Objective reality is being defined as what actually exists in nature and the cosmos. This tri-partite division of reality acknowledges the human quest to know the world as it actually exists. But first, in our quest to know the world, we must be able to interpret image transformations occurring between primary and secondary consciousness. What does this interpretation of sensory image transformations imply for analytic philosophy; that is historically, when analytic philosophy struggled to interpret consciousness as a unitary process.

Colin McGinn[8] believes that the categories of cognition and perception should be extended to include "mental images." In support of McGinn, I'm arguing that "mental images," especially since "mental images" are transformative, are critical to understanding human consciousness and subjectivity. Try to explain how we each create a virtual, phenomenal-self without referencing "mental images." Further, it is manipulation of "mental images" that offers elimination of nightmares, "ghosts," possession, and mind control by other sources, such as OCD, paranoia, and addictions. Extending the effectiveness of cognitive-emotional and related therapies requires knowledge of how to manipulate "mental images" as much as requiring knowledge of brain chemistry and biological structure.

I experience my dreaming brain as it integrates and consolidates memories that become part of that vast 95-98 percent of my "collective unconscious," to use a term from Lakoff and Johnson[9]. I more fully understand the automaticity of everyday activities from bicycle riding to reaching for my coffee cup. And for me, the automaticity of will and the autonomy of free will are no longer mysterious things.

I'm now at a level of understanding that permits me to control subjective states of consciousness. I have become the master of my own neuroses. I can even control subjectively generated images of "ghosts," control feeling possessed, as well as prevent feeling controlled by sidewalk cracks, my nefarious neighbor, alien abductions, or debilitating effects of PTSD.

Critically, I suspect that whatever I can't explain in my dreams and hallucinations is probably associated with biological maintenance of non-conscious dynamic core processes that support my physical and emotional wellbeing. Selectively, core dynamic processes in our evolutionary "old brains" have constant two-way exchanges with our new brains—our higher cognitive centers. Two-way exchange between primary and secondary consciousness does not mean conscious awareness is taking place. Multiple functions are being performed at each level of brain activity and, especially with trauma, the communication across brain modules can get a bit messed up.

Listen quietly in the night for your dreams are talking! Listen quietly in the day for your hallucinations are revealing.

Primary sensory imaging at the dynamic core level becomes color, vibrations in the air become sound, and pressure on my skin gets translated into touch. These are all invisible processes taking place in my brain, not where my body meets its external environment. We often forget the complexity of transformative sensory imaging that automatically takes place in our brains and is invisible. Human subjectivity depends on transformative imaging, and the vortex of human secondary imaging is the phenomenal-self.

Qualia and Consciousness

Changes in our sense of balance is a stark reminder that our relationship to gravity is slowly learned by a toddler, and subject to revision as our brains continue to deteriorate with age. A somewhat fancy term from philosophy, "qualia" is often used to define how our brain is connected with our physical senses. We could describe qualia as sensory knots and say that our brains tie or bind sensory input into useful neuronal connections that let us subjectively experience the world.

Nevertheless, these knots represent the first steps in the brain's most basic image transformations. This discussion about qualia has a purpose: to help explain how image transformations occur--our eyes don't take pictures, and our ears don't hear sound. Sensory knots get tied, bound together in complex interactions across various modules of brain. This knotting process adds emotional content (also experienced as neuro-bio-chemical imprints). Sensory imaging means that we always feel something. Consciousness requires feeling. When the brain is bio-chemically processing sensory input, we feel and are conscious of things. I like Max Tegmark's uncluttered definition of consciousness, ". . . consciousness is the way information feels when being processed[10].

Sensory imaging (making knots) underlies all states of consciousness. Most importantly, this is a major part of the real "unconscious" –the neuronal processes that transform primary sensations into secondary images that, in turn, support human-level subjective awareness.

Now, if I didn't confuse you with my "knot" metaphor, I want to make another distinction between dynamic core and our higher cognitive centers. If dreams are one of the brain's methods of integrating and consolidating sensory input; then, dream imagery reflects processes by which qualia as primary image transformations get processed. But recall the two-way image transformations that can also occur across the brain's hierarchy.

At our higher cortical levels, language is used to attribute meaning to a subjectively defined "something." Words represent objects and elements in the environment that have acquired specific meanings. Once we have individually attached a specific meaning to words, the brain automatically and unconsciously creates the meaning counterpart in our dreams and hallucinations. For example, "hole" substituted for "hold" in my five-year-old linguistically limited vocabulary became a virtual "hole" in a dream Japanese submarine.

Top-down in terms of the brain's hierarchy of image transformations, the linguistic meaning attributed to "hole" creates a virtual cavity in an imagined Japanese dream submarine. Further, note that the phenomenal-self treats automatic and virtual creations of the brain as subjective reality. This automatic image transformation process remains invisible to the self unless dream and altered state image transformations are observed lucidly. However, with dream programming (scripting), the self can actively and automatically intervene in dreaming or hallucinatory processes to substitute its own pleasant transformed imagery.

Following the above analysis, image transformations in dreams represents the brain maintaining support for all of our physical and emotional needs. I suspect that infants and young children remember little of their dreams because basic functions of walking, talking, learning about their physical environment, etcetera, are the majority of their daily tasks. It's much like eating in one's dreams. Daily habits of lifting fork or chopsticks are constantly maintained and need not be continuously reinforced by our multi-tasking, dreaming brains.

Personal Case Study: Dreaming eating with chopsticks, 9 August 2013

Let me attempt to clarify the connection between habitual actions and dream function. Using chopsticks has not been a habitual action for me. Note that whenever I engage in non-habituated behaviors, these behaviors tend to enter my dreams, and are often dramatized as well. Try to get Freudian disguise, censorship or wish-fulfillment out of this dream. More importantly, how do neurons know when behaviors such as chopstick use, bike riding, or glass cutting skills need to be reinforced, or modified? Perhaps this question has an easy answer.

The Phenomenal-Self's Relationship to Qualia

Now let me shift focus from primary transformative imaging (qualia) to secondary image transformations. Primary sensory images (percepts) such as balance and color get re-imaged as concepts at our secondary level of consciousness. Reimaging primary sensory images permits the self to mix and match primary sensory objects in any combination of choice. Thus, balance becomes balancing my checkbook, or balancing life's demands. Color gets reimaged as the color of love, and heat gets reimaged as my mother's warmth. In terms of this analysis, remember that both primary and secondary image transformations generally remain below waking consciousness. I only identify these image transformations in lucid dreaming, or when programming (scripting) hallucinations such as my Genesis Journey.

I conceptualized the working relationship between core dynamics and higher-order consciousness within a model of Transformative Dynamic Integrated Systems (TDIS)[11]: Noting that all our brain's modular parts functionally work together as a whole, TDIS pays homage to systems biology and systems psychology.

And TDIS acknowledges transformative imaging across hierarchical brain levels. The self's re-imaging of self-generated body sensations are the "ghost," and the source of paranoia. The self's job as an active organizer of meta-consciousness is the creation of subjective meaning. In sum, TDIS recognizes the special metacognitive relationship between the self and the brain's core dynamics. I assume that this special transformative imaging relationship is responsible for the emergence of human-level subjectivity—being aware of our own consciousness. At the secondary level of image transformation, our higher cortical centers generate and experience a "felt" entity we call ego or self.

As a transformative image of sustained duration, the self is experienced as being just as real as any other sensory transformation, such as the color red or the touch of your hand upon my shoulder. The color red or my sense of your hand touching my shoulder is just as much illusion as is self, or the color red. However, if I told you that my experience of your hand on my shoulder was an illusion, you might think that I've lost my marbles.

If I were to separately study the body's various systems—vascular, nervous, or endocrine, I would never understand how you can read this book. When I put all of the brain's working parts together as a system, I get human subjectivity generated through image transformations, creative works, and my ability to hold conversations. Physiologically, I get blood flow, electro-chemical discharges in my neural networks, and autoimmune reactions. Thus, my emphasis on the importance of top-down, subjective research being combined with bottom-up, objective research if we wish to more fully understand how the self emerges and functions as part of secondary consciousness[12].

My higher-order cerebral centers reimage primary images (emotions), which permit me to experience bio-chemical changes in my higher cortical centers as feelings. I turn emotions generated in my "evolved old brain," which supports primary consciousness into objects in my dreams. And in similar fashion, I turn thoughts generated in my "evolved new brain," which supports secondary consciousness into visual, auditory, and tactile objects in my dreams and hallucinations. Thus, we notice that transformative imagery is being generated both bottom-up at a primary level of consciousness and top-down at a secondary level.

There has been an ongoing debate as to the source of emotions in the mind sciences. The argument centers around whether emotions are generated at the secondary or primary level of consciousness. In my experience with transformative imagery, Freud got it wrong. Panksepp and Biven sort out the main issues in Chapter 2 of *The Archaeology of Mind* using A. Damasio, LeDoux, and Rolls as major sources of the debate. In that transformative imagery identifies emotional transformations top-down and bottom-up the argument feels to me to be a bit exhausting. In other words, secondary consciousness at the human level bidirectionally addresses this debate. According to my Transformative Dynamic Integrated Systems Model (TDIS), feeling at both the secondary level of consciousness and emotion at the primary level is bidirectionally transformative for humans.

My higher-order self's ability to create virtual, felt objects allows me to concretize "ghosts" and sidewalk cracks, or my mind manipulating neighbor (paranoia). Processes of transformative imagery permit my phenomenal-self to subjectively grow or shrink. Thus, I recognize that transformative imagery can change my physical and/or self-perception from day-to-day. These transformations are fluid, dynamic processes that belie attempts to explain dynamic, psychogenic processes in linear terms of cellular or biochemical causation. Top-down transformative imaging acknowledges an active role for the self. I'm proposing that *TDIS* acknowledge the self as a functional, autonomous, transformative mechanism that synergistically enhances our discussion of human consciousness.

My passion for a new love is the transformative re-imaging and integration of biochemical pressures that creates feelings of emotional longing, which is both subjectively real and physically felt. In the next step of transformative imaging, my higher-order consciousness transforms primary, metaphorical images of the Lakoff and Johnson[9] variety into love as a journey.

For clarification, note that Lakoff and Johnson's metaphors— inside/outside, up/down, front/back, etc.—are subjective elements that represent an intrinsic relationship between neurons and the brain's biochemistry. In other words, I cannot speak of emotions and feelings without referencing the cellular transformative mechanisms responsible for primary and secondary imaging.

I'm using the concept of free will, self as active agent, to recognize my brain's ability at higher cortical levels to reconfigure primary images. Free will as I perceive it, also takes into consideration the primary images (Lakoff-Johnson metaphors) from which reconfigured images (abstractions) are generated. Primary images as metaphors are neuronal building blocks of the brain. And biochemistry is an active process that generates transformative imagery with the neuronal support of primary image metaphor.

In this analysis, I'm attempting to make clear that transformative imaging at the secondary level underlies our sense of freedom of choice. Once reconfiguration of primary images emerges in the course of evolution with our enlarged brains, endless combinations of newly reconfigured neuronal sets become possible: The TDIS model views the phenomenal-self as emerging with secondary image transformations; along with all manner of higher-order virtual images. Contrary to conceptions of the immaterial soul, we acknowledge the evolutionary emergence of mind, self, and consciousness as processes that depend on neurons. And looking across the animal kingdom, we recognize that we are not the only higher order sentient animals on this planet[13,14].

Vetting primary and secondary transformative imaging, we recognize that a virtual, functional self can supervene over materialistic and deterministic interpretations of behavioral biology, and behavioral psychology. My interpretation of transformative imagery directly confronts Sam Harris's denial of free will[15]. Further, my transformative imaging interpretations support virtual and phenomenal models of the self presented by Edelman[16,17], Metzinger[18], and Kandel[19].

Love is an "abstraction" of newly integrated biochemical circuits at ever increasing levels of complexity. But all of this detail is unimportant to my waking consciousness, and mostly goes on below my conscious level of awareness. Consciously being in love means that I'm just enamored, and my landscape trajectory is one of first-order, primary sensory consummation.

Third-order sensory constructs are at the level of my being aware that I am aware of being in love. Second-order constructs are love as a journey. Primary images are those felt at the core level where biochemistry creates sensations of attachment, color and sound. This process of hierarchical associational order eventually becomes complex thought. I string constructs derived from various patterns of neuronal circuit combinations into frames of time, movement, and relationship to my total environment, as well as relationship of these constructs to "Me."

Notice that in terms of all the historical, philosophical, and theological interpretations of time, time as a concept with past and future is being generated by the biology of secondary consciousness. Consciousness is a "now" state as it is required to be for any living organism. As commonly discussed in philosophy, the "Arrow of Time" only exists for human beings as an extension backwards and forwards from the "now". The self is understood as an emergent entity in a transformative process called secondary consciousness, that is, as an entity that is aware of its own organismic passage through space. Movement through space permits the self to know that change has occurred and will continue into its future. Thus, human-level, subjective time is a product of secondary consciousness.

Time is a product of self being aware in a "now" state. This interpretation also follows King[13], and Panksepp and Biven[14]. From the self's position in space, one line extending into the future, and also into the past, places the observer at point zero. Point zero is our "now" state of being. Thus, time and mathematical constructs are generated by the self's active role in secondary consciousness.

Critically, metaphorical constructs of the Lakoff and Johnson[9] variety represent primary sensory constructs that underlie secondary image transformations. In Lakoff and Johnson terminology, the meaning of "up/down" for fetal protoconsciousness is its developing relationship to gravity; "inside/outside" as a metaphor we live by is physical self as container. Read *Saint Augustine's Confessions* in order to appreciate how convoluted historical concepts of time were without a contemporary scientific understanding of self.

Virtual Image Transformations Enhance Sensation

Evolution has given humankind a wonderful, phenomenal world. I don't understand all the fine details, nor do I understand all the micro-physiology involved, but I can mentally, subjectively, move across this dynamic landscape of neuronal elements to understand why I behave and dream the way I do. Physical passion is one form of rapture, while cognitive passion driven by understanding adds an additional dimension of rapture-on-rapture, or the psychology of subjectivity added to physiology. If secondary consciousness with its emergent phenomenal-self did not exist there would be no rapture-on-rapture, no mental orgasms, and no Genesis Journeys.

Awareness of how the phenomenal-self emerges in the course of evolution is a huge advance over my early school years of Descartes' "soul," Freud's "unconscious," and Skinner's "behaviorism." Having additional insights derived from dreams and neuroscience adds more magic to passion rather than less. I now understand how I can experience "mental orgasms," and how as a music-illiterate I can play my dream piano.

Knowledge is not just power, it is enhanced feeling, and enhanced feeling undergirds compassion. Cognitive imaging in dreams and hallucinations can be as intense as orgasm. Cerebral mentation when combined with nature's brute physiological responses, explode like Fourth-of-July fireworks in our fictive Genesis Journeys to the beginning of time.

Fully engaging the compassionate potential that resides in our phenomenal-selves, feelings that can be shared with all humanity, offers a vision of civilization that rises above the world's petty dogmas. Perhaps it is time to put a biology-based self back into science's equation of consciousness and dismiss it as illusion.

For a final comparison, let me ask the reader: "When was the last time you had an orgasm that lasted three or four days? Now I subjectively understand the rapture of hallucinatory visions— the rapture of a Genesis Journey, or the appeal of one's religious spirit. Hopefully, I have also made clearer that human subjectivity is a new level of achievement, a phase change in biology that goes beyond those found in physics and chemistry, in the self-discovered trajectory of evolution that must be taken seriously. In terms of complexity theory, I've just given evolution's trajectory the emergent capacity of purpose. Oh wait! That's reference to you and me as sentient beings.

In that elephants appear to exhibit secondary consciousness by mourning their dead, and dolphins exhibit an individual sense of self by calling each other by name, does this mean they share our human-level of sentience?

Consilience: Altered States and Subjective Inquiry

Structural realism

Continued refinement of brain imaging technology allows us to triangulate first-person observations with real-time neuronal activity[20]. In other areas of advanced technology, we image the atom—electron tunneling microscopes, and view the beginning of the universe through new telescope technology. And for the first time in human history, we have imaged the universe's grid that aligns our galaxies. Brain-imaging technologies are neuroscience's new telescopes. How does brain-imaging technology differ from imaging technology in any other area of science?

Let me tie together some basic concepts in the philosophy of science by using one of my favorite analytical philosophers, John Searle. I have two objectives: to discuss technical terms in everyday language, and to stress the importance of integrating objective-subjective research in the study of consciousness as this combined research also heuristically sets the stage to reanalyze mental health in another work. I will use the transformative language of dreams for my example.

What is it—ontology? How do we find out about it—epistemology? What does it do—causation? I'm following the normative straightforward language of John Searle using these terms[21] while fielding examples that the reader should now be familiar with. "It" in the language of ontology, epistemology, and causation is the image transformations of the self.

Ontology: What is the metaphorical language of dreams? Metaphorical language is transformative sensory imaging that occurs primarily across the human visual, auditory, and tactile senses; although sensory transformations can and do occur with taste, smell, and one's relationship to gravity as well. Examples: my 5-year-old mind transformed "hole" in the Japanese submarine as an actual hole in which my phenomenal-self could hide; pressure on my healing broken ankle was visually transformed into bad guys torturing me; self-induced back sensations were transformed into a "ghost" attempting to possess me. Consequently, these examples specify that transformative imaging can and does occur across states of consciousness. An observation that is critical to understanding select forms of pathology related to our mental health. Transformative imaging requires an active self; conceptually, self doesn't work as an illusion.

Epistomology: How do we find out about it? I have argued that metaphorical dream image transformations are only observable first-person. Additionally, modification of dream imagery through the use of suggestion, hypnosis, or self-hypnosis reveals bidirectional linkages between the brain's higher cortical centers and core dynamics. Controlling bidirectional sensory image transformations between the brain's higher cortical centers and affective image transformations in the dynamic core is a path to overcoming various mental health pathologies[22].

For the hard-core materialist who believes that only objective, third-person science is real, rejection of this book's first-person research is probably automatic. Yet, it is only in a dual state of lucid dreaming that we can experience and directly control these transformations.

Causation: What does it do? Metaphorical image transformations permit our brains to create a subjective, functional, and behavioral relationship to our external environment. The brain has no direct contact with its environment. Primary transformative imaging changes light waves into colors, air vibrations in sound, and pressure on our bodies into touch. Material attempts to reduce these subjective imaging transformations to wavelength, vibration, and pressure doesn't make sense if our goal is to understand human consciousness—physics and chemistry support consciousness but do not define it.

Structural realism says that we must focus on the relationship between things. Consciousness emerges as a relational process that is dependent on physics and chemistry; secondary levels of consciousness from my interpretation cannot be directly attributed to correlates in physics, chemistry, or cell biology per se. The critical neuronal correlates of secondary consciousness occur through transformative imaging but, of course, are always dependent on chemistry and physics.

Recall that the primeval energy that cooled to form quarks, gluons, and electrons that created atomic particles from which everything else in the universe has evolved: physics to chemistry, chemistry to biology, and biology to human-level subjectivity. Each phase change requires analysis at its own level. Thus, I'm arguing that human subjectivity and its related processes that create the self must be studied at each level as a separate evolutionary emergent.

Searle says that materialism inherits assumptions of dualism and vocabulary. "It accepts the idea that if we think consciousness exists we accept dualism[23]." I can't equate phase changes in the course of cosmic evolution with illusions. Cosmic phase changes include the emergence of atoms, chemistry and biochemistry, life forms, and human consciousness. At what cost does objective science exclude analysis of the most recent phase change—human consciousness?

Everything that is observable in our known universe only accounts for 4-percent of its contents. Dark matter and dark energy account for the other 96-percent. There is active debate in physics as to whether the perceived universe is a virtual creation, an illusion. Max Tegmark[24] thinks there are multiple universes and that ours is possibly not just an illusion but a mathematical entity. Physics dares to entertain mind-bending conceptions of reality. Simply put, entertaining the improbable can help us rethink mind-limiting paradigms. The Tegmark mind-bending paradigm stretches our minds a lot further than the phenomenal-self as causative agent.

In my analysis of dreams and other altered states, we discovered that "different neurophysiological states can equal same mental states[25]". Attribution of meaning (semantics) transforms the "hole" of a submarine; concretizes "ghosts" and mind-controlling sidewalk cracks and makes phenomenally real our sense of being possessed by "demons." Thus, we acknowledge that human level "mental states" only exist as subjective, first-person phenomena[26].

My model of "Transformative Dynamic Integrated Systems" (TDIS) incorporates an evolutionary perspective and acknowledges that consciousness is dependent on physics and chemistry. Nevertheless, I have observed that analysis of relational properties within and between atoms is necessary for an understanding of chemistry. That relationship between chemicals in cells is fundamental to a living thing so that it can persist and replicate. In terms of human consciousness, TDIS insists that dumb modular components of the brain create human consciousness through processes of transformative imaging. Lastly, that researchable methodologies exist that can tease out the neurobiological and neuro-generative processes that lead to an autonomous, acting self.

Dream Self

Dream consciousness creates a dream self. In fact, it can create many selves, as there are many virtual selves to be had. Some dream selves are bizarre and capable of actions I would never engage in in waking consciousness—like public sex with strange beautiful women, flying as a superhero, or having the strength of a dozen men.

My dream self is less socially and emotionally confined than my waking self, but my dream self, like all aspects of consciousness, is a process that can be created moment-to-moment. Being aware of this process permits me to understand how my dreaming self can morph so quickly around functional physiological and neuronal needs, and how time can change abruptly. Dream forms also require that I acknowledge that access to my memory-dependent self occurs in a "now" state, and is manifested differently in various states of consciousness.

The memory accessed by the self is from a "now" state. My dream self pulls stored memories from throughout its library and uses them in the construction of dream stories and for most other dream-like elements. This process of accessing memory directories is clearer for me in dreams than during waking consciousness[27]. I can also mix and match faces from memory files as my brain automatically creates dream characters. For some of us, lucid dreaming permits access to never-ending, creative combinations of memories that are not available to our waking consciousness.

Creativity lurks in the shadows of transformative imagery. Self-discovery lurks in the shadows of dreams.

I know that my brain retains concepts of me as mind and body. In terms of monism, I am two entities or things in one. There are always two entities in one that I subjectively experience, and I can make them both active agents when I self-talk. I can also make them both active agents when I lucidly dream or hallucinate. Two entities of subjective experience are not magic but rather the ability to hold content in dual states of consciousness. Holding—as in looking in a mirror--transformed images of dual states of consciousness is what gives you and me an awareness of being aware.

Historical thinkers like Descartes[28] had this dual awareness and took it logically to be a non-material essence. We should and do question historical and traditional logic as we question subjectivity. Today, the scientific community embraces primary and secondary levels of consciousness, and not the dual separation of mind and body held by philosopher-mystics. The mystery of soul as our historically conceived self adds so much confusion to human-kinds' murderous acts, mutual insensitivity, and lustful dehumanization. I continue to emphasize that responsibility to our fellow "creatures" does not end with dogma—secular or sacred dogma. Civil responsibility requires support for a social and economic order that permits individual realization of our biological and cognitive potentials.

Exploring dreams and other states of consciousness highlights our unending quest to explain our relationship to our self, each other, and the external world. Unity of self through image transformations truly transcends the physical and chemical world. But what is meant by "unity of self," and "image transformations" that transcend the physical and chemical world?

Unity of self occurs when emotions at our dynamic core are in harmony with how the phenomenal-self is perceiving and interacting with its world. If I'm emotionally depressed or anxious, my interpersonal relationships are disrupted as is my ability to meet multiple life commitments. Therapeutically, I must regain a homeostatic balance between my emotions of primary consciousness and the conceptual complex of secondary consciousness that guides my everyday behaviors.

Images that we observe in dreams and hallucinations between primary and secondary consciousness represent a transformative process that goes beyond that of cells and biochemistry. For example, when the emotion of fear is concretized and personified in our dreams, neurons and biochemistry create a new level of analysis— virtual entities. Neuronal activity and biochemical actions remain invisible to the phenomenal-self while their transformative output of concretized and personified substances, e.g., dream monsters, take center stage. Thus, transformative imagery between primary and secondary consciousness transcends the world of cell biology and biochemistry.

In my dreams, as in waking consciousness, I am permitted dialogue between my two levels of phenomenal-self and core-self. During waking-hours they interact hierarchically, one on top of the other; and in lucid states and hallucinations, the two levels can be expressed side-by-side. I can also hold the phenomenal-self of "me" and the phenomenal-self of the other in waking-self-talk, or in the self-other social roles of dreams.

In my childhood days, I literally thought my body flew with me to "Heaven" or into outer space. As I matured, I knew this conclusion wasn't the case; but no matter, how I felt was the same. Our conscious brain experiences its own virtual creations as real things. The phenomenal-self believes the color red exists in nature, it believes love is a mystery, and it sometimes believes the "Devil" exists. Our self subjectively believes in the reality of its own metaphorical image transformations while we dream or hallucinate. Understanding transformative image relationships in dreams and hallucinations removes the mystic in mysticism, but it doesn't destroy the wonder. In fact, being able to enter, control, and direct various states of consciousness increases our sense of wonder, as it enhances understanding and our mental health.

It's easy for the self as a virtual entity to talk to the body as a physical entity, or another phenomenal-self. We just say that we talk to ourselves, and we do. We do it in dreams and experience the same phenomena in altered states of consciousness. However, we often attribute this other voice to spirits, gods, or demons. Feeling crazy can be the dark side of how we interpret normal brain processes. Experiencing the same sensations and not feeling crazy can unleash the murderous side of our humanity.

Things happen in my dreams. I lucidly observe various dream scenarios, and I feel all kinds of emotions. Commonly, most people remember dream scenarios filled with fear, anxiety, and related negative feelings. That is, unless we learn to control dream emotion, and how to enter and change dreams lucidly. We come to understand how there can be more than one self in our dreams. We come to understand why people in some African cultures feel that they have more than one soul (self). Amazingly, we can look so radically different between the ages of two and eighty and still feel that we are the same person. We can come to understand how the bisected brain can have two selves. Our moment-to-moment image-transformations, "now" constructions of our phenomenal-self, are our reality.

If you are older, you probably have the same experience I do when I look in the mirror. The guy looking back at me, my physical self, is older than my higher-order, virtual, phenomenal-self. The higher-order virtual-self that I carry around from moment-to-moment is a composite of all my memories: "I must be younger than the image in the mirror." This is one time that I find my brain's automatic, statistical-averaging to be pleasant. But note that we can and do use statistical averaging with our dream characters too and, in this dream process, we can creatively mix and match age. Also, note the brain's neuron-based, inherent-mathematical source of statistical averaging.

Predictive, transformative imaging— composing "now" scenes with memory generates statistical comparisons and probabilities. This interpretation of statistical averaging recognizes that when we dream our neuronal files, or templates, are being rewritten and modified continuously. Neuronal templates are not merely something to which we add images. The brain functions more than only as an adding machine.

Let me briefly revisit the brain's habit of statistical averaging. David Whitney, and Jason Fischer[29] observe that the, "Brain's 15-second [processing] delay' shields us from hallucinogenic experience. This delay saves us from insanity that is being induced by a constantly changing torrent of pictures, shapes and colors. In both virtual and real worlds, the brain filters out information, failing in most cases to notice small changes in a 15-second period of time. What we do see is, in fact, a mixture of past and present. The discovery, called a "continuity field," at first seems to be yet another optical illusion. The continuity field "smoothes" what would otherwise be a jittery perception of object features over time. Essentially, the continuity field pulls together physically but not radically different objects to appear more similar to each other."

For me, the key focus of Whitney and Fischer's research reinforces a number of points that I've been emphasizing:

(a) Sensory processing always employs transformative imaging,
(b) Transformative imaging occurs across all states of consciousness,
(c) The brain does not take pictures,
(d) Higher order cognitive centers are binding sensory input in ways that are still not fully understood and,
(e) Meta-cognitive processes are taking place below waking consciousness at a bidirectional, reentrant neuronal level.

Note that visual statistical averaging at our secondary level of consciousness means that the system's continuity field is sacrificing visual accuracy for stable, continuous perception of environment. Further note that visual "smoothing" of objects appears to support a parallel "smoothing," that of associative memories involved in day-to-day integration and consolidation observed in dreams and supported by imaging technology. Once again, note how "smoothing" calls into question ideas of Libet-determinism.

The Automaticity of Will and the Autonomy of Free Will

Recall, between 95 and 98 percent of our brain's activity occurs below our level of awareness. Psychologist Benjamin Libet's research shows that activity in the brain's motor cortex can be detected some 300 milliseconds before a person feels that he has decided to move[26]. In other words, actions we initiate enter consciousness a split second after the non-conscious part of our brain has set responding neural mechanisms in motion. Once this fact had been established physiologically, it was natural to question the degree to which free will exists. If the non-conscious dynamic core of our brains *act* before we are conscious of willing these actions, how can we say we have free will?

Sam Harris says, "Consider what it would take to actually have free will. You would need to be aware of all the factors that determine your thoughts and actions[30]. I find his "logical" statement to be "illogical" as it subverts a fairly obvious part of human evolutionary history. Automatized behaviors and reflexes are both efficient energy-wise as well as being a necessary part of avoiding predators. Species survival requires competitive functionality. Automatized behaviors provide these competitive functions.

I do not need to be aware of all of my car's working parts to exercise free will driving from my house to the grocery store. The automaticity of my car's "operating system" does equivalent work to the automaticity of my neuronal networks that handle metabolism, structural maintenance, and a plethora of other requirements necessary for my daily survival.

Sam Harris has taken Libet's work and related studies to mean that humans have no free will: "But where intentions themselves come from, and what determines their character in every instance, remains perfectly mysterious in subjective terms[30]". I'm quoting Harris at some length because supporting comments on the book's back flap come from V. S. Ramachandran, Oliver Sacks, Owen Flanagan, and Paul Bloom. These individuals are well-known professionals in neuroscience and philosophy whom I greatly respect. However, I disagree with their support for Harris's interpretation.

In contrast to the above four noted professionals, Gerald Edelman and Guilio Tononi, as prominent figures in neuroscience, leave many areas of human consciousness open to further analysis: "Taking a God's-eye view to observe an individual person from the outside leaves the scientific observer with an impoverished picture of mind. It can lead to the paradoxical conclusion that consciousness is merely a bottleneck in an information-processing cascade, a bottleneck that at any given time can contain "just a few chunks" of information. We have insisted, instead, that the observer must consider consciousness by viewing the brain from within, in terms of what makes a difference to its underlying neural processes"[31].

The individual who best sums up Harris's position is (in my opinion) Eric Kandel, who says, "One cannot infer the sum total of neural activity simply by looking at a few neural circuits in the brain[32]. Kandel also quotes Michael Gazzaniga's more moderate position "Brains are automatic, but people are free[ibid]." Following Gazzaniga's more moderate positions, this last statement can be interpreted to mean that I am partially free because I can stop automatic actions with my freedom to say "I won't." Meaning, I can cancel FAP-like behaviors if I choose. However, while this "won't" interpretation recognizes the brain's neuroplasticity, and responsiveness to higher cortical centers, I think the interpretation only goes halfway.

In earlier analyses, I equated "will" with fixed-action patterns being executed by processes of secondary consciousness. Good examples of our higher cortical centers exercising free will are when a skier consciously modifies fixed-action pattern movement over individual moguls, or when the phenomenal-self automatically intervenes and redirects a nightmare. Scripting, redirecting and controlling nightmares is more than a free "won't." The self as executive agent initiates and programs actions, and my dynamic core executes them. Once my own higher-order FAP had been established, my phenomenal-self observed the automatic, dynamic core image transformations in my dreams after they had already occurred.

Does the reader believe that Libet's research is an example that negates free will? Or does this dynamic, two-way interaction represent a complex relationship between specialized brain modules at the systems level? I submit that Kandel, Edelman and Tononi are closer to the truth than Harris. I'm suggesting that those who say there is no free will have confused a linear, deterministic execution of a fixed-action pattern with a more complex dynamic system of causation. For curious readers—Gerald Edelman's *Wider than the Sky* aptly demonstrates dynamic reentry, bidirectional interaction, across the brain's neural circuits. Also, try Thomas Metzinger's *Neural Correlates of Consciousness* for a more complete understanding of these dynamics.

In my interpretation, meta-consciousness, the ability of the self to function across states of consciousness includes Edelman's re-entrant system dynamics[33]. Also, note the shift in my analysis where emphasis is placed on the self's capacity of meta-consciousness as the permanent system element, and automatized neuronal responses as supporting elements.

Equating FAP movement with "will" might seem strange to some readers. However, when we reflect on how we acquire a skill, such as walking, then, neuronal acquisition of will seems intuitive. Automatized FAPs can seem mysterious as they just seem to happen. Reacquiring balance on my bicycle was closely correlated with my dream imagery. Yet, my higher cortical observations while dreaming lucidly permitted two areas of my brain to be active at the same time[34]. Lucidly intervening in and redirecting a dream, I submit, is an act of free will. Thus, I believe the evidence supports Kandel's dynamic systems interpretation.

Individuals who have lost part of their brains due to stroke, accident, ageing, or disease know how hard it is to re-program a partially disabled brain. Recognizing that the "self" is a special set of dispersed neurons acting back on other sets of neurons takes away much of the mystery of "free-will." Thus, a partially disabled brain can still retain meta-cognitive ability to reprogram fixed-action patterns that I've equated with "will." However, this ability doesn't eliminate the hard work necessary to reprogram the potential of our plastic brains.

When we fail to distinguish between the biology of brain cells and the subjective states of consciousness the cells support, we create the straw men of classical philosophers. Historically, "will" and "free-will" became mysterious entities subject to endless speculation; they were bedfellow with "soul." Throw in the mystical interpretations of free will, and historical speculation fills libraries.

I've previously argued in *Dreams, Creativity & Mental Health* that "dream programming" supports free will in my ability to both preprogram dreams and enter and redirect them when they are in process. Further, the automatic imaging that occurs in dreams reflects cellular maintenance and emotional rebalancing. These are actions of an automaton that represent an earlier level of our evolutionary history. But we also possess higher cortical abilities. Higher-order cortical intervention permits me to control dream content, as well as reprocess physiological and emotional effects from anxiety and depression. In effect, I'm using freedom of choice at my higher cortical levels to modify the automaticity of core brain dynamics.

I've referenced numerous studies in this book that demonstrate that neural networks and brain structures are physically changed with meditation, anxiety, depression, and electrical stimulation.

Modifying the automaticity of core brain dynamics with self-hypnosis is a form of direct control that we can use to counter the spiraling effects of anxiety and depression[35,36,37,38,39,40]. My objection to Harris and those who advocate lack of free will are many. From a therapeutic point of view, Harris's "no free will" position supports biological determinism. Harris's biological determinism, like Sulloway's interpretation of the biological determinism of Freud's unconscious[41] removes the therapeutic potential of an individually controlled active self. Contrary to Harris's position, I have and am arguing that free will is an evolutionary emergent that enables the phenomenal-self to exercise control of bidirectional image transformations between primary and secondary states of consciousness.

The fact that most of our behavior is under control of automatic guidance does not obviate my ability to choose moment-to-moment options. Automatic FAPs can be "self" self-directed and reprogrammed. The automaticity of core brain dynamics does not determine where I ride my bicycle; it just determines how I ride my bicycle.

If emerging research supports my interpretation of fixed action patterns (FAPs) and analysis of image transformations at higher-order cognitive centers, Harris's "perfectly mysterious" conclusion is not quite so mysterious. Intentions are volitional acts of our higher-order cognitive centers. Biological evolution creates an emergent level of secondary consciousness that becomes focused like a "searchlight," which is capable of volitional actions. For a succinct contemporary review of the "Defense of Free Will" see Volk[42] and Nahmias[43]. Nevertheless, speaking therapeutically, we are never free until our primary emotions are under control.

SOURCES: CHAPTER 10: SELF, QUALIA, AND FREE WILL

1. Panksepp, Jaak & Biven, Lucy. (2012) The Archaeology of Mind: Neuroevolutionary Origins of Human Emotions. New York: W. W. Norton & Company: 498; Panksepp, J. (1998) The pernicious substrates of consciousness: Affective states and the evolutionary origins of the SELF. J. of Consc. Studies, 5, 566-582.

2. Tye, Kay M. DOI: http//dx.doi.org/10.1016/j. neuron.2014.08.022

3. Irwin, H. J. (2000) The Disembodied Self: An Empirical Study of Dissociation and the Out-of-Body Experience. Journal of Parapsychology. 64(3):261-277.

4. Shevrin, H., Bond, J.A., Brakel, L.A., Hertel, R.K., and Williams, W.J. (1996) Conscious and Unconscious Processes: Psychodynamic, Cognitive, and Neurophysiological Convergence. New York: The Guilford Press.

5. Metzinger, Neural Correlates of Consciousness (2000); Being No One (2003): The Ego Tunnel (2009).

6. Edelman, Gerald. (2004) Wider than the Sky: The Phenomenal Gift of Consciousness. New Haven: Yale University Press.

7. Nedergaard, Maiken & Goldman Steven A. Brain Drain. March 2016, Scientific American.

8. McGinn, Colin. (2004) Mindsight: Image, Dream, Meaning. Cambridge: Harvard University Press.

9. Lakoff, G., & Johnson, M. (1999) Philosophy In The Flesh: The Embodied Mind And Its Challenge To Western Thought. New York: Basic Books.

10. Tegmark, Max (2013) Our Mathematical Universe. New York: Knopf Doubleday Publishing Group.

11. Just, Glen A. (2012) Dreams, Creativity & Mental Health. Mankato, MN: Eagle Entertainment USA.

12. Just, G. A. (2015) "Convergence of Subjective and Objective Methodologies in Consciousness Research", in Advances in Psychology Research, Vol 103, Hauppauge, NY: Nova Science Pubs. Inc.
13. King, B. J. "When Animals Mourn." Scientific American; July, 2013.
14. Ibid, Panksepp and Biven, 2012.
15. Harris, Sam. (2012) Free Will. New York: Free Press.
16. Edelman, Gerald. (2003) Being No One: The Self-Model Theory of Subjectivity. Boston: MIT Press.
17. Edelman, Gerald. (2004) Wider than the Sky: The Phenomenal Gift of Consciousness. New Haven: Yale University Press.
18. Metzinger, Thomas. (2003) Being No One: The Self-Model Theory of Subjectivity. Boston: MIT Press.
19. Kandel, E. R. (2006) In Search of Memory: The Emergence of a New Science of Mind. New York: W. W. Norton & Company.
20. Voss, U., Holzmann, R., Tuin, I., & Hobson, J. A. (2009) Lucid Dreaming: a State of Consciousness with Features of both Waking and Non-Lucid Dreaming. Sleep, 32 (9), 1191-1200; Voss, U., Frenzel, C., Koppehele-Gossel, J., & Hobson, J. A. Lucid dreaming: an age-dependent brain dissociation. Sleep Research. 2012 Dec; 21(6): 634-42.
21. Searle, John R. (1994) The Rediscovery of the Mind. Cambridge, MA: A Bradford Book, The MIT Press.
22. Just, G. A. (2016) "Phenomenal Methodology: Toward an Egosyntonic Psycho-Neuro-Dynamic Model of Mental Health. In Advances in Psychology Research, Vol. 118 (Ed.) A. M. Columbus. Hauppauge, NY: Nova Science Pubs., Inc.
23. Ibid, Searle, 54; Ibid, 40; Ibid, 70.
24. Tegmark, Max (2013) Our Mathematical Universe. New York: Knopf Doubleday Publishing Group.

25. Mesulam, M.M. (1998) From sensation to cognition. Brain, 121: 1013-1052.

26. Libet, B. Neural time factors in consciousness and unconscious mental functions. In Toward a Science of Consciousness: The First Tucson Discussions and Debates (S. R. Hameroff, et al, Eds.). Cambridge: MIT Press, 1996, pp. 337-347.

27. Kandel, E. R. (2006) In Search of Memory: The Emergence of a New Science of Mind. New York: W. W. Norton & Company: 390.

28. Descartes, R. (1637) The Philosophical Works of Descartes, rendered into English by Elizabeth S. Haldane and G. R. T. Ross, vol. l. New York: Cambridge University Press (1970).

29. Whitney, David, & Fischer, Jason, et al., (posted online Apr. 07, 2014). Brain '15-second delay' shields us from hallucinogenic experience. Reuters/Eddie Keogh.

30. Harris, Sam. (2012) Free Will. New York: Free Press: 8.

31. Edelman, G. M. & Tononi, G. (2000) A Universe of Consciousness: How Matter Becomes Imagination. New York: Basic Books.

32. Kandel, E. R. (2006) In Search of Memory: The Emergence of a New Science of Mind. New York: W. W. Norton & Company, 390.

33. Edelman, Gerald. (2006) Second Nature: Brain Science and Human Knowledge. New Haven: Yale University Press; (2003) Being No One: The Self-Model Theory of Subjectivity. Boston: MIT Press: 217.

34. Voss, U., Holzmann, R., Tuin, I., & Hobson, J. A. (2009) Lucid Dreaming: a State of Consciousness with Features of both Waking and Non-Lucid Dreaming. Sleep, 32 (9), 1191-1200.

35. Just, Glen A. (2012) Dreams, Creativity & Mental Health. Mankato, MN: Eagle Entertainment USA.

36. Schupp, C. J., Berbaum, K, Berbaum, M., & Lang, E. V. Pain and anxiety during interventional radiologic procedures: effects of patients' state anxiety at baseline and modulation by nonpharmacologic analgesia adjuncts. J. Vas. Interv. Radiol. 2005 Dec;16(12):1585-92.

37. Lang, E. V., et al. Adjunctive self-hypnotic relaxation for outpatient medical procedures: a prospective randomized trial with women undergoing large core breast biopsy. [PubMed] 2006 Dec. 15; 126(1-3):155-64. Epub 2006 Sept 7; Lang, E. V., et al. Beneficial effects of hypnosis and adverse effects of empathic attention during percutaneous tumor treatment: when being nice does not suffice. [PubMed} J. Vasc. Interv. Radiol. 2008 June: 19(6):897-905. doi: 10. 1016/j.jvir.2008.01.027. Epub 2008 Mar. 17.

38. Benson, H., et al. Treatment of anxiety: a comparison of the usefulness of self-hypnosis and a meditational relaxation technique. An overview. [PubMed] Psychother Psychosom. 1978;30(3-4):229-42.

39. Patterson, David R. Treating Pain with Hypnosis. Current Directions in Psychology Research. Vol. 15, (6), 2004.

40. Bowers, Kenneth A. The relevance of hypnosis for cognitive-behavioral therapy. Clinical Psychology Review. Vol. 2. Issue 1, 1982, pp. 67-78.

41. Sulloway, Frank J. (1979) Freud, Biologist of the Mind: Beyond the Psychoanalytic Legend. London: Burnett Books.

42. Volk, Steve. In Defense of Free Will, Discover; November 2013, pp. 52-57.

43. Nahmias, Eddy. Why we have Free Will. Scientific American (Jan. 2015, 77-79).

CHAPTER 11

✵

Transformative Imaging, Virtual Entities, and Free Will

Ability to dream lucidly and enter and redirect dreams while they are in process draws attention to the distinction between the automaticity of will and the autonomy of free will. The imaging dynamics that accompany consciousness operate automatically when we dream. Dreaming, after all, is a state of consciousness—a time when the brain's neurons are very busy. Nevertheless, the self can actively intervene in and redirect these normally automatic processes. Self-help books demonstrating how to employ lucid dreaming are becoming their own genre and are mostly a separate development from empirical work in neuroscience and mainstream psychology.

Ability to control autonomic functions with hypnosis has been well established[1]. Conscious manipulation of dreams, hallucinations, or automatic body functions such as pain, calls attention to a higher-order neural network being able to intervene in and manipulate a lower-level neural network. For me, the use of self-hypnosis has been a key factor in achieving quality mental health[2,3,4].

I believe that my personal history, along with research documented by authorities such as Baars and Gage, and trauma specialists like Bessel van der Kolk[5,6,7], demonstrate ability to activate causal two-way interaction between levels of neural networks to control psychogenic pathology that is intertwined with neuronal and biochemical functions. Therapeutically, higher cognitive functions and self-control disappear when our individual emotions are out of control. Loss of free will is the traumatized child or adult in the throes of anxiety and depression struggling to become whole.

While awake, neuronal functionality creates the impression that we are in direct contact with our environment. In other words, all the intervening steps between sensory input and output remain invisible to us. In reality, we are responding to the sensory images formed by our brains that actually mediate our relationship to the outside world. I have and am arguing that dream imaging supports functional movements in our external environment. Hence, dream imagery feels as real in the self's "now" dream state of consciousness as it does in the self's "now" waking state of consciousness. However, the self in a "now" dream state primarily draws input from memory and other internal sources.

Virtual generation of these sensory images occurs at an unconscious level with core brain dynamics. Our sense of being in direct contact with our external environment--not core brain dynamics--creates the subjective impression that will and free will are non-material things. We don't feel our brain's busy neurons; we feel their electro-chemical products. Consequently, we subjectively and historically interpreted products of our brain's imager as "immaterial" things. This conundrum of human subjectivity, that is the automaticity of sensory imaging, has plagued philosophers throughout history.

Our sense of being in direct contact with our environment is the real illusion, not the virtual entities created in our brain to represent our world.

My brain treats the virtual contents of consciousness as something that is just as real as my toe. And because one set of neurons can act back on another set of neurons, the virtual contents of consciousness, such as my beliefs, have emotional and behavioral consequences. Next. I want to tie together automatized neuronal expressions of the brain's core dynamics with will (automatized core-brain actions), free will, and transformative imaging.

Again, note that fixed action patterns (FAPs) at the level of core-brain dynamics are executed automatically and are highly efficient energy-wise. The same efforts executed at the FAP level occur without normal tiredness, as is the case with automatic writing or Zen-driving, but leave us exhausted at a conscious level. For comparison, ask anyone who writes furiously and automatically for an hour or two in trance. Automatic behaviors controlled by the brain's core dynamics are a marvel of energy-efficiency crafted by evolution.

The skier says, "My skis handle the moguls on their own." Thus, in a manner similar to Richard Dawkins, *The Selfish Gene*, a similar agent controlling thinking skis handles hundreds of moguls on their own. How easily we personify and project the self onto our world.

The lucid dreamer says, "Erotic dream partners appear on their own, and my brain does it all by itself." The *Ouija* Board player says, "The planchette moves by itself." Note the non-conscious relationship between core dynamics and the self if FAPs are expressed automatically: it feels as if a mysterious force or spirit is at work. Additionally, image transformations in neuroses and psychoses remain invisible as is the case with dreams and nightmares, possession, hallucinations, and such disorders as OCD. Automatic execution of FAPs by the brain's dynamic core, combined with transformative imaging, has been a perennial source of mystery in humankind's attempts to understand mechanisms of the mind.

If we consciously initiate action, we have a sense of personal control. However, in contrast to secondary consciousness, the dynamic core operates automatically as a "dumb" processor, so to speak. Trauma and/or long-term dysfunctional habits such as excessive alcohol consumption can interrupt the functional relationship between core and autobiographical (secondary) brain mechanisms. Also, note that environmental context commonly triggers the automatic execution of core behavioral expressions. For example, the automatic expression of gambling behavior as the gambler enters the casino.

Keeping informed is the work of our left brain "Interpreter" according to Gazzaniga[8]. Our self as "Interpreter" is always trying to make sense of its sensory experiences. Thus, sidewalk cracks come alive and take control! Thus, Zen-driving seems magical. It is functional, however, not to think of the automaticity of "will" as a mysterious, non-physical something that lives in the nether world. The self as active agent uses free will with Zen-driving. The self can also be mystified by attributing non-consciously executed behaviors to spirits moving the planchette on the *Ouija* board game; that is, until we are able to control trance with the lucidity engendered through self-hypnosis or other means. Can the reader imagine our species not inventing "spirits?" At what stage of evolution does humanity stop inventing the supernatural? At what level of self-awareness do "spirits" stop controlling us?

As an undergraduate student, I willed myself to stay alert for up to eight hours without a break and digest hundreds of pages of university text. This lengthy study routine usually occurred after work between the hours of 10:00 p.m. to 6:00 a.m. After a couple university terms, my total reading attention was so focused that I had to be touched to reenter physical space. Attention is an acquired neural circuit patterning; I might say it is behavioral structuring of brain cell networks that support focused neuronal activity.

Thinking requires me to subjectively manipulate neuronal activity between sets of brain neurons. I'm engaging and disengaging various neural circuits as I consciously problem-solve. Conversely, embedded FAPs act like reflexes and don't require conscious attention. They operate on their own, as is the case with muscles when we walk down the street without thinking about foot movement. However, walking must still be consciously activated or controlled by free will. The automaticity of core brain dynamics simply means that we do not need to pay attention to moving one foot at a time. We think about foot movements after the fact. Libet determinism!

Revisiting Free Will

Subjectively, I know that I make choices. "I'm going to have fish tonight instead of hamburger." "I'll major in psychology rather than physics." We make decisions constantly and with every decision we have this sense of exercising free will. Free will is the self intentionally directing our brain's core dynamics to acquire new behavioral routines and execute them on demand. Free will is my phenomenal-self choosing one set of neuronal options over another. It is my self acting back upon a seemingly endless combination and re-combinations of neuronal sets, choosing A, not B, or B not C. Free will is finding and comparing neuronal sets as well as abstracting commonalities. In these acts of free will, I recognize the embryonic source of my math and probability calculations, as well as the creative use of language.

Free will does not permit behavior that is totally relative; we are limited in choice by real life options, experiences, and genetics. I must find food to survive, but I can dig clams rather than fish. Free will is something that I just seem to have, but it took a long period of evolutionary time to acquire. Developmentally, I had to acquire all those FAPs before I could walk or talk. Once mastered, walking and talking was something I just willed. Once willing became automatic, I could reimage all these FAPs at my higher cortical levels. Higher cortical reimaging permits my higher-order cortical centers to rearrange and manipulate primary sensory images. And at the secondary level, transformative imaging lets me visualize a whole new universe of possibilities. I call these processes thinking and I freely will (arrange) these options within my acquired repertoires.

Behavioral repertoires are like the "ABCs" upon which all languages are written. Once evolution gives us human-level, higher cortical centers, we can rearrange the letters of transformative imagery, so to speak, to create the magnificent artifacts of world cultures. Thus, we are able to navigate through life by endlessly recombining the contents of our neuronal networks. It seems logical that some people have a wider range of choices than others. Some people have larger vocabularies than others; that is, both letter vocabularies, FAP vocabularies, and related dynamic neural networks.

Neuronal combinations are not built in a vacuum; they are as complex as our individually combined experiences and genetics permit. You might be able to hold an object in memory and, an hour later draw it perfectly. I sit and draw parts, look up, draw other parts. The structure and capability of our brain-minds has great variability.

Like any abstraction, free will just seems to exist out there in the space of Descartes' dualistic universe. That is, until we stop and think about the mind as electro-chemical processes supported by brain tissue. Once "self" fully comes to "mind," I have a sense of unity. Once self is sufficiently mature, I can learn to control states of consciousness. Every time I learn to control another state of consciousness, I experience a more complete sense of unity. With unity and control, I can more effectively direct my life with purpose and design[9].

I know higher-order consciousness can orchestrate this complex set of biological processes. Biologically, billions of new neurons in my fetal brain were creating a virtual architecture to process sensory input. And by 30 weeks of gestation, REM emerged as a sign that sensory processing was proceeding as it should. Proto-consciousness and proto-self, those twins of biological development, began to appear. And in agreement with Hobson and Friston[10], ". . . sleep and dreaming lays the foundation for waking perception."

Neuroscience makes us painfully aware that our memories represent dynamic processes; hence, awareness of the constancy of change amongst neurons, dendrites[11] and memories. Damasio's "Autobiographical-Self" emphasizes the importance of accumulating memories over time. Dreams remind me that the further back in time I go, the greater is the total number of modified neurons in my brain. Existing neural connections are constantly being broken, and new connections are being formed. Extrapolating Dawkins' "The Selfish Gene," this is cellular romance at the most exquisite level.

In advanced Alzheimer's enough brain cells are lost that coordination across brain modules is fractured like hammer against glass. That dancing cloud of neurons we call the self no longer lights up our brains and secondary consciousness gradually disappears forever. Llinas's "i of the Vortex" winks dimly and then ceases to be. Processes of memory acquisition and loss speak directly to the dynamic plasticity of the brain. In parallel fashion, a changing self is continuously transformed as the brain's neuronal base is constantly modified.

Nevertheless, my self feels as permanent as the Columbia or Mississippi Rivers, and others can know and experience its character too. My self might not be as long-lasting as one of these rivers, but my phenomenal-self also has a history built from memories, and my self exists through time. Like a damn on the river, neuronal structures control the fluids that generate the electricity that runs all of our biological circuits.

Unlike the electro-chemistry of the river, the eddy called self can make it all the way to the ocean. If self is the eddy, then the river's moving water is consciousness. Self and consciousness, water and eddy, flow to their respective outlets. Drought can destroy the eddy, and the river--as dementia or trauma—can destroy consciousness and self. Flow is such an appropriate metaphor for *Becoming and Being*—Csikszentmihalyi[12].

Neural circuits representing complex, reflexive learned patterns of behavior emerge at a fairly early stage of mammalian evolution. Neural circuits representing higher order-cognitive processes come later, interact with and guide this earlier, neural-sensitive architecture. If this were not the case, I would be unable to script my own dreams. Complex thought emerges in the course of evolution, and complex cognitive processes (higher-order thought) permits mastery over older brain structures. This interpretation challenges self and free will as illusions. Demonstrating that self is an active agent also challenges the interpretation that cell functions in neural circuits alone, and not complex system dynamics, guides a sentient being of our complexity.

The fact that I can enter my dreams or other states of consciousness and exert control supports this free will interpretation. The fact that nightmares automatically discontinue with insight supports self's active role in creating and interpreting meaning[13,14]. When needed, higher-order cognitive processes come into play. What an efficient evolutionary development this is, and it's still not over[15,16].

Free will is thus a product of our dynamically integrated modular brain. Free will is thus interpreted as a dynamic product of systems biology. Free will is an electro-chemical process that emerges in the course of evolving complex life forms. Building on Gerald Edelman's[16] "self-model of subjectivity," free will is control over neuronal sets in charge of human behavior that are not automatized; free will is active control over complex, bidirectional, interacting, re-entrant neural networks.

I take this position on free will because I experience control over my mind and body in waking consciousness, and I experience and often practice this control with dreams and hallucinations. I practice free will in dreams when I take control of imaging processes. I practice free will when I execute a Genesis Journey to the beginning of time. I execute free will when I control anxiety and depression or extend my attention span to eight uninterrupted hours.

Free will is a subjective state that exists as clearly as my sense of the color red, and both derive from the same neural processes embedded in my brain and body proper. But note, at our stage of human evolutionary development there is also considerable re-patterning of active neural circuits that goes on at a non-conscious level; pattern iterations are executed by our brain's core dynamics contrary to our conscious intentions (addictions). Fortunately, when these processes go awry, we can learn to actively intervene. And we can embrace new treatment strategies that knit up the torn pieces of our individual developmental and traumatic histories.

Brain plasticity is active at both our brain's dynamic core and higher cortical levels. Ordinary dreams are examples of ongoing memory modifications, as are dreams across the spectrum of many different creative minds. Quoting Restak: "Today neurologists speak of a 'duality of motor function' when describing the distinction between willed and involuntary action[17]." In the above paragraphs, I have been interpreting this duality of motor functions. For example, stroke patients cannot smile voluntarily when asked, but smile spontaneously. There are different neural circuits activating these motor responses.

What I do with self-hypnosis is to consciously take control over automatic processes, such as heartbeat and pain. Or I reverse the control process with self-hypnosis and let my dynamic core lift my arms or legs without direct commands. As a child, I let my dynamic core mystically move the *Ouija* Board's planchette. It is my intent that these examples draw distinctions between automatic and conscious brain actions.

Why do these automatic processes seem mysterious to so many in the medical community? Why not teach OCD victims how to consciously and directly control the mechanisms under discussion? Why not teach individuals suffering from PTSD to control nightmares and flashbacks by learning how to modify acquired FAPs. I do not know the extent of brain plasticity in these areas, but through personal experience and the evolving literature I quote, brain plasticity is considerable.

In Zen-driving, my automatic control system steers the car by itself, while my executive brain relaxes and enjoys the ride. I suspect that opening these neural circuits to alternative controls changes my dreaming consciousness as well. Control of these processes lets me look at dream and hallucination activation from a different perspective. This analysis suggests cognitive-emotional controls that aren't being fully utilized by the medical/clinical communities— controls that were ignored by 20th Century Freudians.

Shaman/priests alter the phenomenal-self by controlling

subjective states of consciousness. Traditionally oriented psychiatrists might object to my interpretation of states of consciousness, but I think the meaning is clear. The outcomes are even clearer.

I observe and experience a feedback loop between automatic brain functions and consciousness states that most people don't seem to notice. I experience a feedback loop between thought processes while dreaming and problem solving that most people don't, although artists, writers, and scientists for generations have discussed their use of these creative mechanisms. I suspect similar feedback loops develop for long-term lucid dreamers. At a minimum, as lucid dreamers, we are more conscious of these reentrant neuronal loops driving creativity.

The concepts of will and free will have been endlessly dissected in classical philosophy and semantics, rather than as operational concepts that can be researched. Unfortunately, free will has mostly been left in the black box of historical mysticism, along with altered states. The two have much in common. Hopefully, my position is clear. Human subjectivity must be studied at its own level of evolutionary development; and the emergent self must be acknowledged as a causal entity that can act back upon other sets of neurons. That is, if we wish to go beyond the greed of pharmaceutical companies, the *Ouija* Board, and spirit possession.

I think we have researchable psychological methodologies to study these mechanisms at a level that articulates with that of the neurosciences[18]. Dream and sleep research is central to these informative neuro-psycho-dynamic methodologies. Existing brain imaging technologies have greatly furthered understanding of related brain processes.

In my experience, only when we observe dream forms and the transformative imaging contents of dreams simultaneously, can we identify memory acquisitions such as fixed action patterns. But without the dream lab work of many researchers such as Ursula Voss and Allan Hobson, documentation of dual brain states and dream forms would not enter this discussion.

If I can consciously reach into my autonomic nervous system and control outputs that are normally under automatic control, why can't other PTSD-suffers reach across their neural circuits and change one-way neuronal activity to bidirectional activity? Granted, long-term physical damage to neurons limits these options.

In 1958 as I experimented on myself and my dreaming brain, I recognized that the Skinnerian model of behaviorism was incomplete. But in that time period, these basic paradigm shift discussions were not possible at the University of Minnesota, nor were they possible at Mankato State University in the 1970s. Today, denying the reality of the "mental," subjective states of consciousness, might be more expensive than our ready coin can afford.

SOURCES: Chapter 11: Transformative Imaging, Virtual Entities, and Free Will

1. Baars, Bernard B. J. & Gage, Nicole M. (2010) Cognition, Brain, and Consciousness, 2nd Ed. New York: Elsevier, Academic Press: 296.

2. Just, Glen A. (2009) Autobiography of a Ghost. Mankato, MN: Eagle Entertainment USA.

3. Just, Glen A. (2017) "Clinical Advantages of Self-Hypnosis," in Advances in Psychology Research, vol. 119, ed. Alexandra M. Columbus. Hauppauge, NY: Nova Science Publishers, Inc.

4. Hobson, J. Allan. (2014) Ego Damage and Repair: Toward a Psychodynamic Neurology. London: Karnac Books, Ltd.

5. van der Kolk, Bessel. (2014). The Body Keeps the Score: Brain, Mind, and Body in the Healing of Trauma. New York: Viking.

6. van der Kolk, B., et al., Nightmares and Trauma: A Comparison of Nightmares After Combat with Lifelong

Nightmares in Veterans, American Journal of Psychiatry 141, no. 2 (1984): 187-190.

7. Van der Kolk, B., et al., A Randomized Clinical Trial of EMDR, Fluoxetine and Pill Placebo in the Treatment of PTSD: Treatment Effects and Long-Term Maintenance, Journal of Clinical Psychiatry 68 (2007): 37-46.

8. Gazzaniga, M. S. (1998) The Mind's Past. Berkeley: University of California Press.

9. Ackoff, Russell L., & Emery, Fred E. (2006) On Purposeful Systems: An Interdisciplinary Analysis of Individual and Social Behavior as a System of Purposeful Events. New Brunswick, USA: Aldine Transaction.

10. Hobson, J. A., & Friston, K. J. (2012) Waking and dreaming consciousness: Neurobiological and functional considerations. Progress in Neurobiology, 98(1), 82-98.

11. Smith, S. L., Smith, I. T., & Hausser, M. "Dendritic spikes enhance stimulus selectivity in cortical neurons in vivo". [PubMed] Nature. 2013 Nov. 7; 503(7474): 115-20. doi: 10.1038/nature12600. Epub 2013 Oct. 27.

12. Csikszentmihalyi, M. (1997) Creativity: Flow and the Psychology of Discovery and Invention. New York: Harper Perennial.

13. Just, G. A. (2009) Autobiography of a Ghost. Mankato, MN: Eagle Entertainment USA.

14. Just, G. A. (2016) "Phenomenal Methodology: Toward an Egosyntonic Psycho-Neuro-Dynamic Model of Mental Health. In Advances in Psychology Research, Vol. 118 (Ed) A. M. Columbus. Hauppauge, NY: Nova Science Pubs., Inc.

15. Deacon, T. (2012) Incomplete Nature: How Mind Emerged from Matter. New York: W. W. Norton & Company.

16. Edelman, Gerald. (2003) Being No One: The Self-Model Theory of Subjectivity. Boston: MIT Press: 217.

17. Restak, R. (1994) The Modular Brain: How New Discoveries in Neuroscience are Answering Age-old Questions about

Memory, Free Will, Consciousness, and Personal Identity. New York: Scribners: 39.

18. Just, Glen A. (2015) Convergence of Subjective and Objective Methodologies in Consciousness Research. In Advances in Psychology Research, Volume 103, Hauppauge, NY: Nova Science Publishers, Inc.

CHAPTER 12

✻

Lucidity, Autonomy, Determinism, and Self-Hypnotic Trance

In this chapter I will discuss the operational steps and method that I developed in order to use self-hypnosis to control automatic processes in my brain's dynamic core. Manipulating content in consciousness states exemplifies an autonomous-self controlling cellular and biochemical actions across the brain's global workspace. Lucidly employing self-hypnosis drives home the point that mechanisms of secondary consciousness virtually create dynamic, changing models that become the phenomenal-virtual-self as well as the phenomenal-physical-self[1,2,3,4]. Additionally, recall that belief and suggestion influence both the conscious and unconscious creation of content across states of consciousness that can be influenced or controlled by an autonomous-self.

Self-hypnosis is a critical part of the method that I've used since 1957/58[5]. Hypnosis in the hands of another person or clinician subverts clients establishing autonomous self-control between primary and secondary-levels of consciousness. From personal experience using hypnosis and self-hypnosis in the last half of the 20th Century, psychiatrists, especially psychoanalysts, emphasized the dominant role of the therapist. Freud himself frequently admonished his clients, whom he referred to as patients, for not accepting his diagnoses[6].

Authoritarian, "I'm in control," clinical postures both create dependency on the therapist as well as eliminating development of direct client interventions in the client's own consciousness states. Direct client intervention in situationally triggered anxiety, depression, addictions, and OCD is critical. The therapists at these moments of need are absent. However, as referenced in the last chapter, self-hypnosis can be fruitfully guided in a joint relationship with a hypnotist[7,8].

In fact, direct intervention in our own consciousness states was anathema to Freudian psychoanalysis[9]. Self-hypnosis begs a shared and guided relationship with the therapist. Thus, in the late 1950s, I developed direct means to control dreams, hallucinations, nightmares, anxiety, and depression without guidance from the prevailing models in psychiatry and psychoanalysis. Even attempts to discuss my methods with members of the psychiatric profession were met with disbelief. Those of us who grow up with symptoms of posttraumatic stress develop many different kinds of self-destructive behaviors. We also experience excessive anxiety, depression, and nightmares that prevent the maintenance of stable physiological brain and body states, which in turn disrupt healthy social lifestyles.

Over the course of my undergraduate university year of 1957/58, I learned to use self-hypnosis to gain control over automatic physiological processes such as blood flow, heart rate, and attention; additionally, I programmed exotic dreams to substitute for nightmares, and eliminated test anxiety and depression. My primary objective as a college student was to directly access and control these brain networks.

When I began experimenting with hypnosis, I didn't know how the various modules of my brain worked. I did know, however, that some Hindu practitioners of yoga could control what are normally autonomic processes. My first steps to gaining similar capabilities was to learn how to control pain, heartbeat, blood flow, and focused attention. Understanding mechanisms of image transformations related to feeling the "presence" of "ghosts," and controlling sidewalk cracks was a later accomplishment.

Ability to enter hypnotic trance varies greatly between

individuals[7,8,10]. Some of us take to this altered state easily, and others have great difficulty or resist the very idea. Through most of the 20th Century, hypnosis was ignored by a majority in the medical community[11]. Publicly, we are more likely to experience hypnosis as a form of entertainment than as an avenue to better health. Subject to Freudian theory, self-hypnosis in the 20th Century was even less well known and practiced as an aid to improved mental health. Allan Hobson states general agreement with this position in a more recent work[9].

Let me quickly go through the steps I followed as I learned self-hypnosis and point out the implications self-hypnosis has for potential control of consciousness states when awake or dreaming. Note that direct control of consciousness states, and the content of consciousness states, exemplifies the role of an autonomous-self. Learning to control consciousness states and their contents is health promoting as well. Additionally, once we individually learn to control states of consciousness and their contents, phenomenal self-manipulation across shamanic cultures no longer seems mysterious.

Steps to Acquiring Self-hypnotism

First, I relaxed quietly where there were no interruptions. I then practiced letting my hands and feet rise without volition or conscious intervention. Initially, I felt gently nuanced sensations in my hands and feet as core brain centers gradually became accustomed to acting on their own. Once my arms and legs were capable of rising by merely thinking about their movement; that is, without consciously commanding movement, I went on to the next step—one that I suspect those familiar with *Ouija* Boards follow unconsciously. Another parallel to this step might be riding a bicycle. The dynamic core coordinates seemingly on its own at a non-conscious level such actions as muscles, balance, energy release to muscles, and supporting brain chemistry.

As I experience the trance of self-hypnosis, it is this automatized part of my modular brain that is in control—similar to how we move the planchette on the *Ouija* board. There is nothing mysterious about the brain's dynamic core executing automatic commands. What is mystifying is obscuring automated dynamic brain core processes in the dark cloud of trance definitions, or definitions of the Freudian unconscious.

Next, I used self-hypnosis to gain control over autonomic brain processes controlling heart beat, blood flow, and pain. The procedure I followed to control these three automatic functions was, once again, simple "willing." For example, I placed an imaginary band around my wrists and thought that these virtual items were stopping blood flow. I repeated this induction process over a number of days until blood flow was interrupted and the temperature in my hands was noticeably reduced. The same procedure was repeated with pain control.

In similar fashion, biofeedback and neurofeedback studies are demonstrating methods by which we individually can gain control over automatic brain processes[12,13]. Therapeutically, external electrical stimulation is another method that is used to rewire the brain's neural networks[14]. Electrical stimulation to modify neural networks is another example that contradicts the 20th Century Freudians who abhorred direct intervention in pathology. Hindu Yoga practitioners and Tibetan Buddhists have employed versions of these body and pain controls for centuries. Once I gained waking control over automatic body processes, I implemented similar controls in my dreams. I called controlling the content of my dreams "dream programming."

Lucid self-hypnosis (LSH) allows the phenomenal-self to remain active throughout the trance state. The trance experience parallels that of lucid dreaming. Ability to control states of consciousness means that individually we can become our own therapists. (Allan Hobson discusses my use of self-therapy and hypnosis in *The Self Treatment of Glen Just)*[15].

Physical Brain Modification and Self-Hypnosis

In the following two sections of this chapter, I will provide examples of self-induced trance while dreaming and driving to exemplify the self's metacognitive role in these processes, and to highlight the significance of trance control for the shaping and modification of phenomenal sensory processing. But first, I want to call attention to the fact that brain structure is physically modified with use.

Structural changes of the brain and rewiring of its circuits is being confirmed through careful scientific research[16,17,18]. For example, long-term Buddhist meditators can sustain a particular EEG pattern: "Meditation brings about changes not only in well-defined cognitive and emotional processes, but also in the volume of certain brain areas, possibility reflecting alterations in the number of connections among brain cells"[17].

Brain structures differ between those individuals with high levels of lucid dreaming versus those with low levels: "Neuroscientists from the Max Planck Institute of Human Development and the Max Planck Institute of Psychiatry have compared brain structures of frequent dreamers and participants who never or only rarely have lucid dreams. Accordingly, the anterior prefrontal cortex, i.e., the brain area controlling conscious cognitive processes and playing an important role in the capability of self-reflection, is larger in lucid dreamers"[19]. Future research should reveal potential structural changes in the brain when lucid dreaming is acquired later in life.

I didn't know how the various modules of my brain worked when I discovered how to program my dreams, or to enact and control waking hallucinations. I didn't even know how aspirin worked, but I used it anyway. Note that with trance induction during dreaming that the self is metacognitively enacting trance on its own while lucidly observing.

Hypnotism practiced by a therapist on a client takes control of the trance process. Therapist control of trance leaves the patient at the "mercy" of the therapist (hypnotic transference), so to speak. For better mental health, I'm stressing the importance of clients taking direct control of automatic brain processes. In my experience, maximum self-control requires self-induction of trance states. Self-control enhances "ego strength" in a direct manner; thus, the self skips forming a dependency relationship with a therapist or hypnotist. Furthermore, as noted, when we individually encounter anxiety or addiction promoting environments, the therapist is nowhere in sight; thus, self-control is critical. Thus, the "Clinical Advantages of Self-Hypnosis" suggest rethinking the role of client-therapist transference[20].

Modern research is identifying how the various modular sections of our brains communicate physiologically. One can quickly become familiar with a rather large body of research on the brain's modular communications by reviewing Bernard Baars' Global Workspace Theory[21]; or simply scan the Internet using Global Workspace Theory and Bernard Baars as key search words. For the technically oriented reader, Baars, Banks and Newman[22] have a dense volume that gets into technical aspects of consciousness. Or try Michael Posner[23], paying particular attention to "content" sections dealing with executive brain functions. And, for detailed biochemical and physiological research check out the journal *Neuron*.

You can learn these body controls by spending a few months or years with yoga practitioners or Tibetan monks. Or you can practice self-hypnosis in the confines of your own home. I taught myself to hypnotize others as a high school student. The fun and games approach, which helped me self-learn the process on my own. Let me give you an example of a mature form of self-hypnotic trance application.

Personal Case Study: Zen-driving

I drove from Southern Minnesota to NW Wisconsin weekly when my stepmother was dying of cancer. It's about a 2.5-hour drive over wooded, rolling, lake-peppered landscapes. It's always a pleasant drive, but one that is even more pleasant if someone else is doing the driving. I'd fuse my body with the car (incorporate the car into my behavioral space) and experience a sense of flying two feet off the road.

It's a bit of a trick teaching the self to remain lucid during Zen-driving, as I call it. But a trick that is not at all mysterious. Motorcycle riders phenomenally merge bodily with their bikes and know this feeling. Skiers merge with their equipment and sense touch through their skies. Joggers experience the automaticity of core dynamics as they run in front of oncoming traffic. Even regular users of walking canes feel with rubber tips. Readers probably have their own personal examples. In that the physical-phenomenal-self is a virtual construction, we can incorporate physical objects as part of our self.

This Zen process becomes routine as our core-self automatically takes over the driving. Thus, the phenomenal-self is freed up to relax and enjoy the ride. Overall, I experience Zen-driving as though someone else where at the wheel. This is a different view of how multiple personalities come about, or how we experience states of paranoia. Once an emerging neuronal map that holds an image of self and car as one entity in the brain has been generated, Zen driving becomes a reality. So, what is the science behind this phenomenon?

Individuals suffering from phantom hands continue to feel pain in the missing limb after it has been lost. The brain has a map of the now nonexistent hand and any stimulation of the stump triggers activation of this map. Ramachandran's mirror therapy for missing limbs exemplifies the subjective reality of our phenomenal world[24].

In related experiments, phenomenal identification can be created with fake body parts[25,26,27,28,29,30] or full body images[31,32,33,34] that feel like our own. Simply stroking a rubber hand or full-body dummy that is in visual sight at the same time our real hand or body is stroked out-of-sight, subjectively causes the brain to transfer possession to the rubber hand or full body. These experiments offer insight into the phenomenal construction and related plasticity of the self.

May-Britt Moser and Edvard L. Moser are professors in Psychology and Neuroscience at the at the Norwegian University of Science and Technology in Trondheim. Along with John O'Keefe University College London, they received the Nobel Prize for discovery of the brain's positioning system. A simple interpretation of their work acknowledges structural brain correlates that represent organismic relationships to physical space. Various animal forms create internal maps as a type of sophisticated GPS-like tracking system.

Forming a Habit: Essential to the Process

Zen driving helps demonstrate to us the mechanism involved in habits that are automatically expressed by the brain's core dynamics. Waking up hundreds of miles from home and not knowing how we got there is disconcerting. With practice, acquired skills become automatic. Once a habit is fully mastered, we no longer need to think about balancing the bike to ride it; we just "will" the related skill behaviors, and they occur automatically, as well as remaining invisible to secondary consciousness. Knowing that alcoholics or drug addicts can drive in a blackout state also helps enlighten us about how our modular brain works. Intoxicated, "will" takes us 200 miles down the road without conscious effort. Or, "will," spends $500 dollars at the casino, and our higher-order consciousness asks, "How did that happen?" Individuals who commit murder in their sleep are even more perplexed[35].

Note that the mechanism supporting Zen-driving, driving in an alcoholic blackout, spending money at the casino, or killing relatives in our sleep permits very complex behaviors. In Zen-driving we are metacognitively aware throughout the drive. With casino addictions, we feel the automaticity of our brain's core dynamics as compulsions. Committing murder in our sleep can occur completely below the awareness level of our phenomenal-self[35].

Ann Graybiel at MIT and Kyle Smith of Dartmouth College have been conducting research on how behavior becomes habit[36]. Habit basically means that we act without thinking. We are all familiar with acting without thinking—we walk trails, ski moguls, and lose money at casinos. The point I want to emphasize with Graybiel and Smith's research is related to George A. Miller's idea of "chunking." Simply—chunking is collapsing a sequence of behaviors into one functional unit. For example, numbers are not remembered as 5-5-51-2-1-2 but as 555-1212.

In terms of my casino addiction example, we step through the casino door to get the pre-offered free prize and "chunk." Concurrently, a long sequence of learned gambling behavior is executed as one act, so to speak. Alcoholics know this effect when they enter their favorite bar— "chunk." Our brains efficiently "chunk" behaviors. Complex behavioral routines become invisible as we casually ride our bikes down busy city streets—chunk. You know what I mean—chunk! Thus, "chunking" as a form of complex behavioral conditioning offers insight into obsessive and compulsive actions.

Behavior modification works because behavioral plasticity is the observable part of neuronal plasticity. Neuroplastic maps can represent a single tone, for example, or a complex of tones as Merzenich and colleagues have demonstrated[36]. Or in my example of playing piano or violin in my dreams, our brain can "chunk" a whole piece of music even when we are only listeners and not performers.

As children, we acquire one skill after another. It is efficient for our brains to make complex skills automatic. As adults, we can regain control of these automatic processes for therapy or pleasure. Similarly, automatically, we dream, we hallucinate, and we experience neurotic and psychotic episodes.

Personal Case Study: Revisiting Hypnotic induction while dreaming (Dream: 14 Nov. 2013)

As previously noted, the dream challenge is to exit the classroom by passing directly through a room full of furniture. I'm not permitted to pass over the top of the desks and chairs; hence, I must dissolve their presence. Let me call attention to the specific elements that are active in this dream scenario: Metacognitive awareness: My dream-self is aware that it can fly over the tops of the chairs and desks, but this is not permitted. My dream-self is also aware that the classroom is a virtual construction; thus, subject to phenomenal manipulation. There is an element of meta-consciousness that is occurring dynamically and bidirectionally across dreaming and waking states.

Dual states of consciousness: I am the dream-self actor, as well as the observer. I am aware of being the actor in both dream-roles. My observing-self is aware that phenomenal manipulation of my dream environment is under my immediate control. I concentrate hard, and the desks and chairs begin to dissolve. A passage opens up and I "walk" in a straight line to the door, through an area that was previously full of furniture

The hypnotic induction that I subjectively experience while lucidly dreaming feels the same as it does when I'm awake. Upon waking, I realize that lucidity combined with trance suggestion permits any virtual creation or image manipulations I might desire. But at a more immediate level, I realize that practicing image constructions and transformations eventually leads to on-demand imaging that results in waking control of self-created hallucinations. And that it is this capacity to control the brain-mind's imaging processes that holds so much promise for the mental health practitioners and clients.

Once I enact this dream trance control, I can lucidly manipulate any visual content I choose. As a first-year university student, I employed self-hypnosis to substitute erotic lovers for nightmares. In effect, what I was doing is enacting and "chunking" a similar type of trance control for these dream image substitutions. Note, however, that I employ waking and dreaming controls through self-hypnosis 24/7. Also, note that control over the automaticity of my brain's dynamic core eliminated daytime anxiety and depression, and permitted sound sleep, which in turn would have restored my brain cells biochemical homeostasis.

The night preceding this dream, I reviewed Thomas Metzinger's ideas about the phenomenal-self and consciousness. After 6:00 a.m. following this trance dream, I let my brain drift in a dual state of waking-dreaming free association, letting it connect ideas of mirror neurons with various states of consciousness. I made no attempt to capture the details over the following 45-50 minutes. Nevertheless, I now recall a re-occurring theme as to how non-conscious dreaming and dual state associations could predispose me and others to feel that mind can control matter.

Varieties of Phenomenal-Self Imaging

The self in lucid dreaming can direct its own phenomenal experiences. Thus, the self can hold the larger sensory image in focus as a subpart of the image is intentionally modified. A similar type of image transformation is also practiced by some Tibetan monks. The process of consciously modifying an image's subpart has its counterpart in the automatic construction of characters in our dreams. (Recall my discussion of dram images of spouse Ruby).

Cross-cultural awareness of shamans and shamanic trance states sensitizes us to full-body illusions. Shamanic possession of a totem such as a bear or eagle poignantly emphasizes how the phenomenal-self can be manipulated. We can learn these techniques of phenomenal-self manipulation, and following thousands of years of shamanic practices, enact similar subjective states sitting in our classrooms, for example, as I discussed becoming a shamanic bear in my autobiography.

I realized that as an eight-year-old, I was perplexed by my ability to pass back-and-forth through my bedroom ceiling when I went out flying during the night. In the dream example of manipulating classroom furniture there is the same sensation of manipulating my mind's virtual imaging space—classroom chairs and desks disappear at "will," or a hole in a Japanese dream submarine appears on demand. And in similar fashion, so did my childhood bedroom ceiling disappear. Of course, at that young age I did not understand how we humans subjectively occupy phenomenal space.

Trance enactment in dreams brings home the realization that the mind is always creating a "phenomenal-self model," that lives in phenomenal-world space, as Thomas Metzinger discusses it[31]. Thus, trance enactment permits control of both the phenomenal-self as well as its environment. Dream observations support and resonate with Botvinick's rubber hands being subjectively perceived as part of one's body[25]. Or full-body virtual creations (illusions) created by Bigna Lenggenhager stroking Metzinger's back[33].

Self-induced trance is being defined as the brain's ability to enact a phenomenal-self model (PSM) and employ this PSM to control conscious sensory images by direct access to core brain dynamics. Therapist induced trance is similarly defined with the exception that executive aspects of the therapists' self is substituted for the client's self.

Trance states recognize the brain's ability to hold PSMs in memory while consciously generating sensory images (self-hypnotic induction.) (The brain can also hold in memory sensory images that have been generated non-consciously by a therapist induced trance, as observed in parlor game-type tricks),

Analysis of different self-induced trance states calls attention to the similarities of image transformations across all states of consciousness. I believe that my example of phenomenal content manipulation provides support for the assumption that a common image transformer is operative in all states of consciousness. I conclude that creative content image transformations are inspired by individual perceptual differences, beliefs, and culture.

SOURCES: Chapter 12: Lucidity, Autonomy, Determinism, and Self-Hypnotic Trance

1. James, Wm. (1890) The Principles of Psychology. Available: http://psychclassics.yorku.ca/James/Principles.

2. Gallagher, S. (2000) Philosophical conceptions of the self: implications for cognitive science. Trends Cogn. Sci. 4, 14-21.

3. Metzinger, Thomas. (2003) Being No One: The Self-Model Theory of Subjectivity. Cambridge, MA: MIT Press.

4. Merleau-Ponty, M. (2005) Phenomenology of Perception. London: Routledge Classics.

5. Just, Glen A. (2009) Autobiography of a Ghost. Mankato, MN: Eagle Entertainment USA.

6. Brill, A. A. ((1938) The Basic Writings of Sigmund Freud. Edited and Translated. New York: The Modern Library.

7. Lang, E. V., et al. Adjunctive self-hypnotic relaxation for outpatient medical procedures: a prospective randomized trial with women undergoing large core breast biopsy. [PubMed] 2006 Dec. 15; 126(1-3):155-64. Epub 2006 Sept 7.

8. Benson, H., et al. Treatment of anxiety: a comparison of the usefulness of self-hypnosis and a meditational relaxation technique. An overview. [PubMed] Psychother Psychosom. 1978;30(3-4):229-42.

9. Hobson, Allan. (2014) Ego Damage and Repair: Toward a Psychodynamic Neurology. London: Karnac; (2015) Psychodynamic Neurology: Dreams, Consciousness, and Virtual Reality. Boca Raton, Florida: CRC Press.

10. Baars, B. J. & Gage, N. M.(2010) Cognition, Brain, and Consciousness, 2nd Ed. New York: Elsevier, Academic Press: 296-297.

11. See David Spiegel, MD, Wilson Professor and Associate Chair of Psychiatry and Behavioral Sciences, Stanford University of Medicine's website regarding hypnosis research.

12. Fisher, Sebern F. (2014) Neurofeedback in the Treatment of Developmental Trauma: Calming the Fear-Driven Brain. New York: Norton.
    Ibid, Baars & Gage, 296.

13. The Fisher Wallace Stimulator® is cleared by the FDA for the treatment of depression and anxiety. During each 20-minute treatment session (once or twice a day), the device stimulates the brain to produce serotonin while lowering cortisol (the stress hormone
    Ibid, Hobson (2014), 96.

14. Ricard, M., Lutz, A., & Davidson, R.J. Mind of the Meditator, Science, (Nov. 2014), 39-45.

15. Doidge, N. (2007) The Brain that changes itself: Stories of Personal Triumph from the Frontiers of Brain Science. NY: Viking.

16. Nijeboer, S., et al. "Is meditation associated with altered brain structure? A systematic review and meta-analysis of morphometric neuroimaging in meditation practitioners".

17. Neurosci. Biobehav. Rev. 2014 June: 43:48-73. doi: 10.1016. Epub 2014 Apr. 3.

18. "Lucid Dreams and Metacognition," Neuroscience News (Jan 23, 2015). Contact: Kerstin Skork, Max Planck Institute.

19. Just, Glen A. (2017) "Clinical Advantages of Self-Hypnosis," in Advances in Psychology Research, vol. 119, ed. Alexandra M. Columbus. Hauppauge, NY: Nova Science Publishers, Inc.

20. Ibid, Baars & Gage, 287-291.

21. Baars, B. J., Banks, W. P., & Newman, J. B. Eds. (2003) Essential Sources of the Scientific Study of Consciousness. Cambridge, MA: The MIT Press.

22. Posner, M. I. (2012) Ed. Cognitive Neuroscience of Attention, 2nd Ed. New York: The Guilford Press.

23. Ramachandran, V.S., & Blakeslee, Sandra. (1998) Phantoms in the Brain: Probing the Mysteries of the Human Mind. New York: Harper Perennial.

24. Botvinick, M., & Cohen, J. "Rubber hands 'feel' touch that eyes see." 1998, Nature 391:756.

25. Ehrsson, H. H., Spence, C., & Passingham, R. E. (2004) That's my hand activity in premotor cortex reflects feeling of ownership of a limb. Science 305, 875-877. doi: 10.1126/science.1097011.

26. Tsakiris, M. (2010) My body in the brain: a neurocognitive model of body-ownership. Neuropsychologia 48, 703-712. doi: 10.1016/j.neuropsychologia.2009.09034.

27. Petkova, V. I., et al. From part-to-whole-body ownership in the multisensory brain. Curr. Biol. 21, 118-1122. doi: 10.1016/j.cub.2011.05.022.

28. Tsakiris, M. (2008) Looking for myself: current multisensory input alters self-face recognition. PLoS ONE 3:e4040. doi: 10.1371/journal.pone.0004040.

29. Apps, M. A., et al. (2013) Plasticity in unimodal and multimodal brain areas reflects multisensory changes in self-face identification. Cereb. Cortex. doi: 10.1093/cercor/bht199.

30. Metzinger, Thomas. (2009) The Ego Tunnel: The Science of the Mind and the Myth of the Self. New York: Basic Books: 98-101.

31. Ehrsson, H. H., et al. Threatening a rubber hand that you feel is yours elicits a cortical anxiety response. Proceedings National Academy of Science U.S.A. 104, 9828-9833. doi: 10.1073/pnas.0610011104.

32. Lenggenhager, T., Tadi, T., Metzinger, T., & Blanke, O. (2007) Video ergo sum: manipulating bodily self-consciousness. Science 24, 1096. doi: 10.1126/science.1143439.

33. Maselli, A., & Slater, M. (2013) The building blocks of the full body ownership illusion. Front. Hum. Neursci. 7:83. doi: 10.3389/fnhum.2013.00083.

34. Cartwright, R. D. (2010) The Twenty-Four Hour Mind: The Role of Sleep and Dreams in our Emotional Lives. London: Oxford University Press.

35. Graybiel, Ann M. & Smith, Kyle S. Good Habits Bad Habits. Scientific American, June, 2014, 39-43.

36. Michael Merzenich's website is an excellent source for resources on neuro-plasticity. Following his website videos provides additional support for the autonomy of self.

CHAPTER 13

✿

Protoconsciousness Theory

Protoconsciousness makes a number of assumptions about fetal brain architecture that are related to the entire thematic content of this book. As Allan Hobson has stated in private communications to this author, "It is a theory under construction." In this chapter, I will consider protoconsciousness as a partial and incomplete theory. Nevertheless, I provide support for the theory by combining empirical and first-person evidence.

In the following four sections, I review the theory's 1) basic assumptions, 2) empirical support, 3) how protoconsciousness is related to the construction of the phenomenal-self, as well as 4) the theory's relationship to dreams and hallucinations.

Basic Assumptions of Protoconsciousness Theory

The most fundamental assumption that Hobson makes about protoconsciousness theory is summed up by the following quote: "REM sleep may constitute a protoconsciousness state, providing a virtual reality model of the world that is of functional use to the development and maintenance of waking consciousness. [The] hypothesis . . . suggests that the development and maintenance of waking consciousness and other higher-order brain functions depend on brain activation during sleep. It is also suggested that the brain states underlying waking and dreaming cooperate and that their functional interplay is crucial to the optimal function of both"[1].

Hobson views support for the brain's protoconsciousness architecture with the appearance of fetal rapid eye movements (REM) by 30 weeks of gestation. Recall that REM is a major dream state. Hence, Hobson interprets REM as a sign that a fetal architecture is emerging to support lifelong dream functions, and that dream functions themselves are intimately related to developing and maintaining the brain's waking life-critical capacities.

Hobson follows Immanuel Kant's *Critique of Pure Reason* by assuming that the self begins to feel, experience, and think before birth[1]. Feeling, experiencing, and thinking are interpreted as being very embryonic in both Hobson's and my analyses. Along with Hobson, I assume that fetal REM is associated with the brain's sensory processors coming online, and that REM protoconsciousness mechanisms are supporting early sensory imprints that can be measured after birth. I also assume that fetal protoconsciousness mechanisms are emerging to process movement and a sense of gravity.

Empirical Support for Protoconsciousness Theory

Recall that newborn infants recognize their mother's voice, heartbeat, music, and food preferences[2,3,4,5]. The idea that the brain was a blank slate at birth was not only erroneous, but detrimental to 20th Century research and development for fetuses, infants, and children. I am not assuming that the developing fetus has memory as we understand memory in our everyday use of the term. Hence, the prefix proto, proto-consciousness, and proto-self.

The question for protoconsciousness theory regarding the following sub-sections on phocomelic children, sensory deprived individuals, and people with lost sensory capacities has two parts: 1) What is the evidence for a neural architecture that supports fetal memory? 2) What is the mechanism that allows the brain to create a virtual counterpart of its missing senses and physical body parts?

Experiencing missing limbs in phocomelic children

Phocomelic children are born without some of their limbs. Yet, some of them report experiencing presence of the missing limb. "It seems that these data show that even people born without limbs develop complex body models which sometimes include their missing limbs[6]." Research on phocomelic children begs the question: How can the brain experience a body part that never developed? Phocomelic children experiencing their missing limbs suggests that a proto-template of the physical body exists—a map, so to speak—that fully develops with use. However, for some phocomelic individuals, this neural map appears to be expressed in the brain without use.

Acquiring vision in the vision deprived

"Putting Together a New Visual World[7]" after years or decades of being blind also addresses the questions of the brain's fundamental architecture and processes. Comparing the visually deprived with phocomelic children leads to a similar conclusion: active sensory processing for the developing child builds on the brain's innate protoconsciousness architecture. Let's look at the evidence.

Pawan Sinha, professor of Vision and Computational Neuroscience at the Massachusetts Institute of Technology is in charge of Project Prakash[ibid]. There are 400,000 blind children in India. Many of them have congenital cataracts which the project corrects, anywhere from childhood into their 20s. Initially when sight is restored, a vision-deprived twenty-year-old doesn't immediately see "pictures". Typically, they will see shadows and shapes. A person may be seen as an outlined group of fuzzy, geometric shapes. No fine detail can be detected nor can object recognition occur, for example, that an object is a dancing girl. It takes weeks and months to recognize that what is being seen is a dancing girl.

The visually deprived possess a neural structure that processes geometric shapes; what appears to be a proto-structure that supports sight but is not sufficient for sight itself. Partial restoration of vision after decades without use provides support for the brain's neuroplasticity and, at the same time, acknowledges the existence of a critical formative period for full vision development.

The visual System's Complexity

The complexity of neural structures and related biochemistry is mind-boggling, but progress is steady and substantial. Takao Hensch is a joint professor of neurology at Harvard Medical School and Boston's Children Hospital and a good example of contemporary research on the neurology of vision[8]. Hensch and colleagues are using the neurotransmitter GABA (gamma-aminobutyric acid) to reopen closed visual pathways and fully restore sight after critical periods have passed[ibid]. Application of Hensch's research to human populations lies in the future. Nevertheless, research of the processes and neural structures supporting vision continues to detail the involved mechanisms. (See Elbert and Rockstroh[9] regarding visual plasticity with injury).

Older research by J. P. Shaffery and colleagues found a critical relationship between sleep deprivation in rats and ability to develop their visual system[10]. Triangulating Sinha, Hensch, and Shaffery's research, suggests 1) a critical fetal proto-structure is emerging to process vision before birth, 2) there are biochemical switches turning genes on and off during critical periods of neural development, 3) although brain plasticity is considerable, dynamic factors also determine genetic and neural developmental and, 4) there is a direct relationship between sleep deprivation and visual development.

Once again, I find support for Hobson's protoconsciousness assumptions—a fetal proto-architecture exists to support vision, and ". . . the development and maintenance of waking consciousness and other higher-order brain functions depend on brain activation during sleep[1]." The above examples of vision development take us beyond a speculative conception of proto-fetal brain structure to further detail some of the neural and biochemical mechanisms involved.

Experiencing virtual imaging with sensory deprivation

The following example describes Charles Bonnet Syndrome: "A significant proportion of those who go blind—10 to 20 percent, by most estimates—become prone to involuntary images, or outright hallucinations, of an intense and sometimes bizarre kind"[11]. Additionally, blind-at-birth people sometimes report clear and recognizable visual elements in their dreams[ibid]: "Helder Bertolo and his colleagues in Lisbon, in an intriguing 2003 report, described how they compared congenitally blind subjects with normal sighted subjects and found "equivalent visual activity" (based on analysis of EEG alpha-wave attenuation) in the two groups when they were dreaming"[ibid]. The similarity of EEG alpha-wave patterns for blind and normal subjects also suggests the existence of a genetically given protoconsciousness brain architecture.

Observing Fetal language learning and sensory deprivation

Eino Partanen at the University of Helsinki in current online proceedings of the National Academy of Sciences[12] addresses the importance of fetal language learning. Observations that newborn infants pay special attention to the mother's voice, indicates that fetal sound processing has already been occurring.

Additional support for the fetus being exposed to voice sounds comes from Doctor Betty Vohr at the Warrant Alpert Medical School of Brown University and Women and Infants Hospital in

Providence, Rhode Island[13]. According to Vohr, the fetus hears its mother's voice much like you and I hear voice when someone talks with their hands over their mouth. Vohr's research shows a direct relationship between premature infant language development and how many words are heard in neonatal intensive care (NICU). Fetal language and infant memory research demonstrate that fetal language stimulation is directly related to later language development. Vohr and colleagues' research demonstrates that there is a critical formative period in fetal development that supports language learning. Her research also demonstrates a permanent handicap and reduced child language development if this period is not fully accommodated. Both Vohr and Sinha's research suggests a fetal protoconsciousness neural structure that requires stimulation in order to support after-birth maturation.

Both Sinha and Vohr's research support Hobson's protoconsiousness assumption that the fetus begins to experience before birth. Both lines of research support the emergence of permanent fetal neural networks that support vision and language abilities. Thus, it appears that the fetal brain is forming neural structure and content that represents what might be referred to as a "dynamic unconscious."

For contrast, compare these "hard science" interpretations of protoconsciousness theory for a "dynamic unconscious" with that of the psychoanalytic-guided research of Shevrin and colleagues[14].

They ". . . claim that . . . primary process characteristics can be considered indicative of: (a) unconscious content requiring disguise in order to be consciously acceptable . . ." Protoconsciousness theory discards disguise and censorship of the Freudian psychoanalytic model and the supposed "unconscious conflicts" psychoanalysis assumes.

Virtual imaging with sensory deprivation

One more example of the brain's internal visual constructions discussed by Oliver Sacks before summary analysis: "Jacques Lusseyran was a blind French Resistance fighter. He was blinded in an accident before his eighth birthday. As he gradually accommodated his blindness . . . his mind constructed a "screen" upon which whatever he thought or desired was projected and, if need be, manipulated, as on a computer screen. In Lusseyran's words, "In a few months my personal world had turned into a painter's studio"[11].

For those with missing or lost sensory capacities, as well as for individuals with these capacities, being able to create virtual imaging suggests that a virtual image generator is active for members of both groups. The above examples support an innate image generator being active in all states of consciousness. In support of protoconsciousness theory, sensory neural templates appear to be genetically given and capable of virtual imaging even for individuals born without related sensory capacities.

Research on virtual imaging with sensory deprivation and loss takes us beyond basic cellular and biochemical research in areas such as vision. Virtual imaging research directs our attention to higher order neural system integration and the phenomenal, subjective psychology operating at our higher cortical levels.

Similar to Jacques Lusseyran's "painter's studio," my own mind (described in my Genesis Journey example), constructed a screen upon which I projected my thought or desires. In the late 1950s, I used self-hypnosis to gain control over my brain's innate image generator. (Lusseyran's "painter studio" ability developed after he was blinded). Both of the above examples call attention to fundamental, virtual imaging mechanisms that are being acquired either consciously or non-consciously.

Note the similarity between Lusseyran's vivid imagery and my controlled hallucinations. Note the similarity between his "visual" manipulations and dream programming (scripting). And with the congenitally blind, note the suggestion that a self-organizing neuronal template seems to support vision even when vision has never been realized. The same analysis applies to phocomelic children. The above examples provide substantive evidence for the presence of a protoconsciousness architecture.

Transforming *Primary and Secondary Sensations for Self-emergence*

The Archaeology of Mind is a book title by Jaak Panksepp and Lucy Biven[15]. Panksepp is well known worldwide for his studies of primary process emotions. There are seven fundamental systems found in mammals: "SEEKING, RAGE, FEAR, LUST, CARE, PANIC/GRIEF, and PLAY[ibid]." These seven systems are of evolutionary construction and built into the genome of our species.

In "Toward a Neurobiology of the Soul: The Core Self and the Genesis of Primary-Process Feelings," Panksepp and Biven resort to a brief flirtation with philosophy[ibid]—Descartes, Hume, and Kant. Like Allan Hobson, they quote Kant's *Critique of Pure Reason*: ". . . the mind has *a priori* cognitive powers that provide intrinsic knowledge that precedes experience[ibid]. I'm considering Panksepp's seven systems to be a form of innate biological knowledge. Infants come into the world with these seven biological systems, which are developed and shaped in social and environmental interaction.

Additionally, Panksepp and Biven state that: "The evidence is now overwhelming that all mammals have intense experiences when the ancient networks of their emotional brains are directly manipulated. The core SELF nevertheless seems clearly related to primary-process emotional and other affective processes of the BrainMind"[ibid]. Panksepp has researched and promoted the importance of these seven systems for many years. Combining his seven primary process systems with fetal learning further sensitizes us to how erroneous was the idea that infants are born with a blank slate. These primary emotional processes are part of the brain's dynamic core, Panksepp's "core self," and are created by evolution before higher cortical centers emerge.

I observe and connect this hierarchy of evolution—emotion before higher-order cognition—with my dream characters. Emotions in my dreams are true to character but visual representations can be mixed in any associational combinations. As I earlier observed with my dream examples of spouse Ruby, her dream physical features might change from scene-to-scene, but not my emotional reactions to her.

Panksepp's seven primary processes represent *a priori* systems in the "BrainMind." Protoconsciously, the newborn infant comes into this world with very dynamic and complex cognitive and emotional biology. However, the "BrainMind" is not cognitive and emotional, it is cognitive-emotional. Antonio Damasio supports cognitive-emotional monism by noting that emotional elements are always part of cognitive processes[16]. Damasio also recognizes proto-self as a comparable stage of human development that, in my opinion, is compatible with the above Panksepp-Hobson discussion.

Panksepp and Biven embrace Kant, as does Hobson. All three authors are searching for primary processes and supporting neural structures built into the human genome. All three authors analyze the relationship between primary and secondary consciousness. They are extremely helpful sources as we think through fundamental questions of self and consciousness.

We enter the world as newborns with a built-in architecture that supports primary process emotions. Our genomic architecture transforms aspects of our physical world of electromagnetic waves (light), jiggling molecules (sound), and physical force (touch) into useful, subjective elements that enhance our physical survival. These sensory transformations are fundamental aspects of primary consciousness and represent a distinct set of imagery that we can observe in our dreams and hallucinations.

As I've previously noted in dream analysis, primary sensory images undergo a transformation at our secondary level of consciousness. As we pass through infancy to early childhood, say 5-years of age, brain architecture matures to a level that permits fairly complex role taking. Ability to assume various social roles increasingly defines our own role acquisitions as being unique and different from those of all other persons. Thus, as we become unique Human Beings we also generate unique dream associations and imagery transformations.

I propose that the unique reimaging of primary sensory elements at our secondary level of consciousness is the mechanism that is critical for the formation of the phenomenal-self. Memories accessible to secondary consciousness form the substance from which the emerging self comes to be. No two sets of memories or experiences are ever the same. Michael Merzenich[17] explains this process of self under construction this way: "For every touch, for every moment of vision, for every sound or word heard, for every moment of thought or action, there is a second very reliable concurrent association. That second association is to you".

Secondary sensory image transformations occur at a psychological level—meaning attributed to experience is always a product of subjective interpretation. Neuronal plasticity permits endless variations of attributed meaning to sensory transformations at our secondary level of consciousness. Thus, the social world creates interpretations that become spirits, ghosts, and an endless pantheon of ethereal things. And, the emerging self becomes a unique entity unlike that of any other person.

Primary image generation for all of our senses is built into the genome and expressed automatically. Automatic sensory processes usually occur at a nonconscious level and remain invisible to waking consciousness. Fortunately, image transformations at our secondary level of consciousness can be lucidly observed and studied in dreams and hallucinations.

Protoconsciousness Theory and the Construction of the Phenomenal-Self

Most critically, a self-organizing fetal architecture appears to form proto-consciousness and proto-self. Infant recognition of mother's voice, music preferences, and tastes supports sensory images and related neural structures being formed during fetal development. Research by Vohr on language, and Sinha on vision demonstrate the necessity of fetal-to-infant stimulation for these proto-structures to fully materialize. Proto-to-infant maturation of language and visual structures has lifelong effects for "self" development.

Fetal memory preferences measured in infant and toddler development help shape interactions of the self with its physical and social environments. Protoconsciousness experience, then, acknowledges the significance of fetal learning, which Hobson and Friston[18] have linked with fetal REM in the "Cartesian Theatre of Consciousness."

Research identifying memory functions of sleep[19] and reinforcement of motor skills with sleep[20] demonstrates the active relationship between waking and dreaming. Detection of fetal memories in infancy correlates the beginning of these memory functions with fetal protoconsciousness.

Allan Hobson and Karl Friston refer to the mechanism supporting fetal and waking memory processes as ". . . an innate, a priori virtual reality generator . . . that produces a predictive model of the world. The model of the world is continuously updated and entrained by sensory prediction errors in wakefulness, but not in dreaming. This model, which is most clearly revealed in REM sleep dreaming, provides the theatre for conscious experience"[ibid]. Hobson and Friston's interpretation add a virtual reality generator to the brain's innate self-organizing neural networks. Our virtual reality generator is conceived as always being on and generating a virtual model of the world when we are conscious. Virtual replication of our world is always on when we are conscious, as well as being predictive.

In support of Hobson and Friston, Thomas Metzinger says: "Mental simulation, as an unconscious process of simulating possible situations, may actually be an autonomous process that is incessantly active"[21]. Metzinger refers to autonomous image generation as being part of the brain's "fixed network properties."

Leopold and Logothetis view the brain as a system that is constantly simulating possible realities for our immediate self[22]. They are shifting from "unconscious" network properties to a view of the phenomenal-self that is actively preparing to engage its environment.

Whitney and Fischer's research indicates that visual "smoothing" occurs at higher cortical levels over a 10-15 second interval[23]. What we actually see in this chaos removing process are past, present, and future visual elements. Their more recent research supports Metzinger's older speculation that ". . . the phenomenal model of reality exclusively supervenes on internal system properties[21]. Neural networks are not functioning in linear fashion. These systems are dynamic and bidirectionally transform sensory imagery across brain networks.

Whitney and Fischer have identified a sensory process that removes chaos over a 15 second interval. Their research brings neuroscience one step closer to identifying a brain process of finite duration that is building on the past, experiencing the present, and preparing for the future. A speculative question for neuroscience: Is visual "smoothing" an Edelman-like "Neural Darwinian "mechanism that matures at our secondary level of consciousness to become an integral part of self-processes?

Dreams, Hallucinations, and the Phenomenal-Self

How does the lucid observation of dreams and hallucinations support a view of the self that is able to supervene over lower brain functions? In preliminary summary, I've demonstrated that we can learn to control the content of dreams and hallucinations by remaining lucid. And that in a lucid state, we are able to observe bidirectional image transformations between primary and secondary consciousness. I believe I've demonstrated in previous chapters that the elements of belief, suggestion, and mood can shape the contents of sensory images. And that these subjective elements activate an automatic image generator that is always on in any state of consciousness.

In my experience, phenomenal, first-person observations supporting automatic image generation are overwhelming, as is the reality of the phenomenal-self supervening over sensory imaging processes. In this book, I've provided support for a supervening self with examples of "dream programming," controlled hallucinations such as my "Genesis Journey", the automaticity of pre-and-post, dual state image manipulation, and the manipulation of objects in the enactment of trance during a dream.

Lucidity in dreams and hallucinations permits the self to manipulate content for all of our senses—remove nightmare trauma, enact erotic dream character encounters, remove the effects of gravity in dream flight, visually manipulate our virtual environment, and so on[24]. Thus, dream lucidity brings forth the realization that the phenomenal-self is intimately and bidirectionally entwined with all of our senses. The phenomenal-self cannot only control the contents of dreams and hallucinations, it can control body functions such as pain and heart rate.

I conceive of the phenomenal-self as an entity that emerges with experience. It is a unique epigenetic product of secondary consciousness that co-occurs with our genetic capacity to transform primary sensory images into secondary products. This interpretation agrees with Gerald Edelman's view of "Neural Darwinism"—that is, evolution selects neuronal groups in parallel fashion to how biological structures are selected[25]. From the emerging perspective of protoconsciousness theory, dreaming is a time of consolidation and re-organization of new sensory input that continues a process begun in the womb.

The Permanent Nature of the Self

The self in Luhmann-like fashion develops as a stand-alone entity that can supervene over primary processes in the brain's dynamic core. Shaping of the self's content begins in the womb and continues lifelong through social and environmental interaction. Thus, as a meta-cognitive emergent that forms from all of the brain's primary senses, the self is hypothesized as being formed concurrently with the neural networks of secondary consciousness.

The self draws upon memory to position itself in time and space. The self as a virtual entity is as variable as the cultural contexts of its development. The self is a dynamic, functional and virtual structure that continues to change lifelong. The self creates a phenomenal model of itself and a virtual model of its world. And repeating my agreement with Metzinger, it seems fairly obvious that ". . . the phenomenal model of reality exclusively supervenes on internal system properties." I conclude, then, that we only possess a phenomenal model of reality; objectivity is a construct that we approach through the scientific method, it is not something inherent to the human condition.

Source: Chapter 13: Protoconsciousness

1. Hobson, J. A. (2009) REM sleep and dreaming: towards a theory of protoconsciousness. Nature Reviews Neuroscience 10 (11), 803-813.

2. Busnel, M. C., Granier-Deferre, C., & Lacanuet, J. P. (1992) Fetal audition. Annals of the New York Academy of Sciences, 662, 118-134.

3. Baars, Bernard B. J. & Gage, Nicole M. (2010) Cognition, Brain, and Consciousness, 2nd Ed. New York: Elsevier, Academic Press.

4. Kilisevsky, et. al, 2004) Kisilevsky, B. S., Hains, S. M., Lee, K., et al. (2003) Effects of experience on fetal voice recognition. Psychological Sciences, 14(3), 220-224; Kisilevsky, B. S., Hains, S. M., Jacquet, A. Y., Granier-Deferre, C., & Lecanuet, P. P. (2004) Maturation of fetal responses to music. Developmental Science, 7(5), 550-559.

5. Partanen, Eino. Babies Learn to Recognize Words in the Womb. Brain and Behavior, 27 Aug. 2013.

6. Metzinger, Thomas, Ed. (2000) Neural Correlates of Consciousness: Empirical and Conceptual Questions. Cambridge, MA: The MIT Press: 298.

7. Sinha, Pawan. Once Blind and Now They See. Scientific American, July 2013, Vol. 309, No. 1.

8. Hensch, Takao. The Power of the Infant Brain, Scientific American, Jan. 2016, 65-69.

9. Elbert, T., & Rockstroh, B. (2004) Reorganization of the human cerebral cortex: The range of changes following use and injury. Neuroscientist, 10, 129-141.

10. Shaffery, J.P., Sinton, C.M., Bissette, G., Roffwarg, H.P. & Marks, G.A. Neuroscience 2002 110 431-443

11. Sacks, Oliver. (2010) The Mind's Eye. New York: Alfred A. Knopf: 232; Ibid, 237; Ibid, 215.

12. Partanen, Eino. Babies Learn to Recognize Words in the Womb. Brain and Behavior, 27 Aug. 2013.

13. Betty Vohr, Warren Alpert Medical School of Brown University and Women and Infants Hospital in Providence, Rhode Island.

14. Shevrin, H., Bond, J.A., Brakel, L.A., Hertel, R.K., and Williams, W.J. (1996) Conscious and Unconscious Processes: Psychodynamic, Cognitive, and Neurophysiological Convergence. New York: The Guilford Press.

15. Panksepp, Jaak & Biven, Lucy. (2012) The Archaeology of Mind: Neuroevolutionary Origins of Human Emotions. New York: W. W. Norton & Company; ibid, 389-423.

16. Damasio, A. R. (2010) Self Comes to Mind: Constructing the Conscious Brain. New York: Pantheon.

17. Merzenich, Michael. (2013) Soft-Wired: How the New Science of Brain Plasticity Can Change Your Life. San Francisco: Parnassus Pub. LLC.

18. Hobson, J. A., & Friston, Karl. Consciousness, Dreams, and Inference: The Cartesian Theatre Revisited. Journal of Consciousness Studies. 21, No. 1-2, 2014.

19. Diekelmann, S., and Born, J. The memory function of sleep. Nature Reviews Neuroscience 11, 114–126 (1 February 2010) | doi:10.1038/nrn2762.

20. Hobson, 2009; Walker, M. P., Brakefield, T., Morgan, A., Hobson, J. A. & Stickgold, R. (2002). Practice with sleep makes perfect: sleep-dependent motor skill learning. Neuron, 35(1): 205-211.

21. Metzinger, Thomas. (2003) Being No One: The Self-Model Theory of Subjectivity. Boston: MIT Press.

22. Leopold, D. A., & Logothetis, N. K. (1999) Multistable phenomena: Changing views in perception. Trends in Cognitive Sciences 3: 254-64.

23. Whitney, David, & Fischer, Jason, et al., (posted online Apr. 07, 2014). Brain '15-second delay' shields us from hallucinogenic experience. Reuters/Eddie Keogh.

24. Just, G. A. (2009) Autobiography of a Ghost. Mankato, MN: Eagle Entertainment USA; Just, Glen A. (2012) Dreams, Creativity & Mental Health. Mankato, MN: Eagle Entertainment USA.

25. Edelman, Gerald (1987) Neural Darwinism: The Theory of Neuronal Group Selection. Philadelphia: Basic Books.

CHAPTER 14

Transformative Dynamic Integrated Systems

Major Objectives Revisited

I interpreted transformative bidirectional sensory image transformations (TDIS) between primary and secondary consciousness as the process by which the brain is capable of creating virtual images such as shamanic totems, "ghosts," possession, missing limbs, and a phantasmagoria of dream and hallucinatory images. Analysis of these virtual constructions suggests the origin of the phenomenal-self itself.

Learning to employ lucidity across states of consciousness is a psychological, first-person methodology that can integrate subjective and objective research using contemporary imaging technology. The idea that hallucinations could not be studied with brain-imaging technology is obsolete. Controlled hallucinations of my "Genesis Journey" or that of the "woman who can leave her body at will" provide subjects that are amenable to empirical imaging technology.

Method Revisited

Employing lucidity across states of consciousness permits careful observation of subjective states in the laboratory, as demonstrated by Ursula Voss and colleagues[1]. Anton Lutz and colleagues documented real changes in neural processes for meditators in similar fashion[2].

Lucidity permits controlled construction of content across states of consciousness including dreams, hallucinations, presence, trance, and shamanic trance[3]. Suggestion and belief can generate a huge variety of content imagery that we experience as being totally real. Learning to control imagery content across states of consciousness frees us from our "demons," and I suggest that it is time for the mental health community to bring demon possession, paranoia, OCD, automatic writing, Zen-driving, and a number of other so-called psychological states into the laboratory of combined subjective/ objective methodologies.

There is a paradigm shift[4] underway in consciousness research that is supported by internationally known authorities such as Jaak Panksepp, Allan Hobson, Evan Thompson, Gerald Edelman, and Thomas Metzinger. This paradigm shift requires an integration of psycho-neuro-phenomenal research methods[5]. The brain can be imaged with lucid subjects that remain in interaction with researchers[1,3], and dialogue can occur during these procedures. Content imaging can be correlated with physiological processes across states of consciousness. Thus, intra-subjective analysis of bidirectional imaging similar to those that I report in lucid dreams and hallucinations can be analyzed with contemporary technologies.

Technological imaging of content across states of consciousness represents a necessary and intermediate step to connect cellular and biochemical processes directly with sensory image transformations. Combined methodologies[5] using lucidity can reveal sensory imaging processes between primary and secondary consciousness processes that currently remain invisible.

Reductionism Revisited

A fundamental question in consciousness research is how meaning derives from cellular and biochemical processes[6,7]. Imaging bidirectional sensory transformations of controlled hallucinations and trance in the laboratory offers a strategy to observe psychological content being simultaneously generated by co-occurring physiological processes.

A second question of seminal importance that I've proposed in this book is how conscious (active) and nonconscious (reflexive) image transformations occur between primary and secondary levels of consciousness. Image transformations at our secondary level of consciousness such as the perception of "ghosts" and "demons," paranoid intrusions, presence, obsessive-compulsive impulses, false physical inhibitions, and a host of other conditions determine our responses. Cellular and biochemical changes in the brain support, but by themselves, do not determine secondary image transformations.

As conscious beings, we are continuously imaging sensory visual, auditory, and tactile input. These are functional and automatic processes that permit adaptive movement in our social and physical environments. Nevertheless, we can control related imaging content in dreams, hallucinations, and trance while remaining lucid. Thus, the fundamental question of how to distinguish between automatic processes of primary consciousness (Libet-determinism) and autonomous control of secondary consciousness (free will) can be addressed in the laboratory and not merely through philosophical speculation.

My position is that we are both determined and autonomous. Dichotomizing the argument that human action is determined or free is an over simplification of the brain's hierarchy of primary and secondary consciousness. Hence, I conclude that reducing subjective sensory experience, psychological processes, to cell biology and biochemistry requires the inclusion of a phenomenological strategy of self-process image transformations.

Substance dualism conceives of the mind to be immaterial and distinct from the brain. In agreement with Patricia Churchland[ibid], I reject substance dualism. Neither the lucid method nor empirical research supports substance dualism.

Image transformations between primary and secondary consciousness and secondary to primary processes can fall under control of the brain's higher executive functions of the phenomenal-self. For example, in-process alteration of nightmares, dream programming, and controlled, scripted hallucinations. Lucid observation of controlled altered state content offers additional insight into the construction of subjective reality. The brain-mind virtually creates sensory content that corresponds to its subjective reality. It follows, if my personal history is relevant[3,8], that direct clinical intervention in a variety of DSM pathologies can control sensory content by combining subjective methods such as lucidity and hypnosis.

Physiological research is necessary to specify the cellular and biochemical mechanisms involved. Nevertheless, I've argued that transformative images, including the "self," are emergent system properties. I used the concept of emergent property as it is often interpreted in neuroscience. I quote Patricia S. Churchland[7]: "Emergent property is also used in the neuroscientific literature . . . roughly equivalent to network property."

I demonstrated that conceptually image transformations at our secondary level of consciousness are a reimaging of primary sensations (percepts). Additionally, I've shown that the process of transformative imaging can be reversed when belief and suggestion concretize and personifies culturally acquired definitions. Supporting arguments outlined the central role that image transformations play in the development and maintenance of the phenomenal-self.

Emergent Insights of the TDIS Model

Triangulating sensory experiences across states of consciousness brings forth the realization that the brain-mind can and does create all manner of sensory images *de novo*. The fact that sensory images of sight, sound, and touch can be generated at will without external input acknowledges the brain-mind's capacity to create predictive images in waking states as well as in altered states of consciousness.

The following section reemphasizes nine of this book's major conclusions: That sensory images of sight, sound, and touch can be generated at will without external input. This fact acknowledges the brain-mind's capacity to create predictive images in waking, as well as in altered states of consciousness. Thus, I conclude that less dynamic interpretations of sensory processing that deny "self" autonomy and "free will" have reached premature conclusions[6,7].

Lucidity permits observations of primary percepts in our dynamic core being reimaged as concrete entities and personifications at our secondary level of consciousness. I demonstrated active control of the content of bidirectional image transformations in dreams and hallucinations. Controlled imaging at our higher cortical levels has major implications for mental health strategies and treatment.

Subjective meaning derived from culture is critical in terms of what images the "self" generates in dreams and hallucinations, and how biochemistry of mood affects "self" imaging in similar fashion.

Belief plays a central role in the generation of consciousness content: specifically, belief is the semantic driver in self-attributions called presence, possession, paranoia, and related psychogenic disorders.

Lucid observation of image transformations between primary and secondary consciousness supports a phase-change similar to that which occurs when the elements H and O have been paired and displayed as H_2O. Analysis in terms of "structural realism" supports the transformative nature of imaging processes between primary and secondary consciousness. Specific examples are the brain's common practice of concretizing and personifying primary sensory stimuli.

Bidirectional observations of image transformations can be used to distinguish between levels of consciousness, as well as dual states of consciousness. The automaticity of the brain's dynamic core contrasted with the autonomy of "self" reveals insight into how hierarchical levels of the brain-mind are both determined and free. Arguing that the brain-mind is *only* determined or *only* free ignores the lessons of autonomous "dream programming" and "controlled hallucinations" as contrasted with the automaticity of OCD and addictions.

Protoconsciousness Theory[9] focuses the spotlight on the brain's architecture—memory maps. Image transformations in dreams support the existence of neural maps, including those for prejudice and stereotyping.

Knowing that the brain-mind creates virtual models of its "self" and its environment offers insight into how self-perception of physical size can change from a "dot" to interstellar size. I provided examples of virtual physical size changes in both waking and trance states.

Of most significance, the brain-mind creates all manner of virtual entities *de novo*. Understanding virtual content such as the shamanic possession of a bear, or the creation of a full-body illusion of our physical-self, or even a rubber hand that feels sensations, takes us one step closer to a phenomenal interpretation of how a virtual-self emerges. Combining knowledge of virtual entity creations of the full-body with Whitney and Fischer's research[10] on sensory "smoothing" suggests an evolutionary-step mechanism from which an autonomous "self" emerges.

Concluding Thoughts

I've dropped examples and questions throughout this book about the importance of incorporating transformative imaging mechanisms in human services and clinical practices. I have begun to expand this analysis in other works. However, I hope in some small way that I've supported Allan Hobson's call for a psychodynamic neurology[11].

Jaak Panksepp's has a related vision in his call for a psycho-neuro-phenomenology[12]. I have presented a model of sensory image transformations as being central to the looming marriage between psychodynamics, neurology, and phenomenology.

Subjectivity is a real brain state that is maintained by biochemistry and neurons. Subjectivity is the essence and product of the brain's transformative imaging capacity at a system's networks level[13,14]. It is the essentialism that emerges in childhood. If subjectivity is not real, then, human brains don't create color or art. If subjectivity is not real there are only oscillating atoms, electromagnetic waves, and biochemical reactions in this universe. And—life is sterile.

Seeing is to believe, feeling is to know, truth is to see, believe, and confirm nature.

Sources: Chapter 14: Transformative Dynamic Integrated Systems

1. Voss, U., Holzmann, R., Tuin, I., & Hobson, J. A. (2009) Lucid Dreaming: a State of Consciousness with Features of both Waking and Non-Lucid Dreaming. Sleep, 32 (9), 1191-1200.

2. Lutz, Antoine, et. al. Attention Regulation and Monitoring in Meditation. Trends in Cognitive Sciences 12 (2008): 163-169.

3. Just, Glen A. (2012) Dreams, Creativity & Mental Health. Mankato, MN: Eagle Entertainment USA; (2009) Autobiography of a Ghost. Mankato, MN: Eagle Entertainment USA.

4. Kuhn, T.S. (1962) The Structure of Scientific Revolutions. Chicago: The University of Chicago Press.

5. Just, Glen A. (2015) Convergence of Subjective and Objective Methodologies in Consciousness Research, in Advances in Psychology Research. Volume 103, Hauppauge, NY: Nova Science Publishers, Inc.

6. Churchland, Paul M. (2013) Matter and Consciousness, 3rd. ed. Cambridge, MA: MIT Press.

7. Churchland, Patricia S. (2007) Neurophilosophy at Work. New York: Cambridge University Press; (2011) Braintrust.

Princeton, NJ: The Princeton University Press; (2013) Touching a Nerve: The Self as Brain. New York: Norton.

8. Hobson, J. Allan (2014) Ego Damage and Repair: Toward a Psychodynamic Neurology. London: Karnac.

9. Hobson, J. A. (2009) REM sleep and dreaming: towards a theory of protoconsciousness. Nature Reviews Neuroscience, 10(11):803-813.

10. Whitney, David, & Fischer, Jason, et al., (posted online Apr. 07, 2014). Brain '15-second delay' shields us from hallucinogenic experience. Reuters/Eddie Keogh.

11. Hobson, J. A. (2015) Dreaming as Virtual Reality: A New Theory of the Brain-Mind. Clarendon: Oxford University Press.

12. Panksepp, Jaak & Biven, Lucy. (2012) The Archaeology of Mind: Neuroevolutionary Origins of Human Emotions. New York: W. W. Norton & Company.

13. Edelman, G. M. & Tononi, G. (2000) A Universe of Consciousness: How Matter Becomes Imagination. New York: Basic Books.

14. Lewis, M. D. (2005) Bridging emotion theory and neurobiology through dynamic systems modelling. Behavioral and Brain Sciences, 28, 169-245.

EPILOGUE

PHILOSOPHICAL REFLECTIONS

Philosophy as the "Mother of Science" continues to ask fundamental questions about self, and the cosmos. Patricia and Paul Churchland[1,2], Mark Johnson and George Lakoff[3,] Gerald Edelman[4], Thomas Metzinger[5], and Jennifer Windt[6] are good examples of philosophers who represent the growing integration of philosophy and the basic sciences. We stopped speculating about atoms and the alchemy of metals when physics and chemistry matured. The trend in philosophy seems to be going down this same road.

I believe that neuroscience and philosophy are demonstrating that the logic of a Plato, Socrates, Aristotle, St. Augustine, or Descartes as philosophers isolated from empirical disciplines cannot provide answers to self or consciousness. I have touched on philosophical considerations from a dozen or more internationally known philosophers and philosopher-scientists. Here, I provide a brief review of concepts that I've taken from the book's main philosophical contributors in the context of Protoconsciousness Theory and Transformative Dynamic Integrated Systems (TDIS).

The following analysis as it relates to theory construction is a work in progress. However, the above pages have addressed how the self emerges, the critical difference between image transformations of primary and secondary consciousness, and the method supporting the TDIS model. Following, I address the contributions of the main philosophers who have influenced this book. I end with a brief comparison of the TDIS model and Jennifer Windt's "Immersive-Spatiotemporal-Hallucination Model of Dreaming" (ISTH).

Immanuel Kant's [7] concept of the fetal brain possessing *a priori* knowledge has been supported by research on fetal memory, the acquisition of language by prenatal infants, imaging by phocomelic children, and brain state imaging when blind from birth dream [8].

Rene' Descarte's [9] creation of an immaterial soul set forth a dualistic picture of body and mind. Empirical science provides no support for Descarte's dualism. Empirical neuroscience combined with lucid, phenomenal analysis of bidirectional transformative imaging strengthens the argument against any part of the brain-mind being immaterial.

So-called non-material creations of the brain-mind— "ghosts," "spirits," "demons," shamanic totem-states, and out-of-body experiences are accounted for by the natural processes of the brain-mind's virtual image generator.

George Lakoff and Mark Johnson [10] identify "metaphors we live by." I have incorporated their metaphors as fetal *a priori* neural structures that form the basic building blocks for waking memories. I've presented their work as articulating with Kant's *a priori* knowledge, and Hobson's Protoconsciousness Theory.

John Searle's [11] analysis of the self and intentionality offers numerous analytical insights. In Chapter 2, Searle gives a technical philosophical interpretation of three different gaps that exist between human intention and action.

A dissection of his argument in light of TDIS would take a rather long journal article, hence, I will opt for brevity by oversimplifying Searle's rather brilliant insights. He says: "The gap is the general name that I have introduced for the phenomenon that we do not normally experience the stages of our deliberations and voluntary actions as having causally sufficient conditions or as setting causally sufficient conditions for the next stage. [There is a] . . . gap between deciding to do something, and actually trying to do it"[ibid].

TDIS, in a general sense, identifies the gap as the relationship between the automaticity of the brain's dynamic core and our higher-order executive functions. The invisible neuronal and biochemical processes within and between levels of the brain's hierarchy remain invisible to us; invisibility that is exemplified with addictions or OCD.

Patricia S. Churchland has an excellent review of what is required to reduce one theory to another (2007). Specifically: "If one theory can be explained by another and thus reduced to it, then our understanding of the phenomena described by the theory is greatly enhanced"[2].

I reduced Protoconsciousness Theory and incorporated it in TDIS: First, Lakoff and Johnson's metaphors, such as inside/outside, and up, down, were presented as examples of developing primary fetal neural networks. My analysis of fetal memories and language acquisition identified the necessary existence of such neural structures.

Secondly, I presented an extensive series of self-experiments, which I discussed through the lens of empirical research in order to demonstrate a psycho-neuro-phenomenal level of sensory image transformations. TDIS accepts the assumptions and related research of Protoconsciousness Theory, but places emphasis on the bidirectional generation of transformed image content in dreams and other altered states. As a mechanism, I viewed transformative imaging as the link between the biochemical neuroscience of Hobson, and operative phenomenal elements at the psychological level.

Thirdly, I examined the mechanism of sensory image transformations in terms of creating virtual models of self and world. I concluded that virtual modeling capacity of the brain-mind underlies fictive creations we refer to as "ghosts," "presence," visions, rubber hands that can feel, and other so called illusory entities.

Note: P. S. Churchland rejects an autonomous self supervening over other brain-mind processes [2] that I observe and control in dreams and hallucinations. I suggest that her hidden variables can be identified and technologically imaged by combining lucidity research in dreams and hallucinations with technical imaging of the Voss and Hobson variety.

I conceive combined subjective-objective research methods as the key to unlocking the transformative imaging relationship between primary and secondary consciousness. And I'm assuming that future analysis of image transformations between primary and secondary consciousness can further help clarify how an autonomous, supervening self emerges.

Recall, too, that neuroscientific literature also uses emergent property with an equivalent meaning to network property. I have and am assuming that self is a network and global brain property. Quoting Max Tegmark, "In the philosophy literature, John Worrall has coined the term *structural realism* as a compromise position between scientific realism and anti-realism, crudely speaking, stating that the fundamental nature of reality is correctly described only by the mathematical or structural content of scientific theories" [12].

I depart from Tegmark when he moves focus away from our observed universe to that of a mathematical one. I have presented structural realism as a strategy to link empirical neuro-and-psychological science. "Anti-realism" as the phenomenal flip-side of empiricism has come to possess a negative and prejudicial meaning. Phenomenological analysis of brain-mind processes does not equate with non-material, vital entities—neurons and biochemistry support all the processes that I have discussed in this book.

I did not discuss the brain-mind as a mathematical structure. I use the term structural realism to mean that the relationship between two things might be more informative than analysis of each independently. For example, with H and O becoming H_2O. It is hard to imagine how one could deduce the meaning of H_2O by knowing all the qualities of oxygen and hydrogen separately. In similar fashion to the brain's network properties, I'm suggesting that neuroscience can know all the cellular and biochemical properties of primary and secondary consciousness without ever coming to grips with transformative imaging processes between them.

I've provided a number of examples that support a supervening self that is autonomous. Additionally, I have argued that the key to identifying virtual structural imaging processes of the brain-mind is transformative imagery. Hence, I suggest that the mechanism of biological structural realism of the brain-mind is sensory image transformations. Transformative imaging in the psychology of the brain-mind is similar to the strong force that holds the atom together in physics. Transformative sensory imaging is the biological force field that unites primary and secondary consciousness.

Meinard Kuhlman [13] is a philosophy professor at Bielefeld University in Germany. He discusses the problem in quantum physics with particles and fields. Simplifying fields, they represent a relationship between two things. Kuhlman suggests that studying particles is only part of physics' big picture, that relationships between things, for example, force fields between particles, may be a more fruitful way to understand the natural world. The virtual, phenomenal-self can be viewed as a living force that unites dumb brain modules. From this perspective, the phenomenal-self is a fundamental force field in the biology of life.

In analogous fashion, the brain's neurons can occupy dual states where one set of neurons can act on another set [14, 15, 16]. This dynamic, global brain process generates image transformations that become the virtual content and essence of the phenomenal-self. This process is most clearly evident in dreaming and hallucinating experiences.

Consciousness is the magic of biology creating virtual selves in a fashion similar to particles in physics creating force fields. Analytical similarity does not mean sameness. Kuhlman says: "A growing number of people think that what really matters are not things but the relations in which those things stand. What we commonly call a thing may be just a bundle of properties: color, shape, consistency, and so on" [13].

From the point of view of structural realism, things such as brain cells by themselves are of secondary importance to higher-order consciousness (my words). What is of primary importance is the relationship between cells that generate human subjectivity (again, Kuhlman's logic and my words). Subjectivity and cells are part of a larger, interacting, biological whole: "The whole is more than the sum of its parts [13, 17]."

Niklas Luhmann's [18] interpretation turns the usual presentation of structural functionalism on its head. The brain's structure (memory) is temporary and constantly changing. The phenomenal-self as a functional, dynamic entity develops to become the semi-permanent part of the brain-mind that exists through time. Following Luhmann's thinking, I described the emergent self as a dynamic, autonomous neural structure that is meta-cognitive and capable of supervening over the brain's dynamic core.

Owen Flannagan's "*The Really Hard Problem*" of philosophy is how meaning is possible in a material world [19]. I've considered his views by analyzing the virtual creations of the brain-mind as being a product of bidirectional sensory image transformations. The virtual creations of the brain-mind are always grounded in biochemical and cellular processes. Thus, I attempt to integrate a bio-neuro-psychological level of analysis to explain the creation of meaning in a material world. In contrast, I interpret Flannagan's analysis in *The Really Hard Problem* as emphasizing the social-psychological creation of meaning.

Focus on bidirectional image transformations permits reduction of virtual images to cellular and biochemical processes when we triangulate observed, first-person-image transformations in dreams and hallucinations with modern imaging technology. Thus, I'm in general agreement with Kenneth Aizawa and Carl Gillett [20] in their analysis of "Levels, Individual Variation, and Massive Multiple Realization in Neurobiology" that scientific explanation requires that we articulate levels of analysis. For example, we start with physical properties of individual constituents, articulate with biochemical and cellular levels, and then move to systems interpretations in our overall explanations of the neurobiology of the mind.

System properties that articulate with phenomenal image

transformations become visible and identifiable with combined subjective-objective methods. Imaging technology permit objective, cellular and biochemical localization of subjective brain-mind processes.

Allan Hobson: I've incorporated extensive material from Hobson throughout this book. His life has been filled as a productive researcher and prolific writer. Hobson and McCarley's early research on the biochemistry of dreaming placed emphasis on brain-stem activation and dream form [21]. Recall—dream form means that waking muscles and logic get suspended, and time, space, and character portrayal are routinely violated. However, Hobson [22] has always been interested in the meaning of dreams, and the phenomenology of dream content, contrary to numerous criticisms, such as those of Mark Solms [23].

As previously noted, Hobson has been a pioneer along with Ursula Voss demonstrating dual states of consciousness with brain imaging technology. In the last ten years, he has addressed major issues in psychology and psychiatry with a rather extensive series of publications. His productivity is amazing given a serious brainstem stroke in 2001 and two subsequent heart attacks. Allan introduced me to his research on protoconsciousness and dual states research in 2012 at his home in Brookline. His insights into dual states of consciousness and protoconsciousness theory have been invaluable, and these influences are present throughout this book. His reaction to the first draft of this book (2014) was the major factor in the book' s reorganization and added research components.

Gerald Edelman's [24] "Neural Darwinism" provides support for my analysis of how the "self" emerges from biology. Overall, I agreed with Edelman's idea that evolution appears to select neural networks much the way it selects biological structures. Consequently, I discussed self as an emergent, multimodal, global neural system creation.

Thomas Metzinger [25] has been a major factor in my willingness to reveal and expand on first-person experiences. His work with virtual doubles and virtual modeling exemplifies the significance of combining subjective and objective methodologies in consciousness research. I embrace his admonition that, "Rigorous philosophy must take altered state images seriously." I have made transformative imagining the critical mechanism for the interpretation of dreams and hallucinations, virtual phenomena related to psychogenic pathologies, emergence of the self, and much more.

Let me repeat two quotes from Metzinger that speak to the central message of this book:

"The fact that we can actively design the structure of our conscious minds has been neglected and will become increasingly obvious through the development of a rational neuroanthropology"[ibid]. "And: "There is an enormous number of possible neural configurations in our brains and [a] vastness of different types of subjective experiences. Most of us are completely unaware of the potential and depth of our experiential space. The amount of possible neurophenomenological configurations of an individual human brain is so large that you can explore only a tiny fraction of them in your lifetime"[ibid].

A Limited Dialogue between Jennifer Windt and Glen Just

Jennifer M. Windt's wonderful book *Dreaming*[6] appeared after the initial drafts of *Image Transformations of the Brain-Mind*. It is a must read for all serious students of dreaming. Allan Hobson says: "This magnificent book is the best philosophical study of dreaming, bar none." Here, I will not attempt a comprehensive analysis of Windt's model in comparison with my model of Transformative Dynamic Integrated Systems (TDIS). I will, however, address 13-conceptual items that she lays out in her *Introduction* (xv-xxv). And lastly, I will provide a brief comparison between her ". . . new working definition of dreams as immersive spatiotemporal hallucinations" (ISTH) and TDIS.

Method: Both ISTH and TDIS assume that an interdisciplinary approach incorporating philosophy, psychology, neuroscience, and sleep/dream research is necessary for a minimally adequate interpretation of dreams.

TDIS additionally employs content controls across states of consciousness, e.g. scripting dreams and hallucinations on demand. TDIS initially uses self-hypnosis to enact lucidity in dreams, hallucinations, and other so-called altered states of consciousness— lucid self-hypnosis (LSH). TDIS as a functional model permits the observation of bi-directional image transformations between primary and secondary consciousness.

Self: Windt: "The self, as I use the term, is always (and exclusively) a phenomenal self; the phenomenology of self-experience is the product of information processing in the brain and so should not be confused with the brain" (p. 418). *Just*: I accept Windt's interpretation that the self is a "product of information processing in the brain".

TDIS goes beyond information processing as it is typically used in cognitive science. The focus of TDIS is the transformation of sensory signaling between primary and secondary consciousness that leads to bi-directional image transformations. Thus: TDIS defines self as an epigenetic set of dispersed neurons that has been selected through evolutionary processes in the sense of Gerald Edelman's "Neural Darwinism." In this view, the self begins to form protoconsciously from all manner of sensory experiences in at least the fetus's last trimester. The protoconscious fetal-self is much like a small firefly blinking in the dark. It grows in functional abilities after birth with experience, changes with memory reconfigurations throughout one's lifetime, grows dimmer with age, and finally winks out with dementia and death.

I gave examples of the self as an evolutionary emergent capable of supervening over numerous brain states and capable of autonomous actions, e.g., dream and hallucinatory scripting, control over anxiety and various automatic behaviors associated with primary consciousness, and many other examples reported throughout this text, my autobiography, and in *Dreams, Creativity & Mental Health*.

Embodiment—*Windt*: Embodiment is not necessary for having a self, and ". . . the phenomenology of embodied selfhood is more variable in dreams than in wakefulness" (xxiii). *Just*: I accept this interpretation to mean that our individual sense of physical-self is not always present in dreams as well as some other altered states of consciousness. My text example was that of the self shrinking to an atom-like point during meditative-like states. However, metacognitive, lucid observation across states of consciousness reveals that the self can be an infinitesimal dot or an infinite expansion. It can be solely mental without body, or astronomical in bodily size. The variability of self in altered states was extended in TDIS to possession, presence, shamanic totems, size shape-shifting, and the de'ja vu-self that is carried from dreams into wakefulness, and from wakefulness back into dreams.

Windt: Dreams are functionally embodied states. *Just*: I discussed a number of examples of dream functionality, e.g., bike riding and glass cutting skills, emotional homeostasis, and cognitive integration writing this book.

Belief: *Windt*: Dreams involve belief. *Just:* Not only do dreams involve belief, but I gave a number of examples of how belief drives transformative imaging processes between primary and secondary consciousness. Belief concretizes ethereal entities such as ghosts, spirits, and even the self as multiple selves.

Thought: *Windt:* Dreams can and do contain thoughts as thought is conceived during waking states. "What is interesting and unique about dreaming is not the absence of conscious thought but the close relationship in which it stands to lower-level automatically imagistic cognition" (xxiv). Thus, dream forms of the Hobson variety that stress lack of logical content are seen as being "oversimplified." *Just*: I agree with Windt and provided numerous examples of creative thought taken from my dreams, both in this book and in previous works (2009, 2012).

Phenomenal Core of Dreaming: *Windt*: Is it possible to distinguish a phenomenal core of dreaming—how it differs from standard and altered wake states (p. xxiv). *Just*: According to TDIS, the answer is yes. Lucidly observed, the phenomenal core of dreaming emphasizes the sensory image transformations between primary and secondary consciousness. Sensory information transformations at both the primary and secondary levels of consciousness are invisible to the waking-self. A perennial conundrum for third-party philosophy, neuroscience, and dream researchers. Transformative processes remain invisible to third-party observers. Additionally, brain scans do not reveal sensory image transformations—just dream forms as shadows on Plato's cave wall.

Dreams as Types of Conscious Experiences: *Windt:* Dreams as conscious experiences have been neglected, as have the differences between dreaming and altered wake states (xvii*). Just:* I have discussed phenomenal imaging across dreams and hallucinations in this book, and across numerous other altered states in previous works[14]. My discovery of altered states is chronologically numbered in Appendix I. In Chapter 5 on dream types, I've emphasized how sensory stimuli is transformed as dream types. Thus, I've noted that dream image transformation variability may or may not be integrating multi-sensory experiences in any given dream scenario compared to waking states. As I observe the progression of singularly focused functionality from pre-sleep to post-sleep image transformations, memory integration proceeds from simpler to more complex integration in the dreaming process throughout the night.

Dream Access: *Windt:* "Epistemic access to dreams is twice removed from the actual experience except for lucid dreamers. *Just*: Agree. I've stressed the significance of holding longitudinal, lucid dreaming, and altered state analyses to the flame of the empirical sciences. I believe that I've demonstrated the heuristic value of dreaming and altered state integration with the empirical sciences. Insight, creativity, and theory construction are generated using the TDIS Method. In this respect, I've attempted to support the value of phenomenological research in the vein suggested by Allan Hobson, Jaak Panksepp, and Thomas Metzinger.

Descartes *First Meditation* (Dreams as products of dreams): *Windt:* Referencing Descartes, she states: "What if, for instance, his beliefs about his previous dreams are themselves just the product of a dream?" (p. 7). *Just:* In Chapter 9 I discussed the de'ja vu-self. I demonstrate in this chapter that dream histories exist and influence our daytime experiences of what is commonly called de'ja vu. In turn, our waking de'ja vu experiences can reenter our nighttime dreams. (This example also notes the fun of self-discovery we experience through lucid dreaming).

Trustworthiness of Dreams: *Windt:* In "Chapter I" on "Dream Skepticism," she cautiously supports the validity of dream reports. I have stressed, along with Allan Hobson, the importance of being cautious when interpreting dream content and related phenomenology. However, I think that 60-years of longitudinal dream analysis, using the lucid method, provides reasonably adequate checks on dream interpretations and sensory image transformations. The reader will decide the degree of objectivity on his or her own terms. I suggest that future scientific progress connecting objectively observed brain activity with first-person accounts of dream content will be a necessary step in bringing closure to subjective-objective method integration.

Theory of Mind (TOM): *Windt*—places herself in the camp of TOM. *Just:* Not being a professional philosopher, I find it very helpful to incorporate materials from multiple philosophical sources. I see the study of dreams, dreaming, and altered states as stretching across additional disciplines than those noted by Windt. I have benefited considerably from my work and teaching in anthropology, sociology, psychology, counseling, developing and administering day and group treatment communities, and being a parent. A broader grounding in the empirical sciences is also very helpful.

Oneiragogia—a term coined by *Windt:* The term deals with the imagery formed during our transitions into sleep. *Just:* I provided examples of altering pre-sleep imagery with suggestion. I also discussed multiple forms of post-sleep manipulation and control of dream content. My purpose providing examples of image manipulation from pre-sleep through dreaming and post-sleep stages of consciousness was to stress the likely possibility that the same image generating mechanism was operating in all states of consciousness. I also discussed controlled narrative hallucinations to emphasize this point.

Prediction: *Windt*—references the work of Hohwy [27] and Clark [30]: "Put in greatly simplified terms, the basic idea of predictive processing accounts is that the brain does one single thing: it is continuously involved in the business of hypothesis testing by using prediction to optimize its models of its next expected states and minimize prediction errors [26, 27]". *Just*: As one of the functions of dreaming, I emphasized minimizing predictive error by referencing a number of internationally known researchers [28, 29, 30, 31, 32]. I thereby addressed the predictive brain as a dynamic system that functions to reduce error and eliminate chaos—part of my TDIS Model.

Windt's Immersive Spatiotemporal Hallucinations" Model (ISTH):

As I compare Jennifer Windt's ISTH model with Transformative Dynamic Integrated Systems (TDIS), a reminder that her formulation is designed to provide a conceptual framework for future dream analysis and research. The TDIS Model addresses conceptual questions across states of consciousness. Thus, the scope of the two models is different. I have already begun to use TDIS to address basic problems of mental health [14, 34, 35] shamanism, possession, presence, OCD, as well as the integration of subjective-objective research methods [36] that support related theory building.

The TDIS Model defines self as an emergent process, built on a genetic architecture, that begins to emerge in at least the last trimester of the fetus. I used Hobson's Protoconsciousness Theory as a formative component of TDIS. Self in the TDIS Model is a product of secondary consciousness that emerges through the process of second-order sensory image transformations. Secondly, second-order sensory imaging processes are viewed in TDIS as the reimaging of primary sensory processes that philosophy refers to as qualia. Further, bi-directional image transformations (BIT) between primary and secondary consciousness is presented in TDIS as the mechanism that permits the self to be aware that it is aware. BIT also supports the creation of self as avatar, as multiple-selves, and as shamanic totem object, and our human ability to take the role of the other in social intercourse.

A critical difference between ISTH and TDIS is methodology. TDIS claims first-person methodology reveals image transformations across states of consciousness. TDIS is subject to all the criticism of first-person subjective research. Nevertheless, like any psychological method, TDIS is and must be vetted against interdisciplinary research. Both ISTH and TDIS agree on this point.

Windt's Critique Characteristic Comparison [6] **(p. 515).** Dreaming is not completely independent of body and external inputs. Just: I have given a considerable number of my own examples that support this observation. Thus, agreement between ISTH and TDIS.

The idea that ". . . dreams are deceptive experiences characterized by cognitive deficiency is questioned by Windt. In my various publications, I have noted the creative output of my dreams in writing this and other books [14]. Creative works generated in dreams are well known phenomena that I share with many other dreamers [37, 38, 39]. Personally, I think Freudian Psychiatry's emphasis on disguise and censorship throughout much of the 20th Century was a major factor pathologizing dreams. I find this influence to be present across a number of Allan Hobson's publications. As Allan reminded me during my visit to his Brookline home in 2012, "remember, I am a psychiatrist." Allan was trained on the Freudian model.

Windt: Theoretical accounts of dreaming have been

traditionally overly simplified and stereotypical. I have argued that Freud substituted ideas of disguise and censorship, along with his notion of the unconscious, for processes of image transformation. He substituted convoluted theoretical speculations that were not grounded empirically for processes that are observable to lucid dreamers. Hobson broke away from this tradition, but I believe, struggled with Freudian pathologizing, e.g. *Dreams as Delirium*.

Windt: "[Is] there anything like a single unifying model of dreaming that can accommodate variability on the phenomenal functional level of description." In response to Windt's question, I have argued that the mechanism of image transformation is the "unifying element that accommodates variability on the phenomenal functional level of description". I have given numerous examples of bi-directional image transformations in dreams between primary and secondary consciousness. Further, I have noted how these image transformations are subject to generation through "day residue", suggestion, personal history, and culture. Image transformations in hallucinations and other states of consciousness, such as shamanic-totem possession employ self-other bodily and sensory image transformations as well.

Windt asks: What are the necessary and sufficient conditions for dreams to arise. The TDIS Model views an image generator as always being on across states of consciousness, dreaming, altered or not. I stressed lucid hallucinations across states of consciousness as major observable phenomena to support this position.

Windt: What "sets dreaming apart from sleep-related experiences that do not yet account for full-fledged dreams?" The TDIS Model views image transformation from a functional, neuronal learning and memory perspective. For example, I discussed the difference between gross and fine motor skill acquisition with my glass cutting and bike riding experiences. To be functional, the content expression of dreams only needs to address partial items in one's memory files. Windt notes that ". . . multimodality does not appear to be necessary for dreaming[6] (p. 518)". Many of the dreams that are reported in this book, as well as in other of my publications, stress the singular-to-multimodal focus of dreaming. My dream content analysis addresses dreaming processes as supporting memory construction and pruning, skill acquisition, emotional rebalancing, and ongoing cognitive activities.

My pre-sleep imaging is highly subject to suggestion, as I've noted with my flower example. Dual states of consciousness as one enters sleep is much like the employment of suggestion for lucid dreamers. These examples suggest that image generation is always operative when imaging processes co-occurring with consciousness are present.

Windt says, "I introduce immersive spatiotemporal hallucinations as a conceptual tool for capturing the phenomenal core and the distinctive phenomenal-functional properties of dreaming." Michael Merzenich [33] explains the process of self under construction this way: "For every touch, for every moment of vision, for every sound or word heard, for every moment of thought or action, there is a second very reliable concurrent association. That second association is to you".

TDIS views self as an epigenetic process that emerges and functions across states of consciousness—it is always present to some degree when the organism is conscious and active. Self exists across states of consciousness as is noted by the many cross-state examples of lucidity I've observed. I cautiously use the terms hallucinations, delusion, and psychosis because these terms draw attention away from the self as a real multimodal, multi-cognitive, epigenetic entity. As a multi-sensory emergent, self can be partially expressed, or in full-form, as we encounter real-life functional demands. My emphasis on type of sensory dream stimulation in Chapter 5 emphasizes this point. TDIS notes that the distinctive phenomenal-functional properties of dreaming are observable when we take into account transformative imaging.

Windt instructs us not to assume that there is one distinctive and highly invariant property in dreaming [6] (p. 516). In contrast, I find image transformations of the brain-mind to be such a property. Further, she states that ". . . it should be clear that the phenomenal core of dreaming cannot be identified with any of the features that characterize a majority of dreams[6] (p. 517)". TDIS observes a majority of dreams as being subject to bi-directional image transformations between primary and secondary consciousness.

I have drawn upon dozens of other researchers as I've attempted to support a phenomenological understanding of how a supervening, autonomous self develops and functions. Among others, Jaak Panksepp, Evan Thompson, Paul Nunez, and Antonio Damazio have also been major influences in the formation of this book. I could go on! Nevertheless, the main arguments stand, to be dissected, and revised as time and criticism demands.

Sources: Philosophical Reflections

1. Churchland, Paul M. (2013) Matter and Consciousness, 3rd. ed. Cambridge, MA: MIT Press.
2. Churchland, Patricia S. (2007) Neurophilosophy at Work. New York: Cambridge University Press; (2011) Braintrust. Princeton, NJ: The Princeton University Press; (2013) Touching a Nerve: The Self as Brain. New York: Norton.
3. Lakoff, G., & Johnson, M. (1999) Philosophy In The Flesh: The Embodied Mind And Its Challenge To Western Thought. New York: Basic Books.
4. Edelman, Gerald (1987) Neural Darwinism: The Theory of Neuronal Group Selection. Philadelphia: Basic Books; Edelman, Gerald. (2003) Being No One: The Self-Model Theory of Subjectivity. Boston: MIT Press.
5. Metzinger, Thomas. (2009) The Ego Tunnel: The Science of the Mind and the Myth of the Self. New York: Perseus.

6. Windt, Jennifer M. (2015) Dreaming: A Conceptual Framework for Philosophy of Mind and Empirical Research. Cambridge, MA: The MIT Press.

7. Kant, I. (1999) Critique of Pure Reason, eds. P. Guyer and A. Wood. Cambridge: Cambridge University Press.

8. Brugger, P. et al. "Beyond Re-membering: Phantom Sensations of Congenitally Absent Limbs", Proceedings of the National Academy of Sciences, U.S.A. 97:6167-72 (2000).

9. Descartes, R. (1637) The Philosophical Works of Descartes, rendered into English by Elizabeth S. Haldane and G. R. T. Ross, vol. l. New York: Cambridge University Press (1970).

10. Lakoff, G., and Johnson, M. (1984) Metaphors We Live By. Chicago: University of Chicago Press.

11. Searle, John R. (2001) Rationality in Action. Cambridge, MA: A Bradford Book, The MIT Press; Ibid, p. 50.

12. Tegmark, Max (2013) Our Mathematical Universe. New York: Knopf Doubleday Publishing Group.

13. Kuhlman, Meinard. Quantum Physics: What is Real? Scientific American; August, 2013: 45.

14. Just, Glen A. (2009) Autobiography of a Ghost. Mankato, MN: Eagle Entertainment USA; (2012) Dreams, Creativity & Mental Health.

15. Hobson, J. A., and Just, G. A. (2013) "Lucid Hallucinations." In Hallucinations, Causes, Management and Prognosis, Ed. Sofia Alvarez, NY: Nova Science Publications.

16. Voss, U., Holtzman, R., Tuin, I, and Hobson, J. A. (2009) Lucid Dreaming: A State of Consciousness with Features of both Waking and Non-Lucid Dreaming. Sleep, 32 (9), 1191-1200.

17. Duncan, K., Bradley, B., Nathaniel, D., & Shohamy, D. More Than the Sum of its Parts: A Role for the Hippocampus in Configural Reinforcement Learning. https://doi.org/10.1016/j.neuron.2018.03.042.

18. Luhmann, Niklas. (2013) Introduction to Systems Theory. Ed. Dirk Baecker. Cambridge, UK: The Polity Press: 65.

19. Flanagan, O. (2009) The Really Hard Problem: Meaning in a Material World. Cambridge, MA: A Bradford Book, MIT Press.

20. Aizawa, Kenneth and Gillett, Carl. "Levels, Individual Variation, and Massive Multiple Realization in Neurobiology" in The Oxford Handbook of Philosophy and Neuroscience (2009) Edited, John Beckle. New York: Oxford University Press.

21. Hobson, J.A. (2001) The Dream Drugstore: Chemically Altered States of Consciousness. Cambridge, MA: A Bradford Book, MIT Press: 6; Hobson, J. A., & McCarley, R. W. (1977) "The brain as a dream state generator: an activation-synthesis hypothesis of the dream process." Am. J. Psychiatry 134, 1335-1348.

22. Hobson, J. A. (2015) Dreaming as Virtual Reality: A New Theory of the Brain-Mind. Clarendon: Oxford University Press.

23. Solms, Mark. (1997) The Neuropsychology of Dreams. Mahwah, NJ: Lawrence Earlbaum Associates; Solms, Mark & Turnbull, Oliver (2002) The Brain and The Inner World: An Introduction to neuroscience of subjective experience. New York: Other Press.

24. Edelman, G. (1987) Neural Darwinism: The Theory of Neuronal Group Selection. Philadelphia: Basic Books; (2003) Being No One: The Self-Model Theory of Subjectivity. Boston: MIT Press.

25. Metzinger, T. (2009) The Ego Tunnel: The Science of the Mind and the Myth of the Self. NY: Perseus.

26. Clark, A. Whatever next? Predictive brains, situated agents, and the future of cognitive science. Behavioral and Brain Sciences, 36(03), 181-204. doi: 10.1017/SO140525X12000477.

27. Hohwy, J. (2013) The predictive mind. Oxford: Oxford U. Press.

28. Hobson, J. A., Hong, Charles C.-H., & Friston, K. Virtual reality and conscious inference in dreaming. Frontiers in Psychology, 9 Oct. 2014. doi: 10-3389/fpsyg.2014.01133.

29. Hobson, J. A. & Friston, K. Consciousness, Dreams and Inference: The Cartesian Theatre Revisited. J. of Consc. Studies, 21, No. 1-2, 2014.

30. Clark, Andy (2013) Whatever next? Predictive brains, situated agents, and the future of cognitive science. Behavioral and Brain Sciences, 36 (3), pp. 181-204.

31. Adams, R. A., Shipp, S., & Friston, K. J. (2012) Predictions and commands: Active inference in the motor system. Brain Structure and Function, Epub ahead of print.

32. Whitney, David & Fischer, Jason, et al., (posted online Apr. 07, 2014). Brain's '15 second delay" shields us from hallucinogenic experience. Reuters/Eddie Keogh. S

33. Merzenich, Michael. (2013) Soft-Wired: How the New Science of Brain Plasticity Can Change Your Life. San Francisco: Parnassus Pub. LLC.

34. Just, G. A. (2016) "Phenomenal Methodology: Toward an Egosyntonic Psycho-Neuro-Dynamic Model of Mental Health. In Advances in Psychology Research, Vol. 118(Ed.) A. M. Columbus. Hauppauge, NY: Nova Science Pubs.

35. Just, G. A. (2017) "Clinical Advantages of Self-Hypnosis," in Advances in Psychology Research, Vol. 128 (Ed.) A. M. Columbus. Hauppauge, NY: Nova Science Pubs.

36. Just, G. A. (2015) "Convergence of Subjective and Objective Methodologies in Consciousness Research," Advances in Psychology Research, Vol. 103, Hauppauge, NY: Nova Science Pubs.

37. LaBerge, S., & Rheingold, H. (1990) Exploring the World of Lucid Dreaming. NY: Ballantine Books.

38. Skork, Kerstin, Lucid Dreams and Metacognition," Neuroscience News (Jan. 23, 2015).

39. Love, Daniel. (2013) Are You Dreaming: Exploring Lucid Dreams: A Comprehensive Guide. Enchanted Loom Publishing: www.enchantedloom.co.uk.

APPENDIX I

"Glen Just's altered states timelines"

The following altered state timelines (AST) were appended to Allan Hobson's *Ego Damage and Repair: Toward a Psychodynamic Neurology,* (pp. 165-178). All examples were drawn from my autobiography, *Autobiography of a Ghost.* I have partially modified *Ego Damage and Repair* AST headings and listed them without narrative explanations.

Birth—28 March 1936: July/August, 1937 (**16-17 months**) first out-of-body experience while hospitalized.

1939 (3-years): Start of life-long OBEs and "Spirit Presence."

1941/1942 (5/6-years): Japanese Submarine Nightmare and Active Dream Intervention.

1943 (7-years): Conquering virtual space. First remembered fusing of body with another object (automobile).

1944 (8-years): Interstellar OBE, "Soul" separation and fits.

1947 (11-years): Learning to control obsessive-compulsive behaviors; self-confirmation of presence.

1948 (12-years): Conscious mind-body separation—virtual self-projection as dual state.

1950 (14-years): Sexual trauma as nightmare generator.

1951 (15-years): Long-term nightmares without terminus.

1952 (16-years): Suicidal acts and self-projection into thunderstorms.

1954 (18-years): I began my initial review of Freud.

1957/1958 (21-years): Rejecting Freud, embracing behaviorism, and employing self-hypnosis.

1965/1968 (29-32-years): Virtual shamanic projection of self.

1970 (34-years): Longevity of child demonic "ghost."

1973 (37-years): Discovering glossolalia, and collective drug trips.

1978 (42-years): Controlling "presence," and virtual control of physical self.

1979 (43-years): Nightmares after 20-years of active suppression.

1982 (46-years): Self-generated hallucinations using visual media.

1986 (50-years): Self-generation of waking hallucinations using childhood dogma.

1989 (53-years): Non-conscious memory acquisitions using physical posturing.

1991 (55-years): Virtual control of physical size: A dreaming corollary.

1991 (58-years): The startle response with new forms of hallucinations.

1994 (58-years): Repression requires psychic energy, nightmares can be forever.

1998 (62-years): The whole body as phantom limb.

2000 (64-years): Controlled, multi-sensory waking hallucinations.

2010/2011 (74-75-years): Classifying hypnopompia.

2012 (76-years): Using suggestion with hypnogogia.

2015 (79-years): Discovering self-enactment of trance-like controls while dreaming.

APPENDIX II

Applied Definitions and Abbreviations

Autosuggestion: The term is often used interchangeably with self-hypnosis. I use autosuggestion to mean that one is *willing* something to happen without actually entering trance. Self-hypnosis means that there has been a shift in our consciousness level and we are in trance. (Also, see trance)

Belief: One's individual interpretations of reality, which can include self-created entities such as "ghosts" as well as third-party observable things such as chairs. Our individual belief systems generally treat imagined entities, as well as verifiable world objects, with equal veridicality.

Bidirectional sensory image Transformations: In dreams and hallucinations, we transform primary sensations such as pain into concrete objects such as monsters. And we transform concepts at our secondary level of consciousness, such as the idea of torture, into felt sensations such as pain.

Brain (modular) **plasticity**: Modular plasticity means that one part of the brain can take over functions that are normally performed by another part. For example, functions lost to stroke can be taken over by other neurons and we can learn to speak and swallow again.

Brain (neuronal) **plasticity:** Daily, neural connections are modified in our sleep, and a small number of new neurons are created.

Continuity field: Research by David Whitney and colleagues found that visually we average input over 10-15 seconds. Averaging, thus, "smoothes" a visual field that would otherwise be jittery and chaotic. This mechanism helps control neuronal chaos.

Dream forms: The five common dreams forms distort time, space, logic, characters, and movement. When we dream, times can be mixed from any period from our personal history, we can move from one physical space to another in an instant, characters are commonly composites, logic is suspended and the absurd seems logical when the dream is ongoing, and we move in our dreams but not in our beds. J. Allan Hobson is noted for dream forms—*see 13 Dreams Freud Never Had,* and *The Dreaming Brain.*

Dream logic--examples: I am flying above the clouds without wings, or I have simultaneously dispatched 12 martial arts fighters in one session. My dream ego perceives all of these fantastic events as being real.

Dream memory associations (DMA): Time, spaces, and characters are mixed in any combination. DMA suggest that the brain is recording new experiences by modifying neuronal sets that are already in existence.

Dream movement: Movement in dreams is subject to instant realization, e.g., I'm in interstellar space half-way to the moon and in the next instant in my bed.

Dream Interpretation: The author's key to dream interpretation is how imagery is transformed between primary (affective/core brain dynamics) and secondary (cognitive) levels of consciousness.

Dream suggestion: Pre-sleep suggestion tends to enter and influence the content of our dreams, especially when repeated over a number of days. Dream suggestion can be used to replace negative with positive dream content.

Dream Types (Author's Classifications): Stimuli generating the dream type determines classification.

Somatic: Physical sensations are reimaged at our secondary-level of consciousness where they are personified and concretized. For example, pain is reimaged as torturers, and bloating is reimaged as the dream-self searching for a toilet. Similar examples of image transformations between primary and secondary consciousness are routinely observed in somatic dreams.

Memory Associations: The dreaming brain appears to associate momentary body states with one's entire history; for example, dry winter air is transformed into a dream cigarette smoking scene. Memory associations in dreams support contemporary experiences being incorporated in existing neuronal networks. The brain does not take pictures or create new neural maps from scratch but appears to modify existing neuronal structures to store new experiences.

Fixed Action Patterns (FAPs): Waking functional routines such as bike riding are temporally correlated with dream biking mastery. Acquiring new behaviors and complex behavioral routines are reinforced in our dreams. This is a form of unconscious (Hebbian) learning.

Biochemical: Hormone levels, drugs, alcohol, and pharmaceuticals can generate dream image transformations. For example, sex hormones can generate erotic dream partners.

Pharmaceuticals: Example, oxycodone can be experienced by our dream-self as a series of erratic and disconnected dream fragments that have no apparent interconnections.

Thematic (Metaphorical): The acts of writing this book generate similar but not literal dream scenes. For example, contemporary writing efforts appear in my dreams with associated memories of my teaching history, campuses, buildings, and lecture rooms. I never actually write in thematic dreams.

Thematic (Media): A movie theme such as alien invaders may be reimaged throughout much of the night as interpersonal conflict and portray many types of different characters and physical settings.

Cognitive: Ideas and/or concepts at our secondary-level of consciousness are generating review of related memory associations. For example, a multiple number of out-of-body dream and hallucinatory movements occurred in one of my dreams in quick succession. I became aware that my brain was wrestling with phenomenal-self movement as being distinct from waking movement.

Creative: New associations or ideas emerge from the night's dreams that did not exist at bedtime.

Cognitive-emotional: For example, my spouse's dream image changes repeatedly throughout the night while my emotional reactions to her remain the same. This spousal cognitive-emotional pattern suggests that stereotyping is a reflection of how neurons store information.

Nightmares: Intense dreams with disturbing content that frequently result in waking.

Dual states of consciousness: Half of our brain can be dreaming while the other half is watching. Half of our brain can be hallucinating a dream-like reality while the other half navigates the here and now.

Ego: The component of secondary conscious that permits one to be aware of their own existence. I do not use Ego in the Freudian sense as a biologically dependent Id emergent. I use Ego interchangeably with Self. Ego and Self are treated as metacognitive supervening agents that support free will.

Epigenesis: Genes are modified in fetal and post-fetal development by conditions present in their environment. Epigenetic modification of genes can predispose one to depression and other forms of mental illness.

First-person analysis: Subjective interpretation of experience in lucid dreams, hallucinations, altered states of consciousness, or waking.

Free will: The assumption that one's Ego/Self can act independently of past experience.

Freudianism--examples: *Conceptual interpretations*—direct intervention to control dream content is counterproductive to desired therapeutic goals because it interferes with "latent" dream content. Freudian *clinical interpretations* turn rods and poles in dreams into penis symbols. (Freud changed his theoretical and clinical interpretations over time; thus, earlier, middle, and later Freud interpretations can be in conflict. (See Jonathan Lear's *"Freud).*"

Hallucinations—controlled: Pre-planned and enacted dream-like episodes that can be observed lucidly while they are in progress. I use my "Genesis Journey" as an example. (See Just 2009).

Hallucinations—spontaneous: Spontaneous hallucinations are common misrepresentations of our world, e.g., the lamp mistaken for a person due to one being overly tired.

Hypnotic induction while dreaming: One can learn to lucidly enter trance while dreaming and use trance to modify any aspects of the dream's content while continuing to dream.

Hypnotic trance: A state where primary consciousness is in control of one's actions and behavior. Trance induced by a hypnotist usually results in a state of dissociation where one's secondary consciousness is taken over by the hypnotist.

Illusion: One believes something exists in reality, but that something is only in their imagination, e.g., "ghosts," or being possessed by a "spirit". Illusions differ from other brain-mind virtual constructions because their references are non-existent. (See virtual entities for comparison).

Lucidity: A state of consciousness where one half of the brain is awake and observing while the other half is producing "movie-like" imagery in dreams or hallucinations.

Lucid methodology: A proposed research method where one maintains conscious awareness while dreaming, hallucinating, or experiencing other states of consciousness. (See Just, 2015).

Lucid Self-hypnosis (LSH): One remains aware at a secondary level of consciousness while experiencing trance. LSH is also a therapeutic technique proposed by the author to control anxiety, depression, nightmares, OCD, addictions, and related pathologies.

Metaphorical image transformations (MIT): Image transformations between primary and secondary consciousness. Example—one observes an undifferentiated sense of fear being turned into dream "monsters" The key point of MIT is their symbolic, conceptual, emotional, and non-literal transformations. MITs are bidirectional between primary and secondary consciousness.

Mystical Visions: I define mystical visions as being synonymous with waking, narrative hallucinations.

Naturalized religious experiences: A third way of looking at religious experience as being distinct from theists and a-theists interpretation. It is assumed that natural image transformations of the brain-mind are the origin of a pantheon of "spirits" and imaginary entities. The brain's virtual reality generator is the mechanism that both duplicates real-world sensory experiences and creates a pantheon of ethereal beings *de novo*.

Neurophenomenological Configurations (NPC): Images that are created *de novo* in the brain-mind in dreams, hallucinations, and across different states of consciousness. NPCs can be a virtual representation of a "real" world object, or illusory, i.e., "ghosts." The "neuro" of neurophenomenology emphasizes that sensory images are always being constructed by neurons and biochemical processes in the brain.

Neuro-psycho-phenomenology: The integration of neurology, psychology, and phenomenology as a unified model used to interpret experience. For example, interpreting how one can feel they are possessed by a "spirit."

Now state: A state of consciousness that is focused on the present moment. A now state permits one to project thoughts and memories into the past and future. One's now state generates a time continuum for self-reference.

Ouija **board**: A game were a stylus supposedly moves by invisible forces, but in actuality is being moved unconsciously by the players.

Personality: Five major personality types are formed from macro-level brain structures that are related to the thickness and folding of the cerebral cortex; they are, neuroticism, extraversion, openness, agreeableness, and conscientiousness. Brain structures predispose one to a particular orientation to the world. (See Roberta Ricelli and colleagues research).

Phantom limbs: After surgical or accidental removal of arms and legs one may continue to experience pain in the lost limb.

Phase State Change: In physics and chemistry aspects of the material world change depending on the relationship between constituent components. For example, hydrogen and oxygen, two gases, become liquid or solid when combined into H_2O under different temperature conditions.

Phenomenal-Self: The phenomenal-self is conceived as the semi-permanent neural configuration that oversees our moment-to-moment relationships with our social and physical environments. It is a set of functional neural-biological processes in command of secondary consciousness.

Possession or Spirit-Possession: An individual's assumption that a "spirit" has taken control of their mind and/or body.

Primary Emotions: SEEKING, RAGE, FEAR, LUST, CARE, PANIC/GRIEF, and PLAY are primary process emotions for *Homo sapiens* that exist across the mammalian phylum. In dreams, secondary brain processes transform these emotions into feelings, and concrete, personified images that permit one's dream-self to engage in social interactions. (See Jaak Panksepp's research on primary process emotions).

Primary Image Transformations: For example, in dreams primary emotions such as fear and lust can be transformed at our secondary-level of consciousness into concretized monsters and personified erotic partners.

Protoconsciousness Theory: A theory that is being propounded by J. Allan Hobson. The theory assumes that the self begins to think and feel during the fetuses' last trimester. TFI agrees with Protoconsciousness Theory that the self is reinforced nightly in dreams. The transformative imagery (TFI) model subsumes Protoconsciousness Theory and proposes sensory and cognitive image-transformations as the mechanism that generates self. (See Hobson's Protoconsciousness Theory, *Nature Reviews Neuroscience*, 2009).

Psychodynamic neurology: A theoretical orientation that attempts to integrate psychology and neurology in a unified approach to clinical practices. The term *dynamic* implies multi- and non-linear causality. J. Allan Hobson is one of the major proponents of psychodynamic neurology.

Psycho-neuro-phenomenology: A term used by Jaak Panksepp to represent the scientific integration of psychological, neurological, and phenomenological information. The phenomenology component refers to the subjective representations of one's individual experiences of the world.

Qualia: A term used by philosophers to represent primary sensory images such as color.

Real World: A theoretical assumption that matter and energy actually exist, and that life is not just an illusion, or that the cosmos is not only a virtual creation without substance. (See subjective reality).

Reductionism: In scientific terms, a higher-level of analysis can be reduced to a lower-level. For example, the chemistry of water, H_2O, can be reduced to its atomic components water and hydrogen.

Secondary sensory image transformations: For example, in dreams concepts such as monsters can be reimaged downward to generate a physical, felt sense of fear at one's primary-level of consciousness.

Self: Proto, Core, Autobiographical, and *De'ja Vu*:

Proto-Self: An early developmental process that represents modifications of the brain's neurons. For example, fetal learning in the last trimester results in the infant being sensitized to the mother's language sounds, music preferences, and food tastes.

Core-Self: The brain's basic functional components that permit organismic survival, behavioral conditioning, and development of primary memories in response to one's total environment. At the core-self level, neuronal modification occurs below one's conscious awareness. Core-self neuronal processes occur out of sight, so to speak. Core-self conditioning supports innumerable behaviors; for example, acquiring balance on a bicycle. Core-self is the repository of automatized reflexes and primary emotions.

Autobiographical-Self: Equivalent to phenomenal-self. Terms are used interchangeably.

De'ja Vu-Self (DVS): The dream-self that exists over years and decades and parallels attributes of the phenomenal-self. DVS is experienced in dreams as being semi-permanent. It changes over time as does the waking phenomenal-self and accepts dream "forms" as virtual reality. The DVS has direct access to dream memories that have been placed in working memory. For example, physically my DVS has acquired vulnerabilities with age.

Self-Hypnosis: The ability to put one's self in trance. Lucid self-hypnosis permits one to remain aware of changes in their own states of consciousness, and at the same time use trance to control the contents of dreams and hallucinations. Self-hypnosis also permits control of body functions such as pain.

Shaman: Any individual who practices altered states of consciousness within a cultural worldview that assumes the existence of a supernatural plane of reality. (See Just, 2011).

Shamanic possession: An individual's assumption that he or she has taken control of an animal's mind and/or body, and now possesses its attributes and power.

Shamanism: "The systematic use of altered states of consciousness to make sense of the world and community inhabited by the practitioner and that use contributes to the development and maintenance of social order within the practitioner's community". (See Just, 2011).

Structural-Functionalism: A theory that generally assumes that structure comes before function. For example, neuronal brain structure precedes the acquisition of language.

Structural realism: A theoretical orientation that assumes the relationship between two things is more important than their analysis in isolation. For example, one can fully analyze hydrogen and oxygen separately and never understand H_2O.

Subjective Reality: Homo sapiens do not have direct contact with their environments. (I also assume that other mammals must transform basic sensory experiences, for example, light and sound waves into vision and hearing, and pressure on body surfaces into touch). Thus, any organism with biologically determined senses must enact some type of subjective representation in order to respond to its world.

Subjective world modeling: Our individual interpretation of the world and self. This concept focuses on the fact that we do not experience the world directly. We transform images and sensations through our basic sense organs. Subjective interpretations by the self determines one's perception of reality. Individually, both the self and its environment are subjective models.

Supervening-Self: A belief that the self can learn to control its own destiny. For example, in dreams, nightmares, and hallucinations the self can learn to control content, feelings, and emotions. It is assumed that self as agent has the ability to act independently of past behavioral conditioning.

Synesthesia-type transformations: Synesthesia is a transformative brain process where one type of imaging is transformed into another type. For instance, the number seven may be experienced as the color red. These processes typically occur automatically and below one's level of awareness (unconsciously).

TDIS: Transformative dynamic integrated systems. The author's theoretical model that incorporates bidirectional sensory image transformations of the brain-mind. TDIS assumes that the brain and mind act as one unified, sensory transformative system. And that the *Supervening-Self* can mature to act as an agent of free will.

Therapy (Clinical Goal): The overarching goal of therapy is to harmoniously integrate relationships between primary and secondary consciousness. For example, anxiety and depression are common occurrences that disrupt one's self-flourishing. Lucid Self-Hypnosis (LSH) is proposed as a method to facilitate the integration of primary and secondary consciousness processes. (See Just 2016).

Trance (hypnotist): A primary state of consciousness experienced with a third-party hypnotist where fixed action patterns (FAPs) are expressed reflexively and primary emotions are uncensored.

Self-hypnosis: In self-hypnosis as contrasted to hypnotist trance, the self in trance can actively continue to monitor and direct actions and emotions occurring at both the primary and secondary levels.

Transformative imagery (TFI): In dreams, emotions are concretized and personified, thereby, permitting the dream-actor social intercourse. For example, one has an undifferentiated sense of fear that becomes concretized and personified in their dreams as monsters. TFI also means that concepts at one's secondary-level of consciousness can be turned into percepts such as pain or emotions. TFI is bidirectional between primary and secondary consciousness.

Unity of Self: A theoretical construct that envisions harmony between primary and secondary consciousness. For example, affective emotions at the level of primary consciousness (core-brain dynamics) are brought into harmony with conscious goal seeking behaviors and beliefs of the higher-order self of secondary consciousness.

Veridicality of consciousness states: In dreams, the self of secondary consciousness experiences virtually created dream content as though it represents real-world objects. Thus, a dream monster can elicit panic and related biochemical responses as a real monster would in waking.

Virtual Entities: The brain creates image representations of the self and its external world and gives these representations cognitive and emotional value. In contrast to illusions, virtual entities have identifiable references, e.g., my brain-mind's virtual representation of my body refers to a known entity. An illusion, such as a "ghost" refers to an imaginary entity that does not exist outside of our minds.

Virtual Reality Generator (*waking state*): A set of assumed brain-mind processes that create representations of our self and world. Tactile, visual, and auditory inputs are turned into touch, vision, and sound. We do not experience the world of light frequencies, sounds, and pressures directly—we experience the brain-mind's transformations (interpretations) of these phenomena. For example, light waves of a certain frequency are turned into the colors red, blue, and green in the brain-mind. In waking, the VRG functionally adjusts imaging through self-environment interaction.

Virtual Reality Generator (*dreaming/hallucinating state*): It is assumed that the same brain-mind processes that create representations of our self and world are active in altered states such as dreams and hallucinations. However, in altered states the VRG generates imagery without waking, "real world" corrections.

Virtual reality—body size and image: Individually each person creates a body map, and a subjective interpretation of this map. For example, A six-foot man may feel three feet tall emotionally, or experience himself as an interstellar giant. (See Just, 2009).

Will: The brain's core dynamics that represent acquired and automatic responses. For example, I don't think about moving my feet one at a time, I only think about walking to the mailbox. In contrast, loss of will refers to automatized behaviors being expressed independently of secondary consciousness, for example, addictions or OCD.

Zen-driving: Driving under the influence of self-induced trance where core-self is in command while the phenomenal-self of secondary consciousness relaxes and observes. (See Just, 2009).

ABBREVIATIONS

AST: Altered state timelines are my remembered occurrences of various states of consciousness. ASTs were first appended to Allan Hobson's review of Glen Just's self-therapy in *Ego Damage and Repair:* Toward a Psychodynamic Neurology, (pp. 165-178).

DSM: Diagnostic and Statistical Manual of Mental Disorders

DIS: Dynamic integrated systems.

ECE: Extra-corporeal experience. An etheric double is experienced as existing independently of one's physical body.

EEG: Electro-encephalogram. A brain imaging technology.

LSH: Lucid Self-Hypnosis. One remains aware and in control at a secondary level of consciousness while experiencing trance.

fMRI: Functional magnetic resonance imaging. A brain imaging technology.

NICU: Neonatal intensive care unit

OBE: Out-of-body experience.

OCD: Obsessive-compulsive disorder.

PET: Positron Emission Tomography. A brain imaging technology.

PSM: Phenomenal-self model is the subjective, first-person interpretation that we give to our virtual and physical selves. For example, my phenomenal-self can fly in dreams and hallucinations;

waking, I may see myself as being generous, but others see me as being stingy, or I may subjectively feel three feet tall when I'm actually 6.2.

PTSD: Post-traumatic stress disorder.

REM: Rapid eye movement.

nREM, or non-REM: Non-rapid eye movement.

Printed in the United States
by Baker & Taylor Publisher Services